The Market for Mesoamerica

Maya Studies

UNIVERSITY PRESS OF FLORIDA

Florida A&M University, Tallahassee
Florida Atlantic University, Boca Raton
Florida Gulf Coast University, Ft. Myers
Florida International University, Miami
Florida State University, Tallahassee
New College of Florida, Sarasota
University of Central Florida, Orlando
University of Florida, Gainesville
University of North Florida, Jacksonville
University of South Florida, Tampa
University of West Florida, Pensacola

THE MARKET FOR MESOAMERICA

Reflections on the Sale of Pre-Columbian Antiquities

EDITED BY CARA G. TREMAIN AND DONNA YATES

Foreword by Arlen F. Chase and Diane Z. Chase

UNIVERSITY PRESS OF FLORIDA

Gainesville / Tallahassee / Tampa / Boca Raton

Pensacola / Orlando / Miami / Jacksonville / Ft. Myers / Sarasota

First cloth printing, 2019
First paperback printing, 2023

28 27 26 25 24 23   6 5 4 3 2 1

Library of Congress Cataloging-in-Publication Data
Names: Tremain, Cara G., editor. | Yates, Donna, editor. | Chase, Diane Z.,
   author of foreword. | Chase, Arlen F. (Arlen Frank), 1953– author of
   foreword.
Title: The market for Mesoamerica : reflections on the sale of Pre-Columbian
   antiquities / edited by Cara G. Tremain and Donna Yates ; foreword by
   Diane Z. Chase and Arlen F. Chase.
Other titles: Maya studies.
Description: Gainesville : University Press of Florida, 2019. | Series: Maya
   studies | Includes bibliographical references and index.
Identifiers: LCCN 2018054073 | ISBN 9780813056449 (cloth) | ISBN 9780813080406 (pbk.)
Subjects: LCSH: Indians of South America—Antiquities. | Indians of Central
   America—Antiquities.
Classification: LCC F1434.2.A7 M37 2019 | DDC 980/.01—dc23
LC record available at https://lccn.loc.gov/2018054073

The University Press of Florida is the scholarly publishing agency for the State University
System of Florida, comprising Florida A&M University, Florida Atlantic University, Florida
Gulf Coast University, Florida International University, Florida State University, New
College of Florida, University of Central Florida, University of Florida, University of North
Florida, University of South Florida, and University of West Florida.

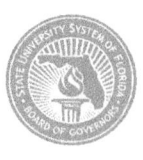

University Press of Florida
2046 NE Waldo Road
Suite 2100
Gainesville, FL 32609
http://upress.ufl.edu

Contents

Illustrations

Figures

Tables

Foreword

Most archaeologists working in Mesoamerica are familiar with the rampant and continued destruction of the artifactual remains of the ancient peoples who once lived there and are concerned about the limitations placed on the interpretation of materials that lack detailed contextual provenience. There are many reasons for the destruction of ancient settlements. In some cases, as in Mexico City, a burgeoning population occupies the same locations that were used in antiquity; modern buildings, roads, and houses now cover the razed platforms and pyramids of the past. Yet, each urban renewal project reveals traces of those past cultures and potentially recovers items that are archaeologically important and artistically beautiful. In other, more rural, situations, land clearing for agriculture and for grazing levels or bulldozes ancient buildings, sometimes by individuals who are not really aware of what is being destroyed. These activities similarly have the potential to produce significant past materials and, while owning registered materials that incidentally result from such activities is allowed in some countries, the intentional excavation of ancient remains is not. Indeed, of most concern to researchers is the purposeful illicit excavation of ancient remains by modern looters attempting to recover artifacts that can be sold to interested individuals and institutions throughout the world. Such activity is prohibited by collaborative and unilateral agreements throughout Mesoamerica but remains a common pastime that results in myriads of open trenches and tunnels at archaeological sites. The destruction of ancient buildings is especially well documented for many of the ancient sites once occupied by the ancient Maya.

This volume is a timely exploration of the market for ancient Mesoamerican antiquities and the issues involved in the tangled web of collecting and academic research. The market for Mesoamerican antiquities is contextualized temporally in order to understand the complex relationships that have emerged between archaeologists, universities, museums, governments, and capitalism. The mores of past times are compared with those of the present in terms of the politics and policies that have been and are involved in the recovery, marketing, and collecting of antiquities. The production of modern materials that explicitly resemble ancient artifacts is also part of this examination. Reproductions have been made and marketed for hundreds of years in Mesoamerica and it is sometimes difficult for an inexperienced eye to know when something is a reproduction and when it is authentic. Thus, cottage industries have arisen in the creation not only of polychrome vessels, complete with figures and hieroglyphs, attributed to the ancient Maya but also of very large and elaborately modeled ceramic sculptures attributed to the ancient inhabitants of the Veracruz region. Because of their value in the art market, a wide variety of other artifactual materials—carved stone monuments complete with texts, elaborately decorated wooden masks, and even paper codices—have also been created and sold to the unsuspecting consumer or bidder. And, as the countries in Mesoamerica have matured, they have done more to preserve their past as a valuable resource, leading in some instances to the return of certain objects from museums and private collections to the country of origin. But despite good intentions, the application of modern policies and practices designed to curb the traffic in Pre-Columbian antiquities has had very uneven results.

Whenever there is a discussion about ancient artifactual materials—whether they have derived from an archaeological expedition, from a museum, or from a private collection—there are also ethical concerns. Mesoamerican archaeologists, in particular, are prohibited by both governments and professional standards not only from selling objects but also from either authenticating materials or placing a monetary value on them. Policies put into place by professional organizations are an attempt to demonetize the antiquities market. What this has meant, however, is that agencies like auction houses have filled this void through authenticating, valuing, and selling objects—all while collecting their own fees. The desire to show that materials are legitimately owned has also led to an increase in false documentation. For instance, fraudulent documentation was produced for a carved hieroglyphic panel from the site of Ceibal (Seibal), Guatemala offered for sale in Miami, Florida almost thirty years ago; even though this artifact had been found, excavated, and recorded by an archaeological project in 1965, the paperwork that accompanied this illegally removed carved stone stated that it had been part of a private collection made before 1920. Definitions of what is considered looting also vary by interest group. For instance, while archaeologists, archaeological institutions, and governments throughout Mesoamerica define looting as the illegal and non-permitted excavation of any and all Pre-Columbian remains, dealers in Pre-Columbian art sometimes conveniently defined looting as the illegal removal of ancient or historic artifactual materials from only churches or museums. Clearly there is a disconnect in these definitions when it comes to any ethical considerations about the ownership of Pre-Columbian antiquities.

The issues surrounding the market for Mesoamerican antiquities are broader than any one country, are not restricted to any single culture, and cross-cut academic disciplines. They are issues of concern to all researchers working with materials from the ancient past in this part of the world, as well as to scholars trying to preserve the past for the future. It is for these reasons that we are pleased to add *The Market for Mesoamerica* to our Maya Studies series.

Arlen F. Chase and Diane Z. Chase
Series Editors

Preface

Pre-Columbian[1] antiquities are among the most popular items on the international antiquities market. Because of the opaque nature of the market and the phenomenal growth of online and alternative sales platforms in recent years, it has become increasingly difficult for the scholarly community to monitor the trade and sale of objects from the Pre-Columbian past. Studies that have been undertaken are generally limited, repetitive, or outdated. Therefore, we may not have a real sense of the nature and function of the current market for Pre-Columbian objects. Without this information it is unlikely that we will be able to positively influence policy in this area or effect substantive change.

This book explores past, current, and future policies and trends concerning the sale of antiquities from Mesoamerica. Chapters have been solicited from experts within a range of fields, from academic research to museums, law enforcement, and policy implementation. As such, *The Market for Mesoamerica* covers topics as diverse as market analysis and forgery detection, policy critique and collection, museum practice, and law enforcement—all within a cohesive theme.

On the fiftieth anniversary of Clemency Coggins's seminal 1969 publication "Illicit Traffic of Pre-Columbian Antiquities," the relevance and impact of this book could not be more timely. It also marks more than 25 years since the publication of *Collecting the Pre-Columbian Past*, a volume edited by Elizabeth Hill Boone from papers presented at a 1990 Dumbarton Oaks symposium. That book, now as a 2012 reprint, represents the only published collections of academic reflections on the role of collecting and the market on our understanding of ancient Mesoamerica. Major shifts in policy, law, ethics, practice, and policing have altered the landscape since the initial publication of Boone's volume. The modern market for Pre-Columbian antiquities is not what it was two decades ago, and our understanding of how the market's past has shaped

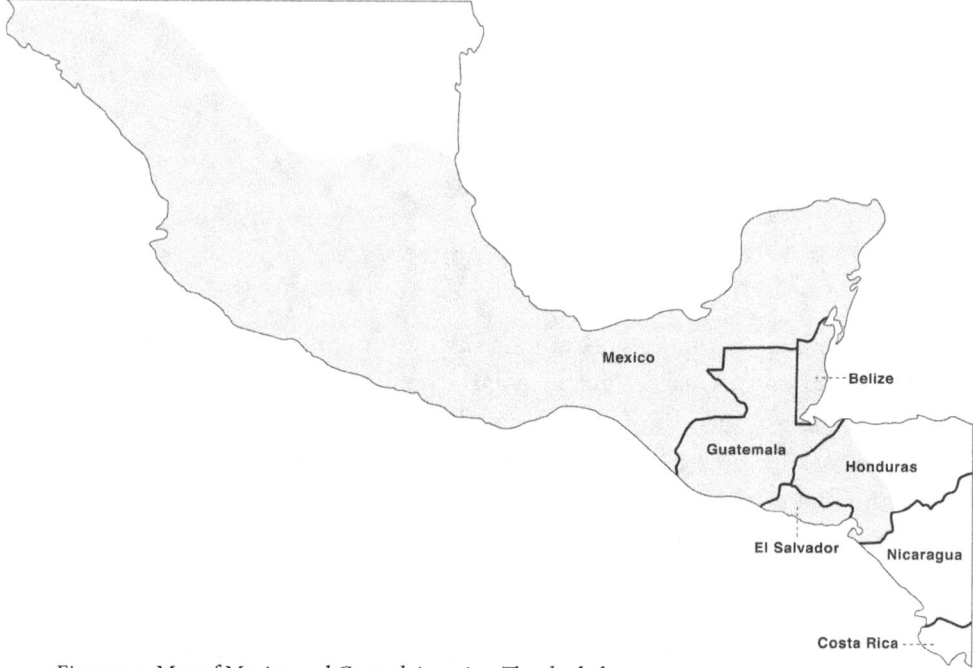

Figure 0.1. Map of Mexico and Central America. The shaded area
indicates the Mesoamerican cultural area. Map created by John Short.

the present and future of our discipline has grown with the inclusion of research from such fields as criminology, law, anthropology, economics, and security studies.

The current volume begins with Rosemary Joyce's commentary on the
chapters herein, and how we might re-envision the idea of a "market" for Mesoamerican antiquities as an "art world(s)" of Mesoamerican antiquities (see
chapter 1). Following this is Allison Davis's discussion of the history of legislation between the United States and countries in Mesoamerica, and how the
Cultural Property Implementation Act (CPIA) creates positive and meaningful relationships (chapter 2). It is our hope that exposing readers to international legislation early in the volume will be a useful and important backdrop
to the chapters that follow. Christina Luke's examination of the movement of
antiquities out of Central America in the late nineteenth and early to mid-
twentieth centuries is an apt ensuing chapter, detailing events that necessitated
the need for protective measures regarding Mesoamerican antiquities (chapter
3). Subsequently, Sofía Paredes Maury and Guido Krempel examine the fate of

cultural heritage in Guatemala in the twentieth and twenty-first centuries and how the country is managing the effects of looting and trafficking of antiquities (chapter 4).

Following Paredes Maury and Krempel's case studies of Guatemalan antiquities is James Doyle's overview of Stela 5 from Piedras Negras, Guatemala (chapter 5). Doyle reconstructs the biography of this monument by tracing its movement from an ancient Maya city to a large New York art museum. The stela is a prime example of the type of object that collectors of Mesoamerican antiquities were looking to add to their repertoire in the mid-twentieth century. What is fortunate, though usually lacking for the art market, is the documentation that accompanies the purchase of the stela. It is far more common for antiquities without provenience to lack detailed paper trails—exemplified by the artifacts studied by Martin Berger in chapter 6. Like Doyle, Berger attempts to reconstruct the biographies of these unprovenienced antiquities but relies heavily on gathering information from auction catalogues, correspondence between buyers and sellers, and archaeological reports to do so.

Similar to Doyle and Berger's concerns with providing context to Mesoamerican antiquities in museum collections, Adam Sellen discusses the creation of an online catalogue of Zapotec urns and his efforts to trace their sale and purchase through time (chapter 7). Sellen also laments the large number of fake Zapotec urns on the market and explains the way in which he and other scholars have attempted to identify them. Pertinent to the issue of inauthentic antiquities is the examination of Pre-Columbian fakes and forgeries by Nancy Kelker in the chapter that follows (chapter 8). In considering the appearance and evolution of the market in faked Mesoamerican antiquities, Kelker outlines the ways in which these objects entered public and private collections and stresses that they remain problematic realities for our discipline.

Touching on aspects of several of the aforementioned chapters (i.e., legislation, the auction market, museums, and collecting), Cara Tremain discusses the quantitative results of the sale of Maya antiquities at a high-end auction house over several decades (chapter 9). By analyzing the public market in this way, we are able to understand the trends and issues relating to the sale of Pre-Columbian heritage and can hope to affect future policy decisions and changes. The volume concludes with Donna Yates's examination of whether cultural property policy is working, specific to the influence of the 1970 UNESCO Convention on the market for Maya antiquities (chapter 10). Just as Davis examines the impact of the CPIA, Yates examines whether legislation has impacted the looting, trafficking, or sale of antiquities. Her recommendations include a focus on object-specific regulations rather than country-specific regulations. What is clear from the chapters in this volume is that we should concentrate on ways we can strengthen policy, increase education, and continue to protect our shared cultural heritage.

We anticipate that the primary audience for this book will be academic archaeologists and museum professionals, but we hope experts from other fields such as criminology and sociology will also benefit from the chapters herein. While this book will be of particular interest to those working on and in the Americas, we hope that it will also interest academics, students, and heritage workers beyond its geographic focus. The looting and trafficking of antiquities and the difficult place of the market for cultural property within our work, is a topic of intense contemporary discussion. This book seeks to contribute to the discussion by identifying the substantive steps that the academic community can take toward effecting transparency, accountability, and ethical practice concerning the Pre-Columbian antiquities market.

Cara G. Tremain and Donna Yates

Notes

1. There are variations in the capitalization of the term Pre-Columbian throughout the volume, depending on the preference of the authors.

References Cited

Boone, Elizabeth Hill (editor). 1993. *Collecting the Pre-Columbian Past*. Washington, D.C.: Dumbarton Oaks Research Library and Collection.

Coggins, Clemency C. 1969. "Illicit Traffic of Pre-Columbian Antiquities." *Art Journal* 29 (1): 94, 96, 98, 114.

1

Making Markets for Mesoamerican Antiquities

ROSEMARY A. JOYCE

The attraction of antiquities from Mexico and Central America, especially from the celebrated urban societies that archaeologists define as Mesoamerican, occupies a special place in the development of modern cultural heritage policy, museum practice, and archaeological ethics. Parallel in many ways to the urgency raised by concerns about the impact of collecting of Mediterranean classical antiquities on cultural heritage sites in that region, for the Americas, the destruction of Maya sites by operators in search of marketable sculptures and more portable objects dramatized threats to heritage in the critical decade leading up to passage of the UNESCO Convention on the Means of Prohibiting and Preventing the Illicit Import, Export and Transfer of Ownership of Cultural Property in 1970.

In their preface to this volume, the editors relate it to two previous landmarks: the publication by Clemency Coggins of "Illicit Traffic of Pre-Columbian Antiquities" (Coggins 1969), and the 1990 Dumbarton Oaks symposium *Collecting the Pre-Columbian Past* (Boone 1993). These represented very different interventions. This volume is indeed a successor that interweaves the somewhat separate concerns of these predecessors. Coggins brought attention to the destruction of sites due to demand for antiquities without concern for how they were obtained, posing an opposition between the interests of the market and of researchers. The Dumbarton Oaks conference took a more nuanced view of the relationships between commerce and knowledge, showing that these had been entangled in myriad ways in the history of study of the region. The contributors to the present volume consider the traffic in antiquities and legislative initiatives to lessen destructive impacts from it, as

well as the ways that researchers and research institutions have been participants in the movement of antiquities from their source countries.

This volume comes at a significantly different moment from either of the
predecessors cited by the editors. The 1969 publication by Coggins preceded
the passage of the UNESCO Convention and was part of the motivation
for the United States to pass specific legislation intended to protect Mesoamerican sites in 1972 (discussed in this volume by Allison Davis and Donna
Yates). While the United States had already passed legislation implementing
the UNESCO Convention before the 1990 Dumbarton Oaks Conference was
held, the impact of this mechanism of intervention on the preservation of
threatened Mesoamerican sites was quite limited when the participants met.
An emergency agreement with El Salvador in 1987 covered material from
the Cara Sucia area, notably the first action under the 1983 Cultural Property
Implementation Act (see Davis, this volume). Emergency protection for the
antiquities of Guatemala's Petén region followed in 1991. A full agreement
with El Salvador was not created until five years after the Dumbarton Oaks
conference was held, and the bilateral agreement covering Guatemala was
only passed in 1997.

In her chapter, Donna Yates makes a case that the implementation of the
UNESCO convention has not had the desired outcome of reducing depredation of Mesoamerican sites. Yet that is not the only way in which the implementation of the convention has operated. Allison Davis demonstrates a number of positive efforts stemming from the U.S. process of reaching bilateral
agreements to implement import restrictions on specific kinds of antiquities.
We can also look at how the implementation of the convention in the United
States has changed the landscape of antiquities collecting in the country.

In the years since the Dumbarton Oaks conference, it has become less ac-
ceptable for art museums in the United States to accept donations of objects
without clear evidence that they entered the United States before the passage
of the 1970 UNESCO Convention. The Association of Art Museum Directors
(AAMD), which covers the most prominent art museums in North America,
eventually implemented guidelines for member museums that have been re-
vised twice since their introduction in 2004, most recently in 2013 (AAMD
2013). Under these guidelines, museums are required to have "provenance
demonstrating that the object was out of its country of modern discovery prior
to or legally exported therefrom after November 17, 1970." While these guidelines can be criticized for allowing museums to substitute "informed judg-

ment" for documented provenance, they represent a major shift from when the AAMD signed on to a friend of the court brief in 1998 arguing in support of a collector accused of violating U.S. law (Lyons 2002).

Major art auction houses have also moved to avoid work with uncertain history, an additional factor possibly contributing to the decrease in Maya antiquities auctioned by Sotheby's since the 1980s, documented by Cara Tremain. Yet in parallel, new forms of marketing facilitated by digital technology have created opportunities for material to be sold directly to buyers in other countries (Brodie 2015). In a few cases, law enforcement actions have successfully identified participants in illegal transactions of this sort, including those trafficking in Mesoamerican works (ICE 2011). Offered for what at times are relatively low prices, such transactions vastly expand the potential acquisition of antiquities by would-be collectors who were not part of the smaller group of patrons of museums discussed by contributors to this volume. At the other end of the spectrum from this small-scale, high-volume threat, the dramatic destabilization of the region as drug trafficking grew has swept under its fold antiquities trafficking, along with other forms of illicit traffic (see Davis, this volume).

This present book, then, takes shape in a very different world from that of the works cited as predecessors by the editors. It postdates any period when archaeologists could reasonably deny the entwined character of aesthetic appreciation and social or historical research. It acknowledges that early museum collections now often treated as completely unobjectionable sources of information often have complicated histories. It seeks as much to understand how collected materials circulated, in order to facilitate new research, as it does to critique the continued ways that markets are supported. The contributors identify the activity of a wide range of participants—excavators, both academic and informal, individual collectors in source countries and outside, agents working for and through galleries, and institutions that work to preserve these things—and trace different ways they interacted to create and satisfy a desire for Mesoamerican antiquities.

In some ways, talking about this solely as a market—with the implication that the important story is about the buying and selling of cultural heritage items—continues to obscure wider systemic issues that affect even those disciplines that have official ethical positions opposing commercialization, like that of the Society for American Archaeology. We might consider whether sociologist Howard Becker's concept of art worlds (Becker 1982, x) might serve us better: "the network of people whose cooperative activity, organized via their joint knowledge of conventional means of doing things, produces the kind of art works that art world is noted for." Thinking about the participants described in this volume as art worlds would allow us to distinguish among the activities involved while recognizing their interdependencies. It would enable us to recognize that Mesoamerican antiquities are produced *as art works* by the art world—not by the ancient crafters and patrons whose intentions resulted in the first manifestation of these objects.

In the conclusion to this chapter, I return to this point, using it as a moment to identify what we might want to single out as a "market" and what we might more broadly want to think about as an "art world" converting things made in the past in this region into antiquities or art works. In order to make those points, I first need to tease out some of the strands that unite the various chapters here around, not a market as such, but an art world or worlds.

Starting in the Middle

An often-told story of the illicit traffic in antiquities from Mesoamerica that appears multiple times in the pages of this volume begins with a crisis of looting of Maya sculptures and pottery in the 1960s (for example, as discussed by Sofía Paredes Maury and Guido Krempel). Certainly the passage in 1972 of protections for sculpture and wall paintings forming part of in situ structures, sparked by this crisis, is a landmark in U.S. legislative history. But as this volume demonstrates, commercialization of Mesoamerican antiquities has a deeper and much more complex history.

Commercialization has historically taken many forms, from the direct exchange of money for goods, to the indirect creation of cultural capital from the acquisition of things explicitly denied the status of mere commodities. Given that early archaeological practices contributed to the commercialization of collecting, we might even reconsider the repeated claim that the market for such things as Maya antiquities reached an unprecedented peak in the 1960s, and include in our analyses earlier peaks of collecting that resulted from archaeological research, in a pattern of shifting modes of acquisition that contributed to creating a continuing Mesoamerican art world (or worlds).

A fundamental part of this story of the formation of art worlds is the way that commerce, museum exhibition, and archaeological explorations together contributed (and continue to contribute) to the creation of a taste for antiquities, and for specific objects. The capacity we have to identify types of objects—Ulua marble vases, Guatemalan carved jade and bone—as fashionable in the market is partly a reflection of the scholarly attention the same categories of objects have attracted.

Perhaps the best illustration of this point in this volume is Martin Berger's exploration of highly targeted looting of a cave or caves in the Tehuacán area. He demonstrates that this occurred shortly after such caves became foci of problem-oriented archaeological research. In his study of the role of Nelson Rockefeller in the mid-twentieth century art world that emerged around Maya art, James Doyle also documents how scholarly investigations fed into the developing taste for Mesoamerican art that market intermediaries supplied.

There is no easy solution to this dilemma: scholarship builds the value of antiquities, but ignoring objects with limited provenience doesn't stop the development of a taste for certain things that fuels the acquisition end of the market. Berger argues that trying to avoid dealing with objects that entered institutions without formal documentation can actually inflict a kind of "double loss" of cultural heritage (citing Levine and Martínez de Luna 2013, 264). Adam Sellen's demonstration of the capacity to assemble a systematic corpus out of objects that mostly did not result from professional excavation exemplifies the challenges posed by the existence of an art world that connects scholars to the antiquities market. He is not alone in finding his academic research cited explicitly in marketing materials; nor is there any way that significant scholarship can be held outside the art world that links researchers and the market.

Of course, the activity of high-profile art collectors created markets in a much more direct and intentional way than the research activities of archaeologists. Specific individuals like Nelson Rockefeller, who James Doyle notes may have been purchasing Maya art as early as the 1930s, were taste makers, not just consumers of commoditized antiquities. Activity by people like this laid some of the groundwork for the upsurge in the market for Mesoamerican antiquities that reached crisis proportions in the 1960s. Such individuals were embedded in networks connected to institutions and museums whose missions they did not just passively support, but actively shaped. A major exhibition held in 1940 at the Metropolitan Museum of Art, championed by Rockefeller, increased the cachet of the works he collected and that others following his example would proceed to collect.

The analyses included here foreground as well the agency of a third group of participants in art worlds, the vendors who were intermediaries in the sale of antiquities. Berger's study is especially revealing, with its precision about ways gallery owners targeted specific items to distinct museums. Multiple galleries are identified as sources for Rockefeller's continuing assembly of his collection by Doyle as well, some overlapping with those identified in Berger's study. This is one way in which the art world is visibly a network: vendors can be conceived of as nodes connecting source countries and the people and institutions to which objects eventually traveled. Here, the research included in this volume shows our continued disproportion of knowledge about the vendors in the collecting countries, and the lack of knowledge we have about those operating in the source countries. The most active roles for individuals in source countries are those for individuals described by Paredes Maury and Krempel for Guatemala, and the uniquely documented producer of forgeries in Mexico, Brigido Lara (discussed by Kelker). Yet as Yates notes in passing, there were already local networks of collecting in the source countries before foreign nationals entered the scene. We actually aren't in a position yet to say how these original collectors of Mesoamerican antiquities acquired and circulated them, before or even after legislation in their home countries was passed to cut off the international trade.

I would argue that we also understand far less than we should about the motivations of museums in collecting countries that entered the art world as buyers during this mid-twentieth century period. The turn taken by Rockefeller in 1970, to negotiate formal acknowledgment of Guatemalan national ownership of a stela from Piedras Negras along with an agreement for its continued custody and display in New York, brings the episode of mid-century collecting that many authors focus on to a close, just as international agreements were being created to combat the destruction of in situ heritage through undocumented excavation intended to feed the art market.

Yet it is in this same period that Sellen shows Zapotec urns once forming multi-urn assemblages were dispersed from a Mexican museum where they had been housed, through art dealers in North America, into private collections and in some cases ultimately into museums.

Berger shows how an assemblage of antiquities from Mexico was scattered across multiple museums through the actions of art dealers at this same time. In this case, gallery agents seem to have pushed museums to acquire materials that would have been much more limited in their immediate visual impact than the large and aesthetically appealing Maya sculptures. Berger's study raises questions about the kinds of pulls that would lead sometimes unlikely museums to participate in a market that was already drawing attention for its links to endangerment of cultural heritage. The desires of the different museums that received parts of these assemblages led them to be open to acquiring materials whose excavation was clearly destructive, evident in the fragmented condition of objects and even the presence of human skeletal remains. These are signs of the violence of removal of these antiquities, not unlike the fragmentation, cuts, and losses from Maya stone sculptures that Yates notes in her chapter must have been evident to museums buying them. The motivating forces that allowed the acquiring museums to overlook such evidence of destruction need to be understood better.

For one museum in Berger's study, the Heye Foundation, there was historical precedent that the curator was attempting to sustain, of leadership in the collecting of turquoise mosaic objects. In another instance, specialist studies of one kind of material, textiles, likely abstracted from a group of objects specifically to increase their marketability, was the apparent pull. But what caused a midwestern art museum to acquire a collection described as composed of "turquoise fragments, ceramics, organic material, and human remains," when it had no history of collection in the area or in the broader archaeological categories of materials included? Here, we must assume an impetus to be part of an emerging appreciation of Mesoamerican art, to be part of an art world that, in the 1960s, the museum aspired to join.

The mid-twentieth-century market makers are in some ways quite clear: individuals of wealth and prestige who could make it tasteful to own Mesoamerican art; museums for which these individuals were benefactors; other museums emulating them; the dealers who moved works into the hands of individual collectors and museums; and the scholars whose research gave specific identity, and thus value, to these works. Yet our accounts of this historical moment demonstrate a blindness, deliberate or inadvertent, to the people who were ultimately supplying these works by removing them from their archaeological contexts. While these people are often subsumed under the identity "looter," the art world we are exploring actually engaged equally complex networks of participants in the source countries as well. Some of the complexity of these participants can be regained by moving our focus back a bit in time, to the moments when what drove the creation of the art world in question were different configurations.

Beginnings

In his study of the collecting of Zapotec antiquities, Sellen characterizes the nineteenth century as a period "when archaeology was still in its infancy but the formation of amateur collections were at their height." Like Sellen, Christina Luke explores a deeper history of the collecting of Mesoamerican antiquities in her study of late nineteenth to mid-twentieth-century Honduras. Here, the growth of international corporations facilitated research by museum and university academics, who developed both museum and research collections and promoted an aesthetic of appreciation of specific things—recognizably contributing to shaping the art world even if they were less clearly participating in making an art market.

This specific history of entangled commerce and research, and others like it, can actually be projected even earlier. This projection is of course implicit in Nancy Kelker's account of forging of Mesoamerican antiquities. Characterizing colonial vessels of the sixteenth and seventeenth centuries as "forgeries" may give too little attention to the generation of hybrid cultural identities, and attributing their use solely to the interest of Europeans in curiosities seems to completely deny the agency of indigenous makers. However, her observation that the travelers who entered the newly independent countries of Central America after independence were provided newly created "antiquities" may well point to a moment when we could begin an account of the emergence of a Mesoamerican art market that continues today. The forces that encouraged the market and the production of forgeries were the same: new nationalisms that used the material past to authenticate somewhat shaky political boundaries (Chinchilla 1998; Joyce 2003).

As my own ongoing research on Honduran collecting shows, the earliest Honduran objects to enter European museum collections arrived even earlier, in the eighteenth and early nineteenth centuries. They were acquired alongside and through the development of projects to extract natural resources, in particular, logging and mining (Joyce 2013). Their sources were local people who had their own interests in collections of such objects.

Repeated failed projects to build a trans-isthmus railway across Honduras that followed in the mid-nineteenth century left little to show for the investments by financiers spanning Europe and North America, except for the ancillary collecting of antiquities by virtually everyone involved in these enterprises. Again, where I can trace their itineraries, these objects came from local

Honduran collectors and owners (Joyce 2013, 2017). These objects ultimately made their way into university and public museums that today adhere to demanding ethical codes that would not allow their acquisition. With the passage of time, they became the basis for studies by scholars who invested effort in detaching their research from these origins.

The sometimes clearly problematic conditions of acquisition of early collections like those Luke and I have investigated in Honduras are seldom acknowledged. In many cases the source countries already had restrictive legislation in place. Contemporary documents may show intentional efforts to minimize the impacts of such laws. For example, in the case of the Harvard-Smithsonian expedition to Honduras that Luke mentions, Honduran law was technically observed, as my research shows that the Honduran national museum did select its choice from the complete vessels acquired by the archaeologists. Yet the bulk of the collected material—in the form of excavated collections—was not subject to the equal sharing called for in Honduran law. Neither Luke nor I have completely clarified why this was so. To account for it, we need to give as much attention to the agency of participants in the art world located in the source country as we have to those in the collecting nations.

My own research on the national attitude toward cultural heritage properties in Honduras in the 1930s suggests that fragmentary pieces were not seen as worthwhile. This is supported by the official Honduran document accompanying the exported collections from this expedition, which described them as of "no value" (included with a letter to Donald Scott from W. D. Strong dated July 28, 1936, in the Peabody Museum archives).

The goal for participants in antiquities collecting in countries like Honduras was to create museums of their own for the education of their population. Lacking a body of trained professional archaeologists who would see value in fragments as scientific specimens, retaining these materials simply would have created preservation and management obligations for which little funding, and often no space, was available.

What is more remarkable than the lack of interest in fragments by these countries at the time is the degree to which the North American archaeologists, purportedly representing science, also prized whole objects most, even when these were of uncertain provenience. The journals from the Harvard-Smithsonian expedition include counts of sherds disposed of on site after being counted, their only apparent scientific value being their quantity. The interests of the museums that archaeologists supplied does account for some of this preference, but not all of it. We probably can assume that the university-affiliated museums that sponsored research in the 1930s would have been less concerned with needing whole objects as a way of attracting visitors than museums in our contemporary epoch. Indeed, most of the antiquities acquired from Central America have never been exhibited in these museums.

Whole objects were desirable in the beginning of this art world because it was organized around such things, not around abstract kinds of information equally evident from broken fragments. Whole objects were abstracted from sets, viewed as duplicates, which could be sent to other institutions, as Sellen shows happened with Zapotec urns, and as I found happened with sherds from the Peabody-Smithsonian Institution, which made their way as far as Tokyo.

The preference for complete objects should be acknowledged as part of an archaeological inheritance, still in some ways operating today. It begins with the elevation of monumental sites over everyday places and ends with the celebration of complete objects over the fragments and sediments that form the matrix of a site (Joyce 2006). As Sellen notes, this emphasis on the singular object often "violates the character of the artifacts, which should be considered together, as a whole, from the perspective of core beliefs in indigenous worldview and ritual practice." This bias toward the singular, complete object is part of the way that archaeology structurally supports the emergence of commercial markets even when the archaeologists involved decry the buying and selling of antiquities.

Archaeologists have endorsed and developed many of the tropes of mysterious, early, and advanced development that create the aura of objects from Pre-Columbian Mesoamerica that are central to a Mesoamerican art world, and thus to the market in Mesoamerican antiquities. As Yates notes, for example, the market for Maya polychrome pottery was expanded by the excitement generated around the decipherment of Maya writing.

While Yates emphasizes the role of continued demand for Maya antiquities after legislation in the United States made import of stone sculpture illegal, the case can also be seen as an example of how structures developed at one point in an art world shape its continuity. The market created by the circulation of now-illegal materials comprised vendors and buyers, and there was as much interest in maintaining the traffic in antiquities by vendors in source countries as by those in collecting nations. Shifting our attention to the ways different networks of participants structured art worlds at different points in time can help us recognize the shared roles of individual collectors, museums, vendors, and researchers in creating structures that support the circulation of certain things as Mesoamerican art works.

Structuring Structures

Perhaps the most significant point to make about the commercialization of Mesoamerican antiquities may be identification of structural conditions that contribute to creating the art world of which the market is a manifestation. Here we need to acknowledge especially those structural conditions that create incentives for people in source countries to supply traffickers. It is hard to characterize the poor and often disenfranchised people who use informally excavated materials as a resource for a meager living simply as participants in the market. As Matsuda's (1998) proposed language shift from "looter" to "subsistence digger" for people in this position reflects, at issue is the precarity of life in highly unequal societies. The more recent development in the so-called Northern Triangle countries (Honduras, El Salvador, and Guatemala) of additional pressures leading to trafficking entwined with the international drug trade, and other forms of illicit trafficking that follow the same routes (touched on by Paredes Maury and Krempel), simply deepens precarity and the structures that make excavating and trading antiquities attractive to some people in source countries.

This is where the discussion by Allison Davis regarding collaborative activities that stem from the current process implementing the U.S. Cultural Property Implementation Act (CPIA) comes in. The CPIA is often viewed as primarily a means of regulating the U.S. market by imposing limits on allowable imports. This is how Yates assesses it, in her critical examination of whether the CPIA has led to less looting. Davis argues that its broader effects have come from encouraging the care for antiquities in source countries. She documents specific ways source countries, with financial and technical assistance from the United States, work to develop a sense of identity with antiquities as cultural heritage among the general population. These efforts address structural conditions, seeking to overcome the incentive that people facing economic precarity have to view antiquities as just (another) exploitable resource.

Cultivating understandings of antiquities as heritage materials, not just as tourism materials, also has the potential to help reinforce civic engagement.

In multicultural situations like those of all the countries under discussion, the recognition of traditional identities and connections to material evidence of past histories can powerfully change the way people regard things as evidence of their own past (Joyce 2005). This can lead newly engaged participants in what had been a circumscribed art world to reassemble the elements of that world into different forms, including framing demands to have a voice in the circulation of antiquities sent as loans to museums in other countries (Joyce 2003). Archaeologists need to accept that antiquities collected for their spiritual power or community needs (as Paredes Maury and Krempel describe in Guatemala) do not derive their primary importance from their use as specimens for research. Ideally, archaeologists would engage in creative approaches to advocate for community voices in the management, curation, and preservation of things that descendant groups see as of specific importance to them.

Such goals can be advanced by the creation of museums in these countries, especially where such museums engage with students. Here, the creation of new art world configurations may involve reexamining some of the lines previously drawn between institutions and individual collectors. In all these countries, in addition to government-sponsored museums, important cultural institutions have been developed by private individuals or groups of citizens who have in their possession collections that might at first glance be viewed as simply commodified products of a market. Such nongovernmental museums build on the existence of forms of private custody of cultural properties uniformly designated as national patrimony in these countries, as discussed most completely by Paredes Maury and Krempel for Guatemala. Such groups and individuals bring capital otherwise unavailable from government to projects that might otherwise never have happened. Under the laws in place throughout the region archaeologists recognize as Mesoamerica, these museums serve only as custodians, not owners, of archaeological objects.

The division between ownership and stewardship is one of the more confusing aspects of heritage management in this region for North Americans used to a regime of property in which portable archaeological objects can be easily alienated in exchange for money. Yet distinguishing between custodians and owners with the power to exchange antiquities in a marketplace is critical for archaeological engagement with broader social groups, not just institutional authorities, to be effective.

In Honduras, for example, efforts of private individuals expanded the presence of museums outside the capital city where the government had manifested its main interest in building institutions (Joyce 2003). Like the examples of selected conservation of items in private museums in Guatemala discussed by Paredes Maury and Krempel, in Honduras, the Museo de San Pedro Sula has been able to provide professional conservation attention to locally recovered objects (Joyce 2005). In addition to reconstruction of Ulua polychrome vessels from registered private collections, the museum has engaged in restoration and exhibition of professionally excavated objects from local sites that would likely have remained stored as fragmented collections without this local interest. The largest part of the museum's visitorship is local school children.

Futures

While the topic of the continued destruction of sites linked to the desire of collectors to own objects of Mesoamerican origin is inherently grim, there are hopeful points in this volume. Not the least is that this kind of detailed, careful research is maturing and going beyond the anecdotal (almost literally) standard that characterized the Dumbarton Oaks conference volume, the only previous work to which this collection should be compared. As new studies continue and the participants in networks forming art worlds are connected by scholarship, we can begin to truly see how these networks have shaped and reshaped over time. In doing this, we need to constantly push our horizon back to avoid various forms of parochialism that would be easy to adopt, such as treating one decade in the late twentieth century as the key to understanding markets that research shows began to emerge much, much earlier.

The pragmatic products that various authors have produced through their research on collections across which materials have been disbursed are also an inspiration for continued research. Whether it is the record produced by Tremain tracking Maya antiquities through one auction house over decades, the corpus of Mixtec turquoise objects Berger has created, the Zapotec urns for which Sellen created a major database, the similar database for Ulua marble vases produced by Luke, or my own construction of a register of more than 1,800 Ulua polychrome vessels (Joyce 2017), research on the circulation of antiquities is yielding new resources for other forms of scholarship.

These new scholarly efforts and products have the potential to extend the art worlds far beyond the traditionally limited circle of wealthy collectors and museums they patronized, or the equally small circle of scholars engaged in research on things like these. Sellen's reported experience is particularly interesting, as it points to new emerging art worlds, if not art markets, that the internet may enable. His online database sees 7,000 visits a month, which he says come from "educators, archaeologists, art restorers and even tattoo artists."

With these new entrants into the art world of Mesoamerican antiquities, our greatest challenge will be to clearly explain why owning objects should not be a desirable goal. We need to develop better arguments directed out to the wider publics so that they understand that our knowledge about the past is not contained in things, but in the relationships of things to each other, and even to the ideally undisturbed sediments where the traces of past activities might be teased out. We need to make the shift to communicating to the broader public that is exemplified by Yates's well-regarded blog, which Sellen singles out for extended discussion. If not, we may well have to look forward to a world in which the technologies that overcome distance serve primarily to extend the art market through auction sites, perpetuating the structure of the art world that came together in the mid-twentieth century. If we are successful, what will emerge may well blur many lines we have treated as indelible, uniting museums whose collecting history is less than ideal with archaeologists to educate broader publics about the importance of protecting heritage sites, and pairing specialist researchers with descendant and source communities, not simply nations, in shared projects of cultural representation. The scope we need to address cannot be contained under the rubric of the market; it is time for us to reimagine the world.

References Cited

AAMD. 2013. *Revisions to the 2008 Guidelines on the Acquisition of Archaeological Material and Ancient Art.* Association of Art Museum Directors, January 29, 2013. https://aamd.org/standards-and-practices (accessed September 30, 2018).

Becker, Howard S. 1982. *Art Worlds.* Berkeley: University of California Press.

Boone, Elizabeth Hill (editor). 1993. *Collecting the Pre-Columbian Past.* Washington, D.C.: Dumbarton Oaks Research Library and Collection.

Brodie, Neil. 2015. "The Internet Market in Antiquities." In *Countering Illicit Traffic In Cultural Goods: The Global Challenge Of Protecting The World's Heritage,* edited by France Desmarais, 11–20. Paris: ICOM.

Chinchilla, Oswaldo. 1998. "Archaeology and Nationalism in Guatemala at the Time of Independence." *Antiquity* 72: 376–387.

Coggins, Clemency C. 1969. "Illicit Traffic of Pre-Columbian Antiquities." *Art Journal* 29 (1): 94, 96, 98, 114.

ICE. 2011. *Cultural Property, Art, and Antiquities Investigations: Salvadoran Maya Artifacts.*

>#>

U.S. Immigration and Customs Enforcement, December 12, 2011. https://www.ice.gov/factsheets/cultural-artifacts (accessed September 30, 2018).

Joyce, Rosemary A. 2003. "Archaeology and Nation Building: A View from Central America." In *The Politics of Archaeology and Identity in a Global Context,* edited by Susan Kane, 79–100. Boston: Archaeological Institute of America.

———. 2005. "Solid Histories for Fragile Nations: Archaeology as Cultural Patrimony." In *Embedding Ethics*, edited by Lynn M. Meskell and Peter Pels, 253–273. Oxford: Berg.

———. 2006. "The Monumental and the Trace: Archaeological Conservation and the Materiality of the Past." In *Of the Past, For the Future: Integrating Archaeology and Conservation,* edited by Neville Agnew and Janet Bridgland, 13–18. Los Angeles: Getty Conservation Institute.

———. 2013. "When is Authentic? Situating Authenticity in Itineraries of Objects." In *What is Authenticity?*, edited by Alex Geurds and Laura van Broekhaven, 39–57. Leiden: National Ethnographic Museum.

———. 2017. *Painted Pottery From Honduras: Object Itineraries and Lives*. Leiden: Brill.

Levine, Marc N. and Lucha Martínez de Luna. 2013. "Museum Salvage: A Case Study of Mesoamerican Artifacts in Museum Collections and on the Antiquities Market." *Journal of Field Archaeology* 38: 264–276.

Lyons, Claire. 2002. "Objects and Identities: Claiming and Reclaiming the Past." In *Claiming the Stones, Naming the Bones: Cultural Property and the Negotiation of National and Ethnic Identity*, edited by Elazar Barkan and Ronald Bush, 116–137. Los Angeles: The J. Paul Getty Trust.

Matsuda, David. 1998. "The Ethics of Archaeology, Subsistence Digging, and Artifact Looting in Latin America: Point, Muted Counterpoint." *International Journal of Cultural Property* 7: 87–97.

2

U.S. Collaboration with Mesoamerican Countries
to Protect Cultural Property

ALLISON R. DAVIS

International agreements are important tools to combat looting and trafficking of cultural property. The Convention on Cultural Property Implementation Act (CPIA)[1] allows the United States to enter into an agreement with another country when pillage threatens its cultural heritage. To date, the United States has entered into 18 agreements under the CPIA, including agreements with the Mesoamerican countries of El Salvador, Guatemala, Honduras, and Belize.[2] What may appear to the public to be paper agreements truly represent ongoing collaboration between countries and specific programming to improve cultural property protection in the region.

Most previous scholarship on the CPIA has focused on the import restrictions created by agreements that allow U.S. law enforcement to better control what enters the American market. Most authors describe the legal provisions and processes to enter into an agreement and establish import restrictions (e.g., Gerstenblith 2017 and Papa Sokal 2006). Some highlight the difficulty of enforcing an agreement's country-specific import restrictions compared with enforcing object-specific import restrictions created by other laws (e.g., Yates 2014, 2015a, 2015b). Relatively little attention has been directed at the cooperative relationships and programming between the United States and partner countries.

This chapter traces the origin of the United States' collaborative approach to protecting the cultural heritage of Mesoamerica, beginning with early recognition by the U.S. government that looting and trafficking of cultural property is an international problem. Although the initial response of the United States did not require engagement with Mesoamerican countries suffering looting at archaeological sites and thefts in museums, the most significant U.S. efforts to combat cultural property trafficking result from the CPIA's use of international agreements to implement part of the 1970 UNESCO Convention on the Means of Prohibiting and Preventing the Illicit Import, Export and Transfer of Ownership of Cultural Property (the Convention). In fact, Gerstenblith (2012, 15) has described the resulting relationships and cooperation between countries as among the most significant impacts of the U.S. approach to implementing the Convention.

Agreements implementing Article 9 of the Convention create cooperative relationships in part because of the efforts the CPIA requires of the United States and the partner country, and in part because of the established practice of undertaking joint activities to increase in situ protection of the types of materials that are subject to U.S. import restrictions. Examples of U.S.-supported programming to support the agreements with each Mesoamerican country highlight how the types of activities have changed over time as cultural heritage protection advances and new threats emerge.

Unilateral and Complementary Actions to Protect Cultural Heritage

At the end of the 1960s and the beginning of the 1970s, looting at archaeological sites increased around the world. This was especially true in the Maya area of Central America, where the most attractive decorative elements were removed by brute force from structures and monuments. At the same time, the types of items taken by looters increasingly appeared on display in U.S. museums and institutions. This trend was famously exposed by Coggins in 1969,[3] and Tremain (2017) has recently documented the complementary trend in sales of Pre-Columbian objects at one auction house that began in the 1960s and peaked in the 1980s.

Most looted objects were acquired or offered for sale outside their countries of origin, and the international community began to realize that the destruction of cultural heritage was an international problem that required an international response. In the 1960s, countries convened at UNESCO to draft an instrument. The United States was the only major market country to participate in drafting and negotiating the text that later became the Convention. While most countries that were losing their cultural heritage to the market viewed the Convention as an opportunity to shift regulatory responsibilities to importing countries, the United States maintained that efforts to prevent import of looted cultural property should be balanced by increased efforts to protect cultural heritage in context (Efrat 2009, 35).

In the end, most of the Convention specified actions that can be taken unilaterally by any country. Yet the Convention also created a window for collaboration among States Parties in Article 9:

> Any State Party to this Convention whose cultural patrimony is in jeopardy from pillage of archaeological or ethnological materials may call upon other States Parties who are affected. The States Parties to this Convention undertake, in these circumstances, to participate in *a concerted international effort to determine and to carry out the necessary concrete measures*, including the control of exports and imports and international commerce in the specific materials concerned. Pending agreement each State concerned shall take provisional measures to the extent feasible to prevent irremediable injury to the cultural heritage of the requesting State.[4] (emphasis added)

Eventually, the most significant efforts by the United States to combat looting and trafficking of cultural property would grow from this collaborative provision in Article 9 into the CPIA. However, the first U.S. domestic legislation to protect the cultural heritage of Mesoamerica took unilateral action that did not engage other countries or require any action from them.

In October 1972, Congress passed the Regulation of Importation of Pre-Columbian Monumental or Architectural Sculpture or Murals (the Pre-Columbian statute).[5] This law applies to any stone carving or wall art that is the product of a Pre-Columbian indigenous culture of Mexico, Central America, South America, or the Caribbean Islands that was, or was part of, an immobile monument or structure. The Pre-Columbian statute prohibits import of these objects when they have been exported from the country of origin without a certification that the export was not in violation of its laws. The logic of the statute is that preventing looted and stolen items from entering U.S. collections and markets will reduce the motivation for future looting in Mesoamerica and other countries in the Americas. The Pre-Columbian statute is a unilateral measure that applies to a few types of cultural property without requiring action from those countries. In this case, the burden falls on only the U.S. government to implement the import restriction.

Shortly before the Pre-Columbian statute was passed, the United States Senate gave unanimous advice and consent to the Convention in August

1972, with the understanding that the Convention was not self-executing and would require domestic legislation for implementation. It was not until 1983 that Congress passed the CPIA to implement some articles of the Convention and the United States became a State Party. The CPIA shares the underlying logic of the Pre-Columbian statute, that preventing stolen and looted cultural property from entering the United States should reduce the incentive to loot in other countries. However, the CPIA is not unilateral. At a minimum, it requires actions by the source country and the United States. To be most effective, the CPIA requires engagement between them.

The nature of actions and engagement varies for stolen and looted cultural property. To prevent stolen cultural property from entering the United States, the CPIA requires relatively minimal action from the source country. The statute prohibits import of stolen material documented as part of the inventory of a museum or religious or secular public monument or similar institution.[6] This provision of the CPIA mirrors closely and implements Article 7(b)(1) of the Convention, which calls on States Parties to undertake "to prohibit the import of cultural property stolen from a museum or a religious or secular public monument or similar institution in another State Party to this Convention after the entry into force of this Convention for the States concerned, provided that such property is documented as appertaining to the inventory of that institution."[7] In order for this import restriction to apply to material from a particular country, the country must take only unilateral actions, including joining the Convention, inventorying cultural property, and documenting thefts.

Paper Agreements Create Collaborative Relationships

The CPIA requires direct engagement and collaboration between countries to prevent cultural property that has not been documented, such as looted archaeological material, from entering the United States. This engagement begins when a State Party to the Convention requests assistance from the United States under Article 9 of the Convention. In order to request assistance, a country must compile and present facts related to four determinations that must be made to enter into an agreement:

(A) that the cultural patrimony of the State Party is in jeopardy from the pillage of archaeological materials of the State Party;

(B) that the State Party has taken measures consistent with the Convention to protect its cultural patrimony;

(C) that (i) the application of the import restrictions . . . with respect to archaeological or ethnological material of the State Party, if applied in concert with similar restrictions implemented, or to be implemented within a reasonable period of time, by those nations (whether or not State Parties) individually having a significant import trade in such material, would be of substantial benefit in deterring a serious situation of pillage, and (ii) remedies less drastic than the application of the restrictions . . . are not available

(D) that the application of the import restrictions . . . is consistent with the general interest of the international community in the interchange of cultural property among nations for scientific, cultural, and educational purposes.[8]

Gathering information related to the determinations is a time-consuming and nearly government-wide effort including cultural officials, police, customs, the judiciary, and diplomats, at minimum. The State Department, including the relevant embassy, works with the requesting government to ensure sufficient information is available to evaluate each determination. During this back-and-forth interaction, the two governments develop important and enduring working-level relationships. In addition, the State Department's Cultural Heritage Center collects input from nongovernmental stakeholders and carries out research and analysis that enhances information provided by the requesting government.

The Cultural Property Advisory Committee (the Committee) draws upon this information to investigate and review each request before making recommendations to the State Department.[9] This process draws insights from all stakeholder groups represented on the Committee, which includes members representing the interests of museums; experts in the fields of archaeology, anthropology, or related areas; experts in the international sale of archaeological, ethnological, and other cultural property; and members who represent the interests of the general public.[10] If the Committee concludes that the four determinations above can be made, it may recommend entering into an agreement. If it concludes that a separate emergency condition exists, the Committee may recommend that import restrictions are imposed on an emergency basis, with or without recommending an agreement.[11] The

Committee may also recommend terms and conditions it believes should be included in any agreement or should be applied alongside any emergency import restrictions.[12]

This extensive information gathering and intensive review leads to a unique understanding between the United States and the partner country regarding specific threats to particular categories of cultural property and the challenges to mitigating those threats. This understanding influences the final text of the agreement and shapes the programming carried out by each country while it is in force. This understanding is most visible to the public in Article II of each agreement, or in a joint action plan, which outlines goals that each country will work toward in order to improve protection of cultural property and to promote the exchange of archaeological and ethnological materials for scientific study or educational or cultural purposes. Luke and Kersel (2013, 17) have discussed the importance of Article II to U.S. public diplomacy.

If the State Department decides to enter into an agreement, U.S. Customs and Border Protection, the Department of Homeland Security, and the Department of the Treasury promulgate and enforce the import restrictions. These import restrictions apply to designated categories of archaeological and/or ethnological material as defined by the statute.[13] Although items that fit the designated categories need not be documented in an inventory or reported stolen for import restrictions to apply, the source country and the United States must take numerous actions and continuously engage to enter into and implement an agreement. The reward for these efforts is an enforcement tool that is highly unusual in the United States. If the U.S. government demonstrates that imported material is designated under the import restrictions, the burden shifts to the importer to demonstrate that an item was exported lawfully or that other statutory conditions are met.[14]

For the United States, significant activity supports the Committee's continuing review of the effectiveness of the agreement.[15] The State Department continues to engage with the partner government and nongovernmental stakeholders to collect information for review. When an agreement is due to expire after a maximum of five years, the Committee and the State Department must once again gather and examine information related to the four determinations, which must be made again to extend an agreement.

For the potential partner country, most activity related to the agreement is focused on improving protection of cultural heritage with an eye toward satisfying the four determinations and with guidance for specific measures outlined in Article II. For example, Determination B, "that the State Party has taken measures consistent with the Convention to protect its cultural patrimony," is brief language that refers to a wide array of actions to monitor and protect cultural heritage, to raise public awareness, and to penalize or sanction persons who violate laws related to the import, export, and transfer of cultural property. It is not possible to list the myriad potential activities enumerated in the 26-article Convention, but some examples include maintaining a national inventory of protected cultural property,[16] prohibiting export of cultural property without an authorizing certificate,[17] and prohibiting the import of cultural property stolen from a museum or public monument.[18]

Guidance for specific measures varies for each country based on the understanding gained during the process to enter into an agreement. Some provisions call on both the United States and the partner country to take action, especially regarding public awareness, law enforcement education, research cooperation, and loans for exhibition. However, many suggested activities could be taken by the source country alone if enough resources were available. For example, El Salvador famously designed and built a new national museum after the 1995 agreement specified that "in order to reestablish public and scholarly access to the collections in the 'David J. Guzman' National Museum which suffered structural damage during an earthquake, the Government of the Republic of El Salvador will use its best efforts to reopen the Museum at the earliest practicable time."[19]

In truth, many of the goals in the agreements require significant undertakings in countries with limited resources. Recognizing this situation, agreements typically call for collaborative programming and assistance from the United States. The following section presents examples of U.S.-supported projects with each Mesoamerican country that has an agreement with the United States under the CPIA: El Salvador, Guatemala, Honduras, and Belize. The subsequent discussion contrasts these agreements with a treaty between Mexico and the United States that precedes the CPIA and has not led to similar programming and engagement.

Decades of Collaborative Programming in Mesoamerica

Over a period of more than two decades, myriad programs and projects have supported the agreements with Mesoamerican countries. Regrettably, it would be impossible to enumerate every activity undertaken.[20] Instead, two U.S.-supported projects have been selected for each country: one early program undertaken shortly after entering into each agreement and one more recent program.[21] These examples demonstrate continued collaborative engagement between the United States and Mesoamerican countries as the review of agreements has identified new threats to cultural heritage and the available sources of U.S. support have changed.

El Salvador

El Salvador was the first country in Mesoamerica to request assistance under the CPIA,[22] and it was the first country in the world to receive it when the United States imposed emergency import restrictions on archaeological material from the Cara Sucia region in 1987.[23] El Salvador subsequently became the first country to enter into a bilateral agreement with the United States to create import restrictions under the CPIA on March 8, 1995.[24]

Early on, review and extension of the emergency import restrictions revealed that cultural property in El Salvador needed to be inventoried to protect items from theft and facilitate their recovery if they were stolen. In 1993, El Salvador passed the Special Law for Protection of the Cultural Patrimony of El Salvador, which required documentation in the Registry of Cultural Property. The United States Information Agency (USIA), which was delegated the President's relevant authorities under the CPIA at that time, sponsored an assessment with the Getty Art History Information Program. Two U.S. experts traveled to El Salvador to advise on what kinds of technical assistance would be helpful to register cultural property, for example designing a record keeping system and establishing procedures. Addressing the same issue, the 1995 agreement specified both that "[the] Government of the United States of America will use its best efforts to facilitate technical assistance in cultural resource management and security to El Salvador, as appropriate under existing programs in the public and/or private sectors"[25] and that "the Government of the Republic of El Salvador . . . will use its best efforts to proceed expeditiously with the registration of cultural property as required by its law."[26]

Review of any agreement typically finds that it remains necessary to publicize it and the associated import restrictions in order to increase effectiveness. Even 20 years after the United States and El Salvador first entered the agreement, the 2015 amendment specified that "representatives of both governments shall publicize [the agreement] and its purposes through appropriate means, including to law enforcement and the public."[27] In 2016, the State Department created a new online platform to help law enforcement and the public identify cultural objects subject to import restrictions. The Government of El Salvador supplied photographs to illustrate the types of materials protected by U.S. import restrictions created by the agreement.[28]

Guatemala

Guatemala was the fourth country to ask the United States for assistance under the CPIA,[29] shortly after newspaper and journal articles on the looting at Rio Azul brought international attention to the depredation of Guatemala's cultural heritage (see Adams 1986; Graham, 1986; Griffin 1986). In response, emergency import restrictions were imposed on Maya archaeological artifacts from the Petén region in 1991.[30] In 1997, the United States and Guatemala entered into an agreement to protect Pre-Columbian materials from throughout Guatemala.[31] In 2012, protections were expanded to include certain types of ecclesiastical material from the Conquest and Colonial periods (examples can be seen in the online platform mentioned previously).[32]

The 1997 agreement specified that "the Government of the Republic of Guatemala . . . will undertake an assessment with regard to improvements in broad areas such as law enforcement, cultural resource management, education, conservation, research, and the national museum system."[33] USIA's Cultural Specialist Program supported some of these goals in 1998, shortly after the two countries entered into the agreement. The Cultural Specialist Program was a U.S. government exchange program that sent American specialists to travel and work with a foreign institution for two to six weeks to address specific needs. Following a request from the U.S. Embassy in Guatemala City, Dr. James Brady went to work at the Institute of Anthropology and History for three weeks to provide consultation and technical assistance regarding establishing an archaeological materials laboratory at the national museum. Among other activities, he worked with an architect on plans and advised on ways in which the lab could be most easily used by scholars.

Over the life of the agreement with Guatemala, it has become increasingly clear that protection of the country's cultural heritage is complicated by the colocation of rich archaeological sites and areas facing intense challenges to governance and law enforcement. This difficult context is captured in the agreement and reflected in programming. For example, the 2012 amendment to the agreement states that "the Government of the United States of America shall use its best efforts to facilitate technical assistance in cultural resource management and security to Guatemala, as appropriate under existing programs in the public and/or private sectors, particularly recognizing the increasing destabilizing influence of drug traffickers in the Central American region."[34]

Since 2002, the U.S. Department of the Interior's International Technical Assistance Program (DOI-ITAP) has worked with the Government of Guatemala to strengthen governance of the Maya Biosphere Reserve, a large protected area in the Northern Petén containing a complex archaeological landscape, including the archaeological sites of Tikal and El Mirador. The reserve is affected by growing criminal activities such as archaeological looting, drug trafficking, illegal logging, human-caused wildfires, wildlife trafficking, and illegal roads and human settlements. The program includes projects that directly address cultural heritage protection, such as training judges and prosecutors on environmental and cultural legislation, strengthening field patrols by park guards, developing tourism, and enhancing field protection at the archaeological sites of El Perú/Waka', La Corona, and El Mirador. These cultural heritage-focused activities take place among an even broader set of projects meant to work together to strengthen environmental governance. The program continues to operate and is financed by the U.S. Congress Direct Apportionment (via the United States Agency for International Development, USAID), and the Department of State under the CAFTA-DR Free Trade Agreement's Environmental Cooperation Agreement. Local partners in Guatemala include the Wildlife Conservation Society, Balam Association, and the Environmental Justice Forum of Petén.[35] The collaborative project leveraged funds from the Guatemalan private sector via Pacunam, a Guatemalan nongovernmental organization providing important in-country leadership.

Honduras

Honduras requested assistance under the CPIA to protect Pre-Columbian archaeological material in 2001,[36] and the United States and Honduras entered into a bilateral agreement in 2004.[37] Similar to the 2012 amendment to the agreement with Guatemala, certain Colonial period ecclesiastical material was added to the U.S.-Honduras agreement in 2014 at Honduras's request due to increasing thefts.[38]

Review of the initial request identified the need to enhance management of archaeological sites, including raising public awareness regarding the importance of their protection. As a result, the 2004 agreement specified that "the Government of the United States of America shall use its best efforts to facilitate technical assistance to Honduras in cultural resource management and security, as appropriate under existing programs in the public and/or private sectors."[39]

By that time, the State Department had created a new grant program dedicated to conserving cultural heritage abroad. The U.S. Ambassadors Fund for Cultural Preservation (the Ambassadors Fund) continues to support conservation of sites, objects, and forms of traditional cultural expression in more than 120 countries around the world. Since the program began in 2001, projects in Mesoamerican countries have received 6.1% of all funds awarded, totaling $4.4 million to support 65 projects in Belize, Costa Rica, El Salvador, Guatemala, Honduras, Mexico, Nicaragua, and Panama.

Prior to the 2004 agreement, the Ambassadors Fund awarded grants to three projects related to indigenous language preservation in Honduras. In 2005, U.S. Embassy Tegucigalpa nominated a project that had the added benefit of supporting the agreement. This project to protect four visitor circuits containing 16 rock art sites in central and southern Honduras was selected for funding, and the project was designed and carried out by the Honduran Institute of Anthropology and History (IHAH). It included a public awareness campaign about the importance of cultural heritage, a personnel training program, and a plan to publicize information about the sites. In addition to conservation activities, the project improved protection of petroglyphs, which were subject to U.S. import restrictions created pursuant to the agreement.

The 2009 extension review noted creation of an inter-institutional commission in 2007 to coordinate protection of cultural heritage, including IHAH, the Ministry of Culture, the Ministry of Tourism, Customs, INTERPOL, the National Police, the Attorney General, the Ministry of Foreign Affairs, the Association of Municipalities, and the Catholic Church. The 2009 agreement specified that "the Government of the Republic of Honduras shall continue to endorse and support the Inter-Institutional Commission for the protection of cultural patrimony; and shall engage agencies and institutions with responsibilities that might affect the cultural heritage, such as the departments of public works, transportation, and housing"[40] and that "the Government of the Republic of Honduras shall continue to apply its best efforts to implement and enforce its Law for the Protection of the Cultural Patrimony (Decree 220–97), and other decrees and legislative measures designed to protect its archaeological heritage."[41]

During the life of the agreement in 2012, the Cultural Antiquities Task Force supported a workshop to address these goals. U.S. Congress created the Cultural Antiquities Task Force in 2004 to promote coordination among U.S. Government agencies and to demonstrate U.S. leadership in international efforts to protect cultural heritage, including through projects that improve cultural property protection in foreign countries. The workshop in Honduras brought together expert instructors from the U.S. private sector, IHAH, the special prosecutor's office, and the International Council on Monuments and Sites (ICOMOS). Workshop participants included IHAH personnel, special prosecutors and investigators, the national police, Interpol, and staff from museum and cultural heritage sites. Participants carried out security needs assessments at seven locations in and around Tegucigalpa that hold objects at risk of looting and trafficking, including museums, cultural institutions, a colonial church, and other storerooms. At each location, students made practical improvements such as locks, alarms, and surveillance cameras.

Belize

Belize was the last Mesoamerican country to request assistance under the CPIA in 2011.[42] In 2013, the United States and Belize entered into an agreement to protect Pre-Columbian and Colonial archaeological material.[43] Investigation of the request for the agreement revealed that the relatively limited government presence in areas with increasing criminal activity leaves many small and medium-sized sites in Belize vulnerable to looting and trafficking. The 2013 agreement recognized the importance of participation by governmental and nongovernmental actors in this context and stipulated that "both Governments shall seek to encourage academic institutions, non-governmental institutions, and other organizations to cooperate in the interchange of knowledge and information about the cultural patrimony of Belize, and to collaborate in the preservation and protection of such cultural patrimony, particularly through best practices in conservation and training."[44] Like the 2012 agreement with Guatemala, it also specified that "the Government of the United States of America shall use its best efforts to facilitate technical assistance in cultural resource management and security to Belize, as appropriate under existing programs in the public and/or private sectors, particularly recognizing the increasing destabilizing influence of drug traffickers in the Central American region."[45]

The earliest programming associated with the agreement addressed both these provisions. In 2014, the Cultural Antiquities Task Force supported a cultural heritage protection project that included a workshop for national law enforcement and three community outreach activities. Participants from around Belize were selected by the National Institute of Culture and History (NICH) and included heritage site managers, government archaeologists, museum staff, and police and customs officers. U.S. expert instructors were drawn from the National Park Service, Federal Bureau of Investigation, Homeland Security Investigations, the Department of State's Cultural Heritage Center, a Department of Justice prosecutor, and Archaeology in the Community (a nongovernmental organization with expertise in community outreach). In addition to training activities, this project identified future needs and potential measures that could be taken to improve cultural heritage management and protection.

Following this program, U.S. Embassy Belmopan and NICH joined with Archaeology in the Community to bring archaeology into schools and communities throughout the country. Mock excavation exercises raised awareness about the importance of maintaining archaeological sites and artifacts intact so that professional archaeologists can excavate, document, and record them. A major component of this program explained national legislation and highlighted the importance of not selling, exchanging, or destroying cultural property because it holds irreplaceable and important information about Belize's culture and history. This project continues Belize's longstanding engagement with young students. Since the 1980s, Belize has used school education programs to promote good stewardship of archaeological cultural heritage (Chase et al. 1988, 60).

Discussion

The agreements between the United States and Mesoamerican countries are more than paper documents. Not only do they underpin U.S. import restrictions, specific programming to support the agreements also improves protection of cultural heritage in context. Review of requests and agreements in force helps to identify existing and emerging challenges in Mesoamerica as well as opportunities to address these challenges, including through U.S.-supported programming in collaboration with partner governments and nongovernmental organizations. These programs embody the "concrete measures" called for in Article 9 of the Convention.

Over a period of more than two decades, the varied characteristics of collaborative programs in Mesoamerica reflect advances in cultural heritage protection, new threats, and available sources of support. The earliest programs in the region supported the agreements with El Salvador and Guatemala and used U.S. government exchange programs to help partner governments assess fundamental needs for managing moveable cultural property, including establishing a national inventory and archaeological materials lab.

Since then, programming themes have shifted to include engaging local communities in site protection and strengthening law enforcement related to cultural heritage crimes. These new themes reflect advances since the 1990s in establishing national services and processes for basic protections such as inventories. They also reflect the growing recognition that conflict and transnational organized crime threaten cultural heritage around the world. In 2004, the Cultural Antiquities Task Force became available to support programs that strengthen law enforcement capacity and coordination related to cultural property protection. In Mesoamerica specifically, many projects that support the goals of the agreements take place as part of broader efforts to strengthen governance in areas with existing and growing criminal activity. These programs are often supported by U.S. foreign assistance programs, for example USAID or DOI-ITAP. Although the U.S. Ambassadors Fund for Cultural Preservation was created in 2001 to conserve cultural heritage rather than combat cultural property trafficking, best practices in conservation typically include documentation, professional development, and community engagement that result in enhanced protection.

Many other U.S. government programs have and continue to support the goals of the agreements, including exchange programs such as the Fulbright Program, the International Visitor Leadership Program, and the National Park Service World Heritage Fellows Program. In 2009, the State Department brought public and law enforcement attention to the problem by supporting the International Council of Museums (ICOM) Red List of Endangered Cultural Objects of Central America and Mexico.[46] As Luke (2012) has noted for Honduras, networks of scholars built during research funded by U.S. government entities, such as the National Science Foundation and National Endowment for the Humanities, enable more successful implementation of many programs undertaken in the framework of the agreements. In addition, nongovernmental organizations and the private sector have carried out significant projects that contribute to the protection of cultural heritage in the region.

Ongoing engagement, working-level relationships, and collaborative programming are unique to agreements entered into under the CPIA. Two agreements with Mesoamerican countries predating the CPIA illustrate this point. Early on, the Treaty of Cooperation between the United States of America and the United Mexican States Providing for the Recovery and Return of Stolen Archaeological, Historical and Cultural Properties was signed in Mexico City on July 17, 1970, and entered into force on March 24, 1971.[47] More than a decade later, the Agreement between the United States of America and the Republic of Guatemala for the Recovery and Return of Stolen Archaeological, Historical, and Cultural Properties was signed in Washington, D.C. on May 21, 1984, and entered into force August 22, 1984. The United States and Guatemala entered into this agreement after the CPIA was passed, but before Guatemala became a State Party to the 1970 Condition on January 14, 1985, a requirement for requesting an agreement under the CPIA.

Both the 1970 treaty with Mexico and the 1984 agreement with Guatemala remain in force, but with very limited effects compared with agreements under the CPIA. Neither called for U.S. import restrictions. Rather, the parties agreed to employ legal means already at their disposal to recover and return stolen archaeological, historical, and cultural properties. More central to this discussion, neither instrument led to sustained engagement or collaborative programming, despite the fact that each agreement contains some provisions related to cooperation. For example, both instruments encourage research by scholars from both countries and the circulation of cultural property for exhibition to enhance appreciation of the cultural heritage of both countries. The most explicit statement regarding ongoing engagement is in the treaty with Mexico, which stipulates that "representatives of the two countries, including qualified scientists and scholars, shall meet from time to time to consider matters relating to the implementation of these undertakings."[48] Even with that provision, such meetings have not taken place. The existence of an international instrument does not guarantee increased collaboration and engagement. Rather, the processes to enter into and extend agreements that are required by the CPIA have resulted in concrete measures to improve protection of Mesoamerica's cultural heritage.

Conclusion

Previous scholarship on the CPIA has focused on the import restrictions created in an emergency condition or by agreements, with little attention given to programming that supports the goals for cultural heritage protection carried out in the framework of the agreements. This chapter provides a glimpse of some projects that the United States has supported in collaboration with partner governments and nongovernmental actors, highlighting the changing focus of programs in Mesoamerica, where some of the oldest agreements remain in force after more than 20 years. Project themes and activities emerge from the unique process required to enter into, implement, and extend agreements under the CPIA. This process sustains working relationships with partner governments and relies on intensive investigation and review by a committee of experts representing U.S. stakeholders from diverse fields.

Ultimately, U.S. support for projects to protect cultural heritage in situ should reduce the burden of policing the market for looted, stolen, and trafficked cultural property from Mesoamerica and other partner countries. However, the effectiveness of programs depends on accurate and up-to-date understanding of the challenges and opportunities particular to each country. In order to identify and support the best projects in each partner country, the U.S. government encourages the public to contribute expertise and knowledge by providing the Committee with information, research, and personal experience related to the determinations outlined in the CPIA.[49]

Acknowledgments

This chapter is dedicated to Maria Kouroupas. I am indebted to her not only for contributions to this work, but also for her wisdom and friendship as I pursued significant professional change. From the earliest agreement with Mesoamerica to her 2018 retirement from the Department of State's Cultural Heritage Center, she has imagined and enacted truly impactful programming that has made the United States a leader in cultural heritage protection and preservation.

Notes

1. *Convention on Cultural Property Implementation Act*, U.S. *Code* 19 (1983), § 2601 *et seq.*

2. The first agreement under the CPIA was with El Salvador in 1995 followed by Canada, Peru, Mali, Guatemala, Nicaragua, Italy, Bolivia, Cambodia, Honduras, Colombia, Cyprus, China, Greece, Belize, Bulgaria, Egypt, and Libya. Each of these agreements remains in force except for the agreement with Canada, which expired in 2002. For more information, see https://eca.state.gov/cultural-heritage-center/cultural-property-advisory-committee/current-import-restrictions (accessed May 15, 2019).

3. For later documentation of looting and trafficking of monumental sculpture predating the Pre-Columbian statute, see Coggins 1972; Reinhold 1973a, 1973b; and Freidel 2000.

4. "Convention on the Means of Prohibiting and Preventing the Illicit Import, Export and Transfer of Ownership of Cultural Property," art 9.

5. *Regulation of Importation of Pre-Columbian Monumental or Architectural Sculpture or Murals*, U.S. *Code* 19 (1972), § 2091 *et seq.*

6. *Convention on Cultural Property Implementation Act*, § 2607.

7. "Convention on the Means of Prohibiting and Preventing the Illicit Import, Export and Transfer of Ownership of Cultural Property," art 7.b.1.

8. *Convention on Cultural Property Implementation Act*, § 2602(a)(1).

9. This chapter describes the process as it is carried out today. Previously, authorities were delegated to U.S. government agencies that no longer exist, including the United States Information Agency and the United States Customs Service.

10. As required by *Convention on Cultural Property Implementation Act*, § 2605(b)(1).

11. *Convention on Cultural Property Implementation Act*, § 2603 *et seq.* For one Committee member's experience, see von Falkenhausen (2016), "Trying to Do the Right Thing."

12. *Convention on Cultural Property Implementation Act*, § 2605(f)(4)(A).

13. *Convention on Cultural Property Implementation Act*, § 2604.

14. *Convention on Cultural Property Implementation Act*, § 2606.

15. *Convention on Cultural Property Implementation Act*, § 2605(g).

16. "Convention on the Means of Prohibiting and Preventing the Illicit Import, Export and Transfer of Ownership of Cultural Property," art 5.b.

17. "Convention on the Means of Prohibiting and Preventing the Illicit Import, Export and Transfer of Ownership of Cultural Property," art 6.b.

18. "Convention on the Means of Prohibiting and Preventing the Illicit Import, Export and Transfer of Ownership of Cultural Property," art 7.b.1.

19. United States, "Memorandum of Understanding, United States and El Salvador," art. II.G; see discussions in Gerstenblith 2017, 11; Kouroupas 1998, 71.

20. Although the agreements with El Salvador, Guatemala, Honduras, and Belize are titled as "Memoranda of Understanding," I refer to them as "agreements" for consistency with the preceding discussion of the CPIA.

21. For contemporary discussions of the earliest activities to support agreements, see Kouroupas (1998), "Illicit Trade in Cultural Objects" and Kouroupas (1995), "U.S. Efforts to Protect Cultural Property."

22. United States Information Agency 1987.

23. U.S. Department of the Treasury 1987.

24. United States 1995; U.S. Department of the Treasury 1995.

25. United States, "Memorandum of Understanding, United States and El Salvador," art. II.C.

26. United States, "Memorandum of Understanding, United States and El Salvador," art. II.E.

27. United States, "Memorandum of Understanding, United States and El Salvador," amend. March 8, 2015, art. II.A.

28. Department of State, Bureau of Educational and Cultural Affairs. "Photo Guides for Import Restrictions." http://culturalproperty.state.gov (accessed December 4, 2018). A photo guide is also available for material from Guatemala.

29. United States Information Agency 1989.

30. U.S. Department of the Treasury 1991.

31. United States 1997; U.S. Department of the Treasury 1991, 1997.

32. United States, "Memorandum of Understanding, United States and Guatemala," amend. Sept. 29, 2012; U.S. Department of the Treasury 2012.

33. United States, "Memorandum of Understanding, United States and Guatemala," art. II.J.

34. United States, "Memorandum of Understanding, United States and Guatemala," amend. Sept. 29, 2012, art. II.C. Similar provisions appear in earlier amendments to the agreement: United States, "Memorandum of Understanding, United States and Guatemala," amend. Sept. 29, 2002, art. II.B; United States, "Memorandum of Understanding, United States and Guatemala," amend. Sept. 29, 2007, art. II.B.

35. U.S. Department of the Interior 2018.

36. U.S. Department of State 2001.

37. United States 2004; U.S. Department of Homeland Security 2004.

38. United States, "Memorandum of Understanding, United States and Honduras," amend. March 12, 2014; U.S. Department of Homeland Security 2014.

39. United States, "Memorandum of Understanding, United States and Honduras," art. II.B.

40. United States, "Memorandum of Understanding, United States and Honduras," amend. March 12, 2009, art. II.J.

41. United States, "Memorandum of Understanding, United States and Honduras," amend. March 12, 2009, art. II.G.

42. U.S. Department of State 2011.

43. United States 2013; U.S. Department of Homeland Security 2013.

44. United States, "Memorandum of Understanding, United States and Belize," art II.e.

45. United States, "Memorandum of Understanding, United States and Belize," art II.g.

46. ICOM previously published a Red List of Latin American Cultural Objects at Risk in 2003 that contained examples of Pre-Columbian and Colonial heritage categories from throughout Latin America.

47. The U.S.-Mexico treaty of cooperation is the only executive agreement regarding cultural property for which the U.S. Senate has approved a resolution of advice and consent to ratification. In other words, it is the only true treaty as defined in the Article II, Section 2, of the U.S. Constitution.

48. "Treaty of Cooperation between the United States of America and the United Mexican States Providing for the Recovery and Return of Stolen Archaeological, Historical and Cultural Properties," art. II.2.

49. See https://eca.state.gov/cultural-heritage-center for information about how to provide information for upcoming requests and reviews of agreements (accessed February 9, 2018).

References Cited

Adams, Richard E. W. 1986. "Rio Azul." *National Geographic* 169 (4): 420–451.

Chase, Arlen F., Diane Z. Chase, and Harriot W. Topsey. 1988. "Archaeology and the Ethics of Collecting." *Archaeology* 41 (1): 56–60.

Coggins, Clemency. 1969. "Illicit Traffic of Pre-Columbian Antiquities." *Art Journal* 29 (1): 94–114.

———. 1972. "Archaeology and the Art Market." *Science* 175: 263–266.

Efrat, Asif. 2009. "Protecting against Plunder: The United States and the International Efforts against Looting of Antiquities." *Cornell Law Faculty Working Papers* 47: 1–87.

Freidel, David A. 2000. "Mystery of the Maya Façade." *Archaeology* 53 (5): 24.

Gerstenblith, Patty. 2012. "United States and Canada Expert Report for Participants in the Second Meeting of the States Parties to the 1970 Convention, Paris, UNESCO Headquarters, 20–21 June 2012." Paris: UNESCO.

———. 2017. "Implementation of the 1970 UNESCO Convention by the United States and other Market Nations." In *The Routledge Companion to Cultural Property*, edited by Jane Anderson and Haidy Geismar, 70–88. London and New York: Routledge.

Graham, Ian. 1986. "Looters rob graves and history." *National Geographic* 169 (4): 452–461.

Griffin, Gillet G. 1986. "In defense of the collector." *National Geographic* 169 (4): 462–465.

Kouroupas, Maria Papageorge. 1995. "U.S. Efforts to Protect Cultural Property: Implementation of the 1970 UNESCO Convention." *African Arts* 28 (4): 32–41.

———. 1998. "Illicit Trade in Cultural Objects." *Conservation: The GCI Newsletter* 13 (1).

Luke, Christina. 2012. "The Science behind United States Smart Power in Honduras: Archaeological Heritage Diplomacy." *Diplomacy & Statecraft* 23 (1): 110–139.

Luke, Christina, and Morag M. Kersel. 2013. *U.S. Cultural Diplomacy and Archaeology*. New York: Routledge.

Papa Sokal, Maria. 2006. "The U.S. legal response to the protection of the world cultural heritage." In *Archaeology, Cultural Heritage, and the Antiquities Trade*, edited by Neil Brodie, Morag M. Kersel, Christina Luke, and Kathryn Walker Tubb, 36–67. Gainesville: University Press of Florida.

Reinhold, Robert. 1973a. "Looters Impede Scholars Studying Maya Mystery." *The New York Times*, March 26, 1973.

———. 1973b. "Traffic in Looted Maya Art is Diverse and Profitable." *The New York Times*, March 27, 1973.

Tremain, Cara Grace. 2017. "Fifty years of collecting: The sale of ancient Maya antiquities at Sotheby's." *International Journal of Cultural Property* 24 (2): 187–219.

UNESCO. 1970. *Convention on the Means of Prohibiting and Preventing the Illicit Import, Export and Transfer of Ownership of Cultural Property.* November 14, 1970.

United States. 1995. *Memorandum of Understanding Between the Government of the United States of America and the Government of the Republic of El Salvador Concerning the Imposition of Import Restrictions on Certain Categories of Archaeological Material from the Prehispanic Cultures of the Republic of El Salvador.* March 8, 1995.

———. 1997. *Memorandum of Understanding Between the Government of the United States of America and the Government of the Republic of Guatemala Concerning the Imposition of Import Restrictions on Archaeological Objects and Materials from the Pre-Columbian Cultures of Guatemala.* September 29, 1997.

———. 2004. *Memorandum of Understanding Between the Government of the United States of America and the Government of the Republic of Honduras Concerning the Imposition of Import Restrictions on Archaeological Material from the Pre-Columbian Cultures of Honduras.* March 12, 2004.

———. 2013. *Memorandum of Understanding Between the Government of the United States of America and the Government of Belize Concerning the Imposition of Import Restrictions on Categories of Archaeological Material Representing the Cultural Heritage of Belize from the Pre-Ceramic (Approximately 9000 B.C.), Pre-Classic, Classic, and Post-Classic Periods of the Pre-Columbian Era Through the Early and Late Colonial Periods.* February 27, 2013.

United States Information Agency. 1987. "Receipt of Cultural Property Request from the Government of El Salvador." *Federal Register* 57, no. 67 (April 8, 1987): 11413–11414.

———. 1989. "Receipt of Request for Import Restrictions from the Government of Guatemala Under the Convention on Cultural Property Implementation Act." *Federal Register* 54, no. 203 (October 23, 1989): 43213.

U.S. Congress, Senate. 1982. *Implementing Legislation for the Convention on the Means of Prohibiting and Preventing the Illicit Import, Export, and Transfer of Ownership of Cultural Property.* 97th Cong., 2nd sess., 1982, S. Doc. 97–564.

U.S. Department of Homeland Security, Bureau of Customs and Border Protection. 2004. "Import Restrictions Imposed on Archaeological Material Originating in Honduras," *Federal Register* 69, no. 51 (March 16, 2004): 12267–12271.

———. 2013. "Import Restrictions Imposed on Certain Archaeological Material From Belize," *Federal Register* 78, no. 43 (March 5, 2013): 14183–14185.

———. 2014. "Extension of Import Restrictions on Archaeological and Ecclesiastical Ethnological Materials from Honduras," *Federal Register* 79, no. 48 (March 12, 2014): 13873–13875.

U.S. Department of the Interior. International Technical Assistance Program. *Strengthening Environmental Governance in the Protected Areas of the Peten, Guatemala.* https://www.doi.gov/sites/doi.gov/files/uploads/doi-itap_factsheet_-_guatemala_overview_-_english_-_final_0.pdf (accessed February 9, 2018).

U.S. Department of State. 2001. "Notice of Receipt of Cultural Property Request From the Government of the Republic of Honduras," *Federal Register* 66, no. 184 (September 21, 2001): 48732.

———. 2011. "Notice of Receipt of Cultural Property Request From the Government of the Republic of Belize," *Federal Register* 76, no. 199 (October 14, 2011): 63985.

U.S. Department of the Treasury, Customs Service. 1987. "Import Restrictions on Archaeological Material from El Salvador," *Federal Register* 52, no. 176 (September 11, 1987): 34614–34616.

———. 1991. "Import Restrictions Imposed on Archaeological Artifacts from Guatemala," *Federal Register* 56, no. 72 (April 15, 1991): 15181–15182.

———. 1995. "Prehistoric Artifacts from El Salvador," *Federal Register* 60, no. 47 (March 10, 1995): 13352–13361.

———. 1997. "Import Restrictions Imposed on Archaeological Artifacts from Guatemala," *Federal Register* 62, no. 192 (October 3, 1997): 51771–51774.

———. 2012. "Extension of Import Restrictions on Archaeological and Ethnological Materials From Guatemala," *Federal Register* 77, no. 189 (September 28, 2012): 59541–59543.

Yates, Donna. 2014. "Displacement, Deforestation, and Drugs: Antiquities Trafficking and the Narcotics Support Economies of Guatemala." In *Cultural Property Crimes: An Overview and Analysis on Contemporary Perspectives and Trends*, edited by Joris Kila and Marc Balcells, 23–36. Leiden: Brill.

———. 2015a. "Reality and Practicality: Challenges to Effective Cultural Property Policy on the Ground in Latin America." *International Journal of Cultural Property* 22 (2–3): 337–356.

———. 2015b. "Illicit Cultural Property from Latin America: Looting, Trafficking, and Sale." In *Countering Illicit Traffic in Cultural Goods: The Global Challenge of Protecting the World's Heritage*, edited by France Desmarais, 33–45. Paris: ICOM.

von Falkenhausen, Lothar. 2016. "Trying to Do the Right Thing to Protect the World's Cultural Heritage: One Committee Member's Tale." In *Obama and Transnational American Studies*, edited by Alfred Hornung, 375–389. Heidelberg: Universitätsverlag.

3

Corporatism, Heritage, and Museums

Rigmarole in Central America, 1899–1950

CHRISTINA LUKE

The exploration of Central America sharpened in the late nineteenth century. Discovery defined this new area of conquest, and its material correlates secured an expedition's success. Among the most prized items from the Republic of Honduras were polychrome ceramics and marble vases attributed to the Ulua Valley. Expeditions also admired the stelae from Copan and nearby environs. The portable vases and casts (from the stelae) became desired objects—yet not without collusion. Dubious practices for exporting objects were also followed in Costa Rica and Colombia. Tweaking of information given on customs forms by archaeologists, museums, and sponsors, many of them corporate, became common practice and with it established patterns for hegemony and acquisition. The web of corporatism and the development of infrastructure that engulfed Central America by the late nineteenth century continued apace through the interwar period, facilitating access to territory and the mobility of artifacts.

Here narratives of place and policy give depth to the networks of travel and business in Honduras. Archaeologists leveraged the infrastructure provided by the Cuyamel Fruit and United Fruit companies: housing, entry into society (i.e., dinners, dances, tennis, golf, and fishing expeditions), transport in-country via plane and train, ship transport to the United States via the Great White Fleet, ease of in-country banking, and strategic influence at the borders (Honduran, Costa Rican, and U.S.) from corporate executives and diplomats. Today these narratives come from the personal correspondence, photographs, and notebooks of archaeologists held by Harvard University, the University of Pennsylvania Museum, and the Smithsonian Institution, as well as those embedded in the photographic collections of the United Fruit Company at the Baker Library at the Harvard Business School. I demonstrate that the heritage of Central America and the privilege afforded to archaeological expeditions moved well beyond the arc of the state and into the realm of the global economy.

Exploration

The archaeologies of place are often defined not by their creators, but rather by those who "discover" them. During the decades of discovery, the infamous explorer John Lloyd Stephens reveled in the monumentality of Copan. He sought to establish a museum in Boston that would rival those of Europe. To realize this goal, his initial plan was to purchase the site of Copan, which he did for US$50 in 1839 (about US$1,372 in 2018). Yet in 1845, a date that corresponded to national legislation aimed at site protection and nation building, the Honduran government revoked the deal (see Joyce 2003; Luke 2006; Molloy 2009; Roberts 2000; Stephens and Catherwood 1854).

Under the auspices of the Peabody Museum, the Harvard expedition to Copan in the late nineteenth century, first directed by John Owens and later George Byron Gordon, took plaster casts of sculptures owing to the impossibility of transporting the original material to the coast (see Hinsley 1985; Joyce 2001a, 2001b). Further to the east, the portable objects of the Ulua Valley lured explorers, archaeologists, museums, and collectors. By the late nineteenth century, polychrome pottery and marble vases were among the most coveted items (see Gordon 1921; Joyce 1986, 1993, 2017; Luke 2002, 2006, 2010, 2011; Luke and Henderson 2006; Luke et al. 2006; Reents-Budet 1994; Stone 1938). In turn, these expeditions ensured that by the early twentieth century northwest Honduras was famous for these material correlates: sculpture from Copan, polychrome pottery, and Ulua marble vases. The fieldwork of archaeologists Sylvanus Griswold Morley, Doris Zemurray Stone (1941), Dorothy Popenoe (Joyce 1994), Alfred Kidder (Ricketson and Kidder 1930), and William Strong (Strong et al. 1938) contributed further to a common understanding of the cultural history of Honduras. Their influence and interest guided the archaeological research agenda as much as it did the spheres of transit through which materials traveled.

Five institutions in the United States showed growing interest in the region: the American Museum of Natural History in New York, the Museum of the

American Indian (the Heye Foundation, the collections of which were later transferred to the Smithsonian's National Museum of the American Indian), the Peabody Museum of Ethnology and Archaeology at Harvard, the University of Pennsylvania Museum of Archaeology and Anthropology, and the Middle American Research Institute in New Orleans. Today these institutions are revered as reputable museums precisely because they put in place strict guidelines for, and/or ceased regular acquisition of, antiquities—at least by the 1970s and 1980s. These decisions corresponded to the global pivot toward discouraging purchase of unprovenanced collections, largely owing to the 1970 United Nations Educational, Scientific and Cultural Organization (UNESCO) Convention on the Means of Prohibiting and Preventing the Illicit Import, Export, and Transfer of Cultural Property. The archives, however, reveal fierce competition among these institutions at the turn of the twentieth century and through the late 1940s. These networks give us insight into the modes of collecting practices, the roles of archaeologists, the influence of museums, and the spheres of corporatism and espionage.

Agents

The late nineteenth and early twentieth century marked the coming out of archaeology as a formal discipline in the United States. Princeton University, Harvard University, and the University of Pennsylvania had among them the most robust programs. Funding flowed from wealthy elite patrons, many eager to source collections for U.S. museums. At first the race was on for material from the Mediterranean and Holy Land, yet interest quickly grew for material from Latin America. Antiquities from the region of Lake Yojoa and the Ulua Valley of northwestern Honduras (fig. 3.1) were of specific interest. Harvard's Peabody Museum, the Smithsonian Institution, and the American Museum of Natural History all began to amass collections—and thus also raised funds for expeditions.

Parallel with the expanding attention to the archaeology of Central America were the growing economic and military interests in the region, especially those of the British, the Americans, and the Germans. The construction of the Panama Canal displayed the growing might of the American arm and the nested relationships between government and business interests. The Germans in the region, too, demonstrated the long-reach game of securing footholds in peripheral areas and in so doing ruffling feathers of the imperial powers (see

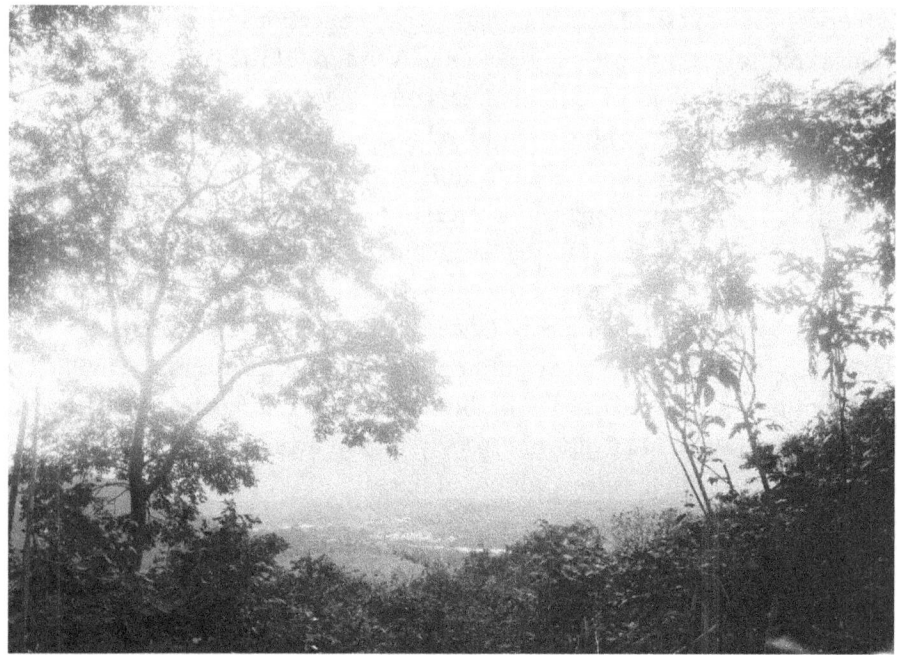

Figure 3.1. View of Pimienta taken from camp on Cerro de Palenque. Image by Dorothy Popenoe. Courtesy of the Peabody Museum of Archaeology and Ethnology, Harvard University, PM# 2004.24.11519.

Langley and Schoonover 2014; Munro 2015; Schoonover 1988; Schoonover and Schoonover 1989). Banana and coffee development as well as infrastructure in railroads, ports, and canals all spurred major investments (fig. 3.2). The railways (United Fruit/Tela Railroad Company and the Standard Fruit railway) along the north coast of Honduras to San Pedro Sula made further development possible. The United Fruit Company (UFCO) and the Cuyamel Fruit Company came to dominate the corporate landscape. The key person was Samuel Zemurray, president of Cuyamel Fruit (1911–1929) and later, president of UFCO (1933–1950).

To keep tabs on the activities of foreigners and to ensure the success of U.S. interests in the region, the U.S. Office of Naval Intelligence (ONI, established in 1882) set up operatives in Central America, among whom were archaeologists. This aspect was in part funded by the Carnegie Institution in Washington, which balanced their investment in science and the academy

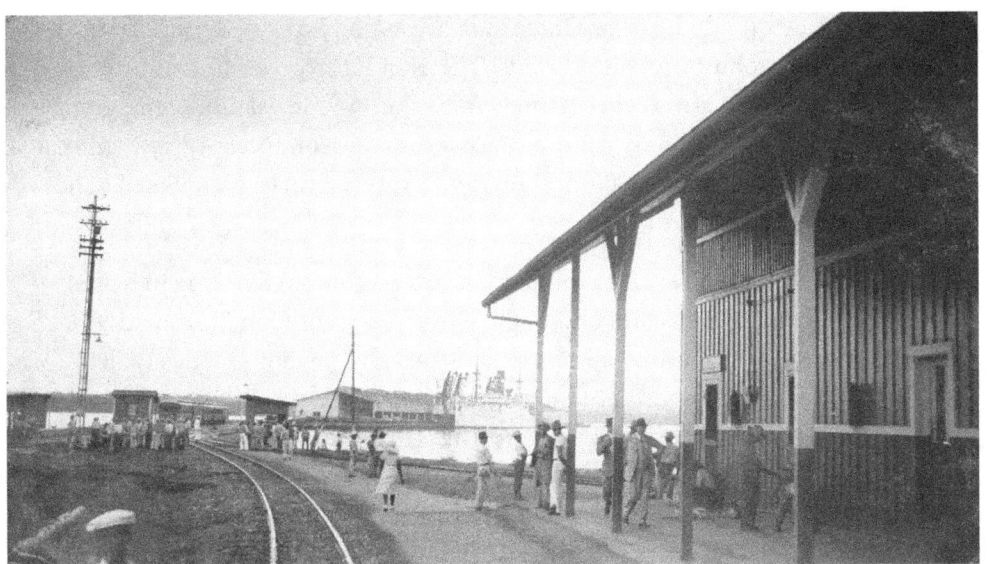

Figure 3.2. Puerto Barrios. The S.S. *Tela* is at dock alongside banana sheds with the railroad ticket office in the foreground. January 17, 1938. Scan of photograph from Judge Burt Cosgrove photo album. © Judge Burt Cosgrove. Courtesy of the Peabody Museum of Archaeology and Ethnology, Harvard University, PM# 2011.24.1.7.3.1.

with intelligence and security (see Castañeda 2005, 2010). These men (and one woman) had solid pedigrees, which smoothed their entry into expatriate business society (see Browman 2011; Harris and Sadler 2003). Archaeologists involved included Sylvanus Griswold Morley, Herbert Joseph Spinden, John Held Jr., and Samuel Kirkland Lothrop, all (save Held) with a Harvard pedigree. In addition, an eminent and well-respected botanist, Fredrick Wilson Popenoe, participated in espionage activities through his post as an Agricultural Explorer for the U.S. Department of Agriculture. He, too, was an associate of the Peabody Museum. Agents moved fluidly throughout the region and were able to recruit additional participants, such as Mr. J. T. Bennett, a U.S. citizen operating a hotel near San Pedro Sula, Honduras.

While many archaeologists such as Dorothy Popenoe (Wilson's wife) as well as members of the William D. Strong Expedition were not directly involved with espionage nor the powerful corporate structure of UFC, they benefited from the respective in-country infrastructure and external transit routes. Over the years, U.S. (and European) interest in the region expanded, and among the results was a robust antiquities trade. The Honduran government responded with increasingly strict legal frameworks. The 1900 legislation came on the heels of the 1899 Peabody Museum–Government Honduras Agreement that gave parameters for excavation, study, and export. Article 4 stipulated conditions for *partage*:

> The objects which shall be found in the excavation shall belong in halves to the Peabody Museum and to the Government of Honduras, with the special reservation that all precious metals and precious stones (jadeite or jade not being considered a precious stone) and any object which shall not have a duplicate, shall belong to the Government of Honduras. The division shall be made in such a way that all the objects of the same material or of a similar class shall be divided equally between the Peabody Museum and the Government of Honduras.

The tenets of the agreement were transformed in 1936 owing in large part to the persistent practices of aggressive export on behalf of Harvard and the Smithsonian (Luke 2006). The expansion of U.S. businesses in Central America between 1900 and 1936 enabled export of antiquities to such an extent that the practice (and the expectation) became the norm, rather than the exception.

Corporate Compounds

To locate our archaeologists in the context of corporate Honduras, I now turn to an overview of these networks. In addition to being a shrewd businessman, Sam Zemurray was a political shark. In 1911 he orchestrated the overthrow of the sitting President of Honduras (Miguel Dávila), putting in place his friend, Manuel Bonilla. This relationship proved very profitable for Zemurray. In fact, the scale of banana production in Honduras can be directly tied to the competitive corporate structure that he fostered. My entry points into the corporate world of bananas are the residential and social compounds at Tela along the Caribbean coast and La Lima near San Pedro Sula, arguably the heart of banana country. Photographic archives at the Baker Library of the Harvard Business School reveal the extensive transformation of Honduran landscapes by fruit companies.

The new rail line infrastructure connected the northern coast to the interior areas of the country, and plantations were connected to each other via rail. Extensive infrastructure was also required for water management, and over the course of two decades, the face of the landscape was embossed with a system of drainage and irrigation canals. Plantations also hosted factories and residential facilities for workers—and often schools, laboratories, and hospitals. Main company compounds, such as those in La Lima and Tela, included airfields for top executives; clubs with bars, game rooms, pools, tennis courts, and golf courses; and elaborate residences (figs. 3.3 and 3.4). The higher an individual was on the corporate ladder, the greater the size of his home, also reflected in ease of in-country and regional travel (i.e., via air rather than land or sea).

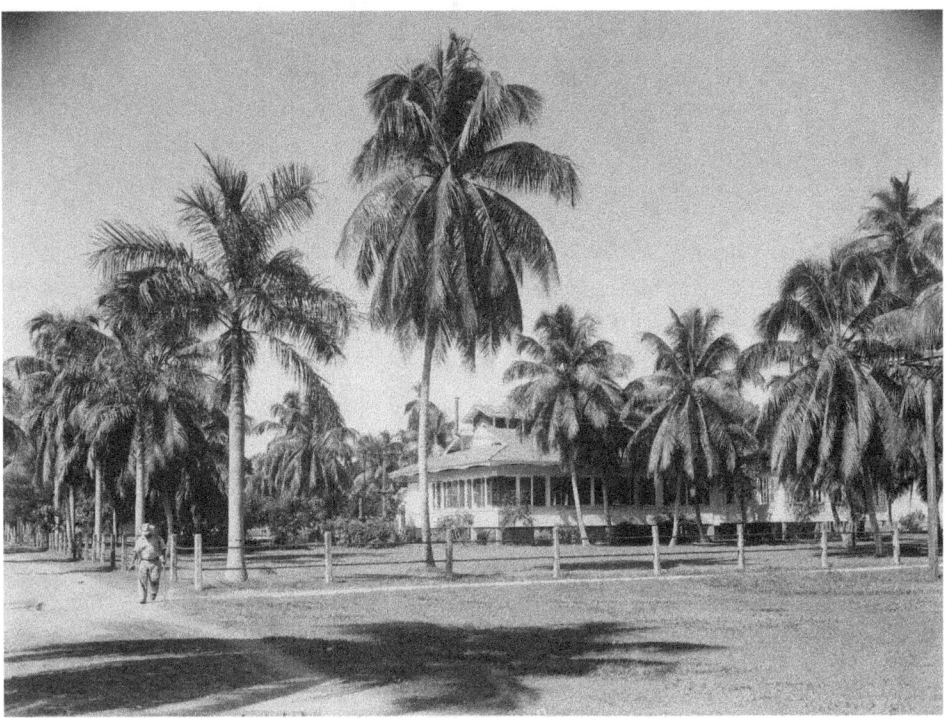

Figure 3.3. Clubhouse at Tela. UF10.067. No. 4245. Baker Library, Harvard Business School, Historical Collections Mss:1 1891–1962 U860.

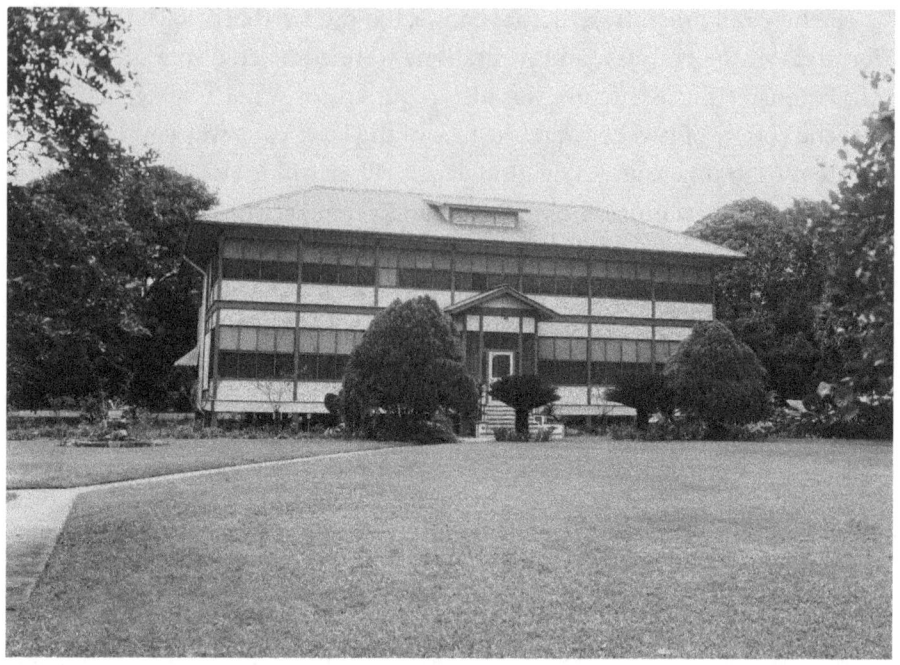

Figure 3.4. Turnbull Residence, 1946, La Lima, Honduras. Baker Library, Harvard Business School, Historical Collections.

Family, business, and politics all served to position archaeology in Honduras at the forefront of privileged access to personal and diplomatic practices. Mr. Aycock, the UFCO general manager, as well as the second in charge at UFCO, Mr. Walter Turnbull, both made inquiries with the Honduran government for archaeological concessions as well as for the shipment of artifacts from Honduran ports to the United States. Wilson Popenoe, too, leveraged his networks to facilitate excavation and export. He was able to track developments along the coast, in the mountains, at the ports, and along rail lines and even keep tabs on air travel. The Strong Expedition benefited from the UFCO plane and pilot. In fact, Strong's letters recount the opportunities to see the archaeological landscape from above during day trips to Costa Rica with Zemurray and Turnbull.

The professional networks of archaeologists with direct personal ties to United Fruit Company ensured access to lands and transit routes. Expeditions were put up in La Lima, and often within the gates of the primary UFC compound; thus their members were woven into the fabric of UFC social occasions: tennis matches, dinner parties at private residences, and dances at the club. These events could take up an entire 24-hour period on a day off (i.e., for the archaeologists):

> Up in time for tennis matches—Mrs. Moore (Tela) beat Mrs. Pierce (La Lima) in 3 swell sets. Went to [Balycarchs] (old Tela) for cocktails and dinner with Kidders and Doubledays. Very good. Dressed for dance— went from Hatches. Swell dance—slow starting but last till 4:30. Ate at club. At guesthouse Mr. Cloward (Mrs. Jewett's bro) insisted on more. To bed at 5:30—25 hours on our feet![1]

Strong emphasizes the importance of the host, the corporate wife, in welcoming and facilitating the entire economic enterprise in Honduras. Conchita Turnbull (Walter Turnbull's wife, see above), especially, appears to have been notably expert at this practice. Ladies favored the evenings with both "western" as well as "native society" dances—the marimba was the most preferred instrument. In sum, through relatively fluid channels, William Strong, Alfred Kidder, Doris Stone, and Dorothy Popenoe were able to situate archaeology within this arc of upper echelon society and corporate authority. To be sure, their work built on the legacy of Harvard's previous research.

Having gone to Honduras in the late nineteenth century to work with Harvard's expedition at the monumental site of Copan, George Byron Gordon confronted disappointment: Harvard's concession was revoked. He turned to the Ulua Valley, owing largely to the lure of the hallmark marble vases.[2] Gordon's interest had been presented in academic publications such as the *Journal de la Société des Américanistes de Paris*, and the collections amassed by Squier, then curated in the Museum of Natural History in New York.[3] In the late 1920s and early 1930s Dorothy Popenoe followed in Gordon's footsteps at the site of Playa de los Muertos.[4] Her fieldwork and scholarship contributed to important advances in approaches to excavation, and after her untimely death in 1932 (Joyce 1994), the director of the Peabody Museum, Alfred Tozzer, adopted her methods (Joyce 1994).

Dorothy's commitment to stratigraphic control can be understood in part by the plunder taking place in the region. She was deeply concerned about the ransacking of archaeological sites by the extensive and intensive development of the UFCO. Both she and Strong noted the destruction from draglines (Luke 2006, 40).[5] In response, they advocated for greater care and attention to preservation. Tozzer had opportunity to see Zemurray on occasion in Boston. In 1932 he wrote to Dorothy and Wilson: "Things are certainly moving in the Fruit Company. We dined with Mr. Zemurray the other night and I think I got under his business hide enough to impress him with the work of the Museum in his lands and the part played there by the Popenoes."[6] While Dorothy may have advocated for mitigation regarding the unregulated destruction, Tozzer's goal was funding for future expeditions. In fact, beginning in 1924, the UFCO made handsome contributions for the excavations at Quiriguá along the Honduran-Guatemalan border.

Through the 1930s and 1940s (i.e., after Dorothy's death), Tozzer continued to assist Wilson Popenoe in collecting documentation from Dorothy's excavations (i.e., details on stratigraphy). Tozzer requested copies of her maps, as well as those held by the UFCO, to provide a contemporary context.[7] While the request for Dorothy's research maps did not pose an issue, Wilson balked at Tozzer's desire to publish the location of UFCO complexes.

> As regards the other map, the Division map of the United Fruit Co. showing the Ulua Valley from the sea to Playa de los Muertos, I rather hesitate to ask the Company's permission to publish this as I know they are usually pretty careful about such matters. I rather feel that it might be best to leave this out. It hardly seems essential to the publication, anyway. If necessary, perhaps someone could draw up a sketch map using this as the basis, showing the location of Playa de los Muertos with relation to the sea and the Ulua valley in general.[8]

Wilson's appointment as an agent for ONI perhaps explains some of his trepidation. Tozzer did finally receive a map of the valley showing the location of the UFCO facilities: "It [showed] the various banana farms and the windings of the Ulua; it [gave] a much clearer picture of the area than one can get from any of the larger maps on smaller scales." The map came from Alfred Kidder, a member of the 1936 Harvard-Smithsonian Strong Expedition to Honduras.[9]

Museum Markets

In addition to his interest of in-country archaeological excavation, Wilson Popenoe also acted as a primary negotiator for acquisitions on behalf of the Peabody Museum. Tozzer appreciated this relationship:

Thanks for sending [a] fine lot of sherds. They round out our collection beautifully and the new "archaic" heads give us the finest collection of these in the world. I want to get a student to work on these, particularly the great variety of dressing of the hair. Again expressing my personal thanks and those of the Museum for your great generosity and kindness, I am, with best wishes.[10]

The Peabody paid well for the finds: "Please remember that we are willing to pay $100 as you suggest for one of those fine bowls."[11] In addition, Popenoe contributed personal funds to the Peabody expedition, often for the purchase of objects.[12] Competition for Honduran material can also be traced in part to Herbert Spinden, who purchased materials for the Museum of Natural History in New York. One dealer in Honduras, Edwards, acted on behalf of various institutions, and a clear rivalry comes through in the correspondences. Alfred Tozzer also knew that Eric Moore[13] was acquiring exquisite material for Toronto: "[the vases] knock out not only one, but both your eyes synchronously and simultaneously."[14] Tozzer was "very envious."[15]

Institutions often worked through middlemen, usually with ties to big businesses and politicians in Honduras, to do their buying and assist in transportation. G. B. Gordon's networks from his days in the field (as a Harvard man) served him well as curator and later director of the University Museum at the University of Pennsylvania. His in-country agent was a businessman in San Pedro Sula, Lincoln Valentine. Over the years the steady interest in purchasing antiquities had generated considerable curiosity. Valentine tried to quell the expanding market and counter reports in local newspapers of high prices.[16] Yet, even so, middlemen traders were keenly aware of the growing U.S. demand, setting prices as high as $10,000 for a single marble vase. Even if the prices were grossly inflated, people paid. The result was unregulated plunder by UFCO businessmen and workers seeking a lucrative find or a precious souvenir.

In an attempt to rectify the situation (i.e., the runaway market) and to redirect rumors, Valentine instructed the Smithsonian Institution to offer a nominal price to a local collector who had recently paid an exorbitant amount for a vase.[17] The plan worked:

A few days since I fell in with Charles Lanz, owner of the fine marble bowl which was turned up here last summer. As I wrote you previously, Charley informed me that he had turned down an offer of two thousand dollars, and that he had the bowl insured for $2,500, and so on; all of which was obviously sales talk. Charley now says he has heard nothing from Fred Jenkins, who took the bowl to the States to sell on commission; and that he would be glad to sell the bowl for $100 if and when he can get it out of Jenkins' clutches. I haven't see the article and don't know just how fine it is. I may get in touch with it later. Doris Zemurray Stone was through here the other day, by the way, and told [me] she was taking one of these bowls up to Tulane. I suspect it is the broken one which was found near La Lima last year and cornered by Don Carlos Turnbull (about which I have written you), but am not sure.[18]

U.S. institutions continued to rationalize their acquisition practices through education paradigms of exhibiting artifacts from distant areas. The Honduran government, however, kept tabs on what people were doing and which institutions were acquiring.[19] With the new 1936 Honduran law that made export illegal, there was growing interest in documented (i.e., legal) collections by U.S. museums, which turned away from the purchase of undocumented (i.e., illegal and likely plundered) materials. Of course, these institutions could also afford to shift their policies—after all, by that point they had established robust collections, even if through dubious practices.

How to reconcile the desire for context, especially given Dorothy Popenoe's methodological approaches, with the expanding market for antiquities from Latin America became a point of contention for Wilson Popenoe. Writing from Colombia, Popenoe expressed to Tozzer the idea that a commitment to stratigraphic control couldn't keep up with the demand, especially from new regions:

He says, what I already know, and you know better than I, that it is much cheaper to *buy* things than it is to *dig* them, but for several reasons I thought it worth while to spend a little money on digging; firstly, we know just where the stuff comes from, and secondly, the market is mighty thin right now and it is very hard to find anything to buy. Hawkins tells me, by the way, that a man out at Dibulla [Colombia] has six small gold frogs which are for sale, and I told him to buy them and deposit them with one of my friends here at the office, for safekeeping. I hope he gets them. He tells me that most of the gold which is turned up around here is being sold to the government, and melted down. That is really a pity. The government is apparently anxious to build up its gold reserve and is buying old jewelry to that end, and even these precious prehistoric things.[20]

The "rescue argument" for the good of history presented a tough ethical point for Popenoe and other archaeologists, especially when the sponsoring government was a major part of the problem. Regardless, with stricter in-country legal instruments that limited the export of antiquities, the academic community had to redefine how to proceed.

Science and *Partage*

Beginning in the 1930s, Harvard sought to cultivate standards for "professional" archaeology, which meant revisiting not only *partage* agreements, but also coming to terms with new partnerships. With funding for research in the 1930s coming through UFCO, another series of negotiations were necessary that did not include the government:

> We talked over the following proposition: He and his position with the United Fruit would contribute a pass to you, automobiles and mules and habitation in Fruit Company stations to the probable value of about $1000; the Bureau of the Smithsonian would contribute $500; and the Peabody Museum $500. This $1000 would pay for the labor which would be practically the only expense not covered by the Fruit Company contribution. We should then regard the Fruit Company as contributing 50–50 with two institutions and the results of the dig will be divided 50–50. If we sent a man down we should expect his expenses would not be taken out of our $500.[21]

Negotiations between Harvard and the Smithsonian ensured that experienced archaeologists would be doing the work and that young professionals would be trained in proper stratigraphic methods:

> We are sending an expedition to the [Ulua] Valley in Honduras this coming February. Dr. Strong of the Bureau of Ethnology is to be in charge. Alfred Kidder is going along as a second man. It would be possible, I think, to attach Paul to this expedition where he would have excellent supervision and would really learn something about archaeological techniques. . . . The day is passed when any scientific institution is interested in mere loot. Archaeological techniques have improved so much within the last decade that training in these is absolutely essential for successful

archaeological investigations. Even Alfred Kidder, who has had two seasons in archaeological work in Venezuela feels he needs additional study on techniques and this is one of the reasons why he is going along with Dr. Strong, who is an experienced field worker."[22]

As these correspondences show, Harvard and the Smithsonian both celebrated their commitment to scientific approaches, a point they made with great pride in contrast to practices followed at Tulane: "Blom and the whole Tulane outfit are out for *kudos* and loot. The scientific aspect of the work is secondary, so far as I can see."[23] Even still, the Peabody rejoiced at the low cost of acquisition, writing to Popenoe,

> The Museum will send you a check on New York for $600. I can't tell you how pleased we are to get this and how cheap it all is. When you come to reckon out the cost of excavating all this material, one can easily see that the price is extraordinarily low.[24]

The arrangement between Harvard and the Smithsonian apparently proceeded without direct engagement with the Honduran government, and on the doorstep of the major changes under the 1936 legislation.

In fact, the formal contract between Harvard and the Smithsonian leaves out any provisions for the division of antiquities for the UFCO and Honduran Government:

> 1. The expedition to the [Ulua] Valley is to be a joint expedition of the Smithsonian Institution and of the Peabody Museum. 2. Each institution is to contribute $750 in cash to the budget. Dr. Wilson Popenoe is to arrange for transportation of Dr. Strong and Mr. Kidder to and from the field with the United Fruit Company and to contribute various aids to the work in the field. . . . 3. All collections will be secured by the expedition area to be divided equally between the two institutions. Dr. Strong has suggested that since he will be most familiar with the material, he divide it so far as possible into two equal groups marked A and B and that these be assigned by lot. This is entirely satisfactory to us. 4. The Peabody Museum is to have the right of publication, which I understand is agreeable to Dr. Wetmore and yourself.[25]

Over the course of the next year, twenty-three boxes of materials were shipped to the United States. The shipment included a map that illustrated "the various banana farms and the windings of the Ulua," despite Popenoe's preference not to provide this directly to Tozzer (see above).[26]

The division of finds between the Smithsonian and Harvard apparently went smoothly, save one item: a ceramic vessel of a type that presents an effigy of a marble vase. Today (2019) their market value is limited (to at most a few hundred dollars per vase), and they are of interest only to a very small academic group. In 1937, the situation was different. The capital imbued in these ceramic vases stemmed not only from their perceived value as antiquities, but also from their stylistic similarities with the much rarer marble vases. The rift between two prestigious U.S. institutions also increased the perception of value. The dispute occurred despite efforts to implement a policy for allocation:

> In arranging for the division, my suggestion would be to divide the collection into two parts, A and B, of presumably equal importance, placing in each part some of the each type and some material from each of the graves. Then a drawing could be made from a hat, you selecting A or B as the part remaining in Washington, we taking the other part. This I think is a much better way than for each side to select one piece in turn.[27]

This option did not include the "one of a kind" effigy vase. A. Wetmore, the Assistant Secretary at the Smithsonian wrote,

> One lone vessel, an earthenware replica of the famous Uloa alabaster jars, a gift from Dr. Wilson Popenoe to the Joint Expedition, remains for consideration. It is the only one in the collection; we have two related pieces from the Bay Islands but none from the mainland. Naturally, we should like to keep this specimen sending Peabody Museum something (a sherd series from the Bay Islands has been suggested) in exchange. Or if you really need the jar, perhaps you can send us something in return for our interest.[28]

The Peabody fired back: "Personally I prefer Plan B as we too would like very much to get the Popenoe vase as we have nothing like it and you have two related pieces from the Bay Islands. We are perfectly willing for you to make the choice between Plan A or Plan B."[29] Alfred Tozzer even suggested shifting the deal such that the Peabody would forgo entire lots in favor of "one or two *whole* specimens."[30] The Smithsonian, too, favored this scenario, provided that they got to keep the ceramic effigy in question:

My conception of a "selection of type specimens" was, as you indicate in your letter, the same as that of Dr. Kidder—"a sherd series" which was both in Plan A and Plan B. . . . In the last sentence of your first paragraph you suggest that this "series" from Bay Islands and "one or two whole specimens" would be an equivalent of our interest in the Popenoe vase. In Plan B we feel you have perhaps overlooked the fact that we give up our interest in the entire [Ulua] sherd collection excepting only a few (200) sherds. . . . It seems to us that the Popenoe vase and the "sherd series" from the Bay Islands represent a fair equivalent for one-half of the [Ulua] Valley sherd collection excepting the type series, shown above. I understand this collection of sherds would fill three or four barrels.[31]

In the end, the Smithsonian refused the offer:

It is a specimen we should like to exhibit, especially since we have none of the [Ulua] alabaster vases. . . . Peabody Museum is to receive half of the entire Uloa sherd collection; we have no desire to retain a larger proportion and for this reason can not consider Doctor Tozzer's proposal. Perhaps you and he can find it possible to give the subject further thought in the near future.[32]

This squabbling between U.S. institutions neglected the perspective of the Honduran government, which eventually trumped both institutions in the implementation of the 1936 law.[33] After this date, permits issued to foreigners for archaeological excavations became much harder to secure, and thus researchers, rather than continue their work in-country and establish suitable storage facilities and exhibitions, moved to new regions, ideally those with softer legal frameworks and vested in-country partners.

Evading Borders

Doris Stone's negotiations for equipment related to archaeological enterprise to be duty-free has a long tradition. Harvard, too, put such measures in place during their first concession at Copan. Less clear was export of antiquities. For all institutions actively engaged in foreign excavations during the period of *partage*, the process of clearing customs became critical. Upon entry into the United States, the boxes were delivered to the respective museum, often without the awareness of the respective director until after the fact. Common were memos such as this one from Helen Whiting, Chief Cataloguer at the Peabody: "Dr. Tozzer has asked me to let you know that the two boxes from Honduras arrived at the Museum today."[34] These shipping and receiving methods worked very well for a period of time—until legal instruments shifted and the relative in-country power of the institution and company began to fade.

In the 1890s Boston was the preferred port of designation, and if this couldn't be arranged, then materials were to be sent to New York. Material would then be shipped via bond to Boston.[35] Gordon had implemented this process beautifully, yet at the cost of endangering his own life. He gave up his space on board ship for additional boxes, making his return trip extremely long via the Pacific Coast or Panama to San Francisco and then via train to Boston.[36] His commitment and success in this process earned him the reputation as the "go to" expert on shipping archaeological materials from Central America to the United States.[37] In consultation with his colleagues at the Peabody, Gordon developed tactics for evading details on customs forms with the conviction that it was best for the object—and that unlike other commodities (he gave the example of smuggling cigars) there was no economic impropriety.[38] Gordon would post notice of the name of the ship and the consignor. Charles Bowditch, a Peabody Museum financier and trustee, served as the consignor of the shipment, and thus also was able to receive it upon arrival in Boston (either direct shipment or in bond from New York).[39]

By the 1930s archaeologists and institutions had become very savvy in working around Honduran and U.S. customs officers and policies, often with assistance from members of the UFCO, including Turnbull, W. Popenoe (especially when shipping from the port at Tela), and/or U.S. diplomats posted to Honduras.[40]

The same was true of archaeology taking place in neighboring countries through similar networks. In 1947 Harvard's Peabody Museum began a new concession in Costa Rica. Again, cultural capital, corporatism, and insider networks clenched the deal. Doris Stone's position as the daughter of Zemurray enabled her to cultivate key arrangements.

Finally here is the Peabody contract for excavations in Costa Rica. It will be noted that there are some slight omissions from what appeared in the original. There will be no tax on cameras. I thought it best to let the permission pass as it now stands than to have to have a law made to pass through congress because of duty-free entries. In reality, after talking over the situation with Sam, there is nothing we will need that is dutiable unless it is a jeep. This I probably can arrange through the company when the time comes, or even through other sources.

The director of the Museo Nacional is very pleased over the idea of Peabody, and I don't believe that there will be any trouble even over "piezas unicas." Unless I hear from you otherwise I am going to present the same sort of contract to Honduras. I'll wait until I hear from you. Best to Dr. Tozzer and to yourself, Very sincerely, Doris.

p.s. All the Peabody has to do when they are ready to dig is to come down and bring the letter with them in case an authority wants to see it. I am getting exclusive rights from the Museum to dig on company property. Several people and even some institutions have wanted to do so, but we've never let them. Perhaps you will want to dig at Palmar or Coto.[41]

The Peabody thanked Stone and "look[ed] forward" to the material—but didn't specify when (or who) would be traveling to Costa Rica.[42]

Correspondence between Donald Scott and Doris Stone focused on how to navigate the border and arrange for shipment. Stone wrote, "Arriving New Orleans September third on board San Jose if possible arrange with port authorities free passage six boxes thanks DORIS." Scott telegraphed her: "ARCHAEOLOGY MATERIAL OVER ONE HUNDRED YEARS OLD CAN BE ENTERED FREE stop IF ANY DOUBT ARRANGE SHIP DIRECT TO US IN BOND DONALD SCOTT."[43] Stone provided detailed guidance for language to be used on customs forms, and Scott dutifully followed:

I am excited by what you say is on the way for us. I hope you have the sort of shipping invoices that our Customs Department requires. There should some statement of value. The following words should be used in the description: "a collection in illustration of the progress of the arts" and a consular invoice should be secured from the Consul saying the materials were made at whatever date you choose to give. I should think that "prior to 1500 AD" is alright. In addition, there should be sworn statement of this antiquity. In going to the Consul with all this, reference can be made to Paragraph 1811 in the United States Customs Tariff.

What all this rigmarole amounts to is this: you can go to the Consul with a list of the shipment which will simply say, two crates of pottery and stone—a collection in illustration of the progress of the arts, value—. The Consul will give you the consular invoices covering the matter and you can swear before him that these objects were made prior to 1850.

I am glad to hear that the Honduran book is going forward

Very sincerely, Donald Scott, Director[44]

Realignment

The narratives told here demonstrate the inter-connectivity of archaeologists, massive corporate entities (i.e., UFCO), diplomats and prestigious U.S. institutions (i.e., Harvard and the Smithsonian) in their quest for antiquities from Central America. This story isn't necessarily different from those in other areas of the world. Networks of power and prestige made archaeology possible throughout the nineteenth century and certainly defined how it became professionalized. In the examples given in this chapter from Honduras, Costa Rica, and Colombia we find tight connections owing to the relative rural nature of these landscapes and structures of development—plantations, rail lines, airfields, roads, and ports—for the extremely profitable sphere of bananas. By the early twentieth century, these networks of U.S. businesses made Central America a priority for U.S. intelligence via the ONI. These two overlapping spheres of influence and key members with ties to places such as Harvard gave archaeology leverage. The secretive networks of the ONI were one avenue, while the more public, elite linkages (and funding) from the fruit and railroad companies were another. Both facilitated the purchase of antiquities in-country for the purpose of filling out U.S. museum collections.

Wilson Popenoe's professional expertise as botanist coupled with his work in espionage allowed him to pursue archaeology and assist in the acquisition of collections for Harvard. Conchita Turnbull's dinner parties and personal interest in ceramics, and Samuel Zemurray's tremendous wealth and power in Central America afforded archaeologists access to these spheres of privilege. When shipping material from the region to the United States, regardless of legislation, William Strong, Alfred Kidder, and Doris Stone deployed their connections, calling on upper-echelon executives and diplomats to pull strings. Beginning in 1936 and certainly after 1947, the ability to conduct "business as usual" for foreign archaeologists in Honduras shifted considerably. Owing to more fluid legal parameters and opportunities in Costa Rica, both business and fieldwork, Stone continued apace. In these ways, there is a rich history to be uncovered regarding the nexus of the antiquities trade, corporatism, and archaeology in Central America and beyond.

Acknowledgments

This chapter draws on research conducted many years ago. The places I once knew have changed, subject to the fierce unrest that has engulfed Central America, especially Honduras, over the last two decades. The people I once knew have also been caught in the crossfire, and in fact, many are no longer with us. The realities of these ongoing tensions and struggles have made the practice of archaeology around La Lima and San Pedro Sula (Honduras) increasingly difficult, if not impossible. Even still, I am reminded of the wonderful memories of working in the Ulua Valley with Honduran colleagues as well as Rosemary Joyce and John Henderson. In addition, the time spent at the Smithsonian and the gracious support of archivists over the years at Harvard's Peabody Museum and the Baker Library at the Harvard Business School have made this work possible. I am grateful for the opportunity to present in this volume.

Notes

1. *Journal of William Duncan Strong, Smithsonian-Harvard Honduras Expedition January 8–Mar. 22, 1936.* vol. 1. Smithsonian Institution. [Strong 1936].

2. Gordon, G. B. 1897 *Report on Honduran Activities.* Accession File: 97–44–2. Peabody Museum of Archaeology and Ethnology at Harvard University (PMAE).

3. Gordon 1897.

4. Popenoe, Dorothy. 1930 Report Playa de los Muertos flanking part of the Farm 11 of the Tela Railroad Company Accession file 30–46. PMAE.

5. Strong 1936.

6. A. Tozzer to Popenoes. December 22, 1932. Accession file 33–18: Pottery of the Ulua Valley, Honduras, Dorothy and Wilson Popenoe, Correspondence 1932–1934. PMAE.

7. W. Popenoe to A. Tozzer. July 2, 1933. Accession file 33–57: Popenoe collection of archaeological material from the Ulua Valley, Honduras. PMAE.

8. W. Popenoe to A. Tozzer April 16, 1934. Accession file 33–57: Popenoe collection of archaeological material from the Ulua Valley, Honduras. PMAE.

9. W. Strong to A. Kidder. March 28, 1936. Accession file 38–45: Collection of pottery from vicinity of Lake Yojoa, Honduras Joint Smithsonian–PM. Exp. PMAE.

10. A. Tozzer to W. Popenoe. October 28, 1933. Accession file 33–57: Popenoe collection of archaeological material from the Ulua Valley, Honduras. PMAE.

11. Ibid.

12. In 1936 Strong gave $500 to the Peabody expedition. Strong 1936.

13. W. Popenoe to A. Tozzer. October 9, 1935. Accession file 38–45: Collection of pottery from vicinity of Lake Yojoa, Honduras. Joint Smithsonian–PM. Exp.–Strong, Kidder. PMAE.

14. Luke 2006, 44; W. Popenoe to A. Tozzer. February 18, 1936.

15. A. Tozzer to W. Popenoe. March 3, 1936. Accession file 38–45: Collection of pottery from vicinity of Lake Yojoa, Honduras Joint Smithsonian–PM. Exp. PMAE.

16. Luke 2006.

17. Luke 2006.

18. A. Tozzer to W. Popenoe. April 16, 1934. Accession file 33–57: Popenoe collection of archaeological material from the Ulua Valley, Honduras. PMAE.

19. W. Popenoe to A. Tozzer. October 9, 1935. Accession file 38–45: Collection of pottery from vicinity of Lake Yojoa, Honduras. Joint Smithsonian–PM. Exp. PMAE.

20. W. Popenoe to A. Tozzer. 1935–1936. Accession file 38–45: Collection of pottery from vicinity of Lake Yojoa, Honduras. Joint Smithsonian–P.M. Exp. PMAE.

21. A. Tozzer to W. Strong. January 11, 1935. Accession file 38–45: Collection of pottery from vicinity of Lake Yojoa, Honduras. Joint Smithsonian–P.M. Exp. PMAE.

22. A. Tozzer to T. Barbour. February 14, 1935. Accession file 38–45: Collection of pottery from vicinity of Lake Yojoa, Honduras. Joint Smithsonian–PM. Exp. PMAE.

23. A. Tozzer to Strong. June 3, 1935. Accession file 38–45: Collection of pottery from vicinity of Lake Yojoa, Honduras. Joint Smithsonian–P.M. Exp. PMAE.

24. A. Tozzer to W. Popenoe. January 21, 1939. Accession file 39–8: Collection of pottery vessels from lake Yojoa and Ulua Valley, Honduras.

25. D. Scott to Stirling. November 22, 1935. Accession file 38–45: Collection of pottery from vicinity of Lake Yojoa, Honduras. Joint Smithsonian–PM. Exp. PMAE.

26. A. Kidder to D. Scott. March 28, 1936. Accession file 38–45: Collection of pottery from vicinity of Lake Yojoa, Honduras. Joint Smithsonian–PM. Exp. PMAE.

27. A. Tozzer to D. Strong. May 27, 1937. Accession file 38–45; Collection of pottery from vicinity of Lake Yojoa, Honduras Joint Smithsonian–PM. Exp. PMAE.

28. A. Wetmore to A. Tozzer. April 18, 1938. Accession file 38–45: Collection of pottery from vicinity of Lake Yojoa, Honduras; Joint Smithsonian–PM. Exp. PMAE.

29. A. Tozzer to A. Wetmore. April 21, 1938. Accession file 38–45: Collection of pottery from vicinity of Lake Yojoa, Honduras. Joint Smithsonian–PM. Exp. PMAE.

30. Graf to A. Tozzer. April 29, 1938. Accession file 38–45: Collection of pottery from vicinity of Lake Yojoa, Honduras. Joint Smithsonian–PM. Exp. PMAE

31. A. Tozzer to Graf. May 5, 1938. Accession file 38–45: Collection of pottery from vicinity of Lake Yojoa, Honduras. Joint Smithsonian–PM. Exp. PMAE.

32. D. Scott to A. Wetmore. May 20, 1938. Accession file 38–45: Collection of pottery from vicinity of Lake Yojoa, Honduras. Joint Smithsonian–PM. Exp. PMAE.

33. The new Constitution Politica of Honduras Adopted April 1936: Titulo VIII, de la Hacienda National, Capitulo I, de los Bienes Nacionales: "Articulo 157: Constituyen el tesoro cultural de la Nacion: 1. Toda la riqueza artistica e historica existente in le pais, la cual estara bajo la salvaguardia del Estado, que podra prohibir su exportacion y enajenacion; en cuyos casos debera adquirirla para el mismo. 2. Las ruinas de antiguas poblaciones y los objectos arqueologicos, los cuales son inalienables y imprescriptibles. 3. Los lugares notables por su belleza natural o por su valor artistico e historico. El Estado organizara un registro de dicho tesoro cultural, aseguara su custodia y establecera las respectivas responsabilidades penales."

34. H. Whiting to W. Popenoe. January 20, 1939. Accession file 39–8: Collection of pottery vessels from lake Yojoa and Ulua Valley, Honduras. PMAE.

35. C. Bowditch to G. B. Gordon. February 25, 1893.

36. C. Bowditch to G. B. Gordon. June 28, 1893.

37. C. Bowditch to G. B. Gordon. May 2, 1896.

38. G. B. Gordon to C. Bowditch. June 22, 1896.

39. G. B. Gordon to C. Bowditch. July 4, 1896.

40. W. Popenoe to A. Tozzer. December 13, 1935. Accession file 38–45: Collection of pottery from vicinity of Lake Yojoa, Honduras. Joint Smithsonian–PM. Exp. PMAE.

41. D. Stone to D. Scott. August 22, 1947. Accession file 48–11: Pottery, stone, etc., from Honduras, Sula Ulua Region. Mrs. Roger T. Stone. PMAE.

42. D. Stone to D. Scott. September 9, 1947. Accession file 48–11: Pottery, stone, etc., from Honduras, Sula Ulua Region. Mrs. Roger T. Stone. PMAE.

43. D. Stone to D. Scott. 1946. Accession file 46–26, folder 2 of 2. PMAE.

44. D. Scott to D. Stone. August 22, 1947. Accession file 48–11: Pottery, stone, etc., from Honduras, Sula Ulua Region. PMAE.

References Cited

Browman, David L. 2011. "Spying by American Archaeologists in World War I." *Bulletin of the History of Archaeology* 21 (2).

Castañeda, Quetzil E. 2005. "The Carnegie Mission and Vision of Science." *Histories of Anthropology Annual* 1: 27–60.

———. 2010. "'Conjunctivitis': Notes on Historical Ethnography, Paradigms, and Social Networks in Academia." In *Prophet, Pariah, and Pioneer: Walter W. Taylor and Dissension in American Archaeology,* edited by Allan L. Maca, Jonathan E. Reyman, and William J. Folan, 333–356. Louisville: University Press of Colorado.

Gordon, G. B. 1921. *The Ulúa Marble Vases.* Philadelphia: University Museum.

Harris, Charles H., and Louis R. Sadler. 2003. *The Archaeologist was a Spy: Sylvanus G. Morley and the Office of Naval Intelligence.* Albuquerque: University of New Mexico Press.

Hinsley, Curtis M. 1985. "From Shell-Heaps to Stelae: Early Anthropology at the Peabody Museum." In *Objects and Others: Essays on Museums and Material Culture*, edited by George W. Stocking Jr., 49–74. History of Anthropology, Vol. 3. Madison: University of Wisconsin Press.

Joyce, Rosemary A. 1986. "Terminal Classic Interaction on the Southeastern Maya Periphery." *American Antiquity* 51 (2): 313–329.

———. 1993. "The Construction of the Mesoamerican Frontier and the Mayoid Image of Honduran Polychromes." In *Reinterpreting Prehistory of Central America*, edited by Mark M. Graham, 51–101. Niwot: University Press of Colorado.

———. 1994. "Dorothy Hughes Popenoe: Eve in an Archaeological Garden." In *Women in Archaeology*, edited by Cheryl Claassen, 51–66. Philadelphia: University of Pennsylvania Press.

———. 2001a. "Instituto Hondureño de Antropología e Historia." *Encyclopedia of Archaeology: History and Discoveries,* vol. III, edited by Tim Murray, 669–671. Denver: ABC-Clio.

———. 2001b. "Peabody Museum, Harvard University." *Encyclopedia of Archaeology: History and Discoveries,* vol. III, edited by Tim Murray, 1006–1010. Denver: ABC-Clio.

———. 2003. "Archaeology and Nation Building: A View from Central America." In *The Politics of Archaeology and Identity in a Global Context,* edited by Susan Kane, 79–100. Colloquia and Conference Papers 7. Boston: Archaeological Institute of America.

———. 2017. *Painted Pottery of Honduras: Object Lives and Itineraries.* Boston: Brill.

Langley, Lester D., and Thomas Schoonover. 2014. *The Banana Men: American Mercenaries and Entrepreneurs in Central America, 1880–1930.* Lexington: University Press of Kentucky.

Luke, Christina. 2002. "Ulúa Style Marble Vases." Unpublished PhD dissertation, Cornell University.

———. 2006. "Diplomats, Banana Cowboys, and Archaeologists in Western Honduras: A History of the Trade in Pre-Columbian Materials." *International Journal of Cultural Property* 13 (1): 25–57.

———. 2010. "Ulua Marble Vases Abroad: Contextualizing Social Networks between the Maya World and Lower Central America." In *Trade and Exchange: Archaeological Studies from History and Prehistory,* edited by Carolyn D. Dhillon and Carolyn L. White, 37–57. New York: Springer.

———. 2011. "Materiality and Sacred Landscapes: Ulúa Style Marble Vases in Honduras." *Archeological Papers of the American Anthropological Association* 21 (1): 114–129.

Luke, Christina, and J. S. Henderson. 2006. "The Plunder of the Ulúa Valley, Honduras, and a Market Analysis for Its Antiquities." In *Archaeology, Cultural Heritage, and the Antiquities Trade,* edited by Neil Brodie, Morag M. Kersel, Christina Luke, and Kathryn Walker Tubb, 147–172. Gainesville: University Press of Florida.

Luke, Christina, Robert H. Tykot, and Robert W. Scott. 2006. "Petrographic and Stable Isotope Analyses of Late Classic Ulúa Marble Vases and Potential Sources." *Archaeometry* 48 (1): 13–29.

Molloy, Sylvia. 2009. "Translating Ruins: An American Parable." In *Telling Ruins in Latin America,* edited by Michael J. Lazzara and Vicky Unruh, 51–62. New York: Palgrave Macmillan.

Munro, Dana G. 2015. *Intervention and Dollar Diplomacy in the Caribbean, 1900–1921.* Princeton, N.J.: Princeton University Press.

Reents-Budet, Dorie. 1994. *Painting the Maya Universe: Royal Ceramics of the Classic Period.* Durham, N.C.: Duke University Press.

Ricketson, Oliver, and Alfred V. Kidder. 1930. "An Archeological Reconnaissance by Air in Central America." *Geographical Review* 20 (2): 177–206.

Roberts, Jennifer L. 2000. "Landscapes of Indifference: Robert Smithson and John Lloyd Stephens in Yucatán." *Art Bulletin* 82 (3): 544–567.

Schoonover, Thomas. 1988. "Germany in Central America, 1820s to 1929: An Overview." *Jahrbuch für Geschichte von Staat, Wirtschaft und Gesellschaft Lateinamerikas* 25: 33–59.

Schoonover, Thomas, and Ebba Schoonover. 1989. "Statistics for an Understanding of Foreign Intrusions into Central America from the 1820s to 1930." *Anuario de Estudios Centroamericanos* 15 (1): 93–118.

Stephens, John L., and Frederick Catherwood. 1854. *Incidents of Travel in Central America, Chiapas, and Yucatan.* London: Arthur Hall, Virtue [and] Company.

Stone, Doris. 1938. *Masters in Marble* (No. 8). Department of Middle American Research, Tulane University.

———. 1941. *Archaeology of the North Coast of Honduras.* Cambridge: Harvard University, Peabody Museum of Archaeology and Ethnology.

Strong, William D., Alfred V. Kidder, and Anthony J. D. Paul. 1938. *Preliminary Report on the Smithsonian Institution–Harvard University Archeological Expedition to Northwestern Honduras, 1936* (Vol. 97). Washington, D.C.: Smithsonian Institution.

4

There and Back Again

Looting, Trafficking Culture, and the Management of Cultural Heritage in Guatemala

SOFÍA PAREDES MAURY AND GUIDO KREMPEL

The present chapter focuses on the case of Guatemala, a country with a long history of looting and illicit trade, particularly during the twentieth century, when archaeological discoveries took place within the context of the civil war (1960–1996). Although this topic has been addressed by several authors or shared informally as field anecdotes,[1] very little has been written about how unprovenanced archaeological material is de facto managed in Guatemala.

Notably, since the implementation of the Law for the Protection of the Cultural Patrimony of the Nation (Decree 26-77)[2] in 1977, the State allows the existence of collections of Pre-Columbian art in private hands. Such collections are considered legal only if duly registered in the Registry of Cultural Property. Since all kinds of archaeological heritage are considered "property" of the State, objects in private collections are generally considered as being "in custody." Therefore, we also address existing modalities of custodianship within the country, although legislation does not necessarily apply to each case in similar ways.

Finally, we address the issues of recovery and repatriation of Pre-Columbian art. For this purpose, we present certain case studies that reflect the particularities and difficulties faced by the country (governmental and nongovernmental institutions), both legally and logistically, and how it copes with recovered material once the objects have been returned to their country of origin.

Looting and Illicit Trade in the Maya Area

Looting is one of the most widespread illegal activities among the inhabitants of Mesoamerica which, as is well known, affects the documentation and conservation of archaeological sites. Objects from the Maya region have been specifically sought for the international art market, as evidenced by, for example, the demand for ceramics from the Northeastern Petén region (Tremain 2017). The same is the case for a variety of objects from the Usumacinta River region, or monuments from specific sites like Cancuén, Dos Pilas, and La Corona, to name just a few, all standing out for their extraordinary artistry. Pre-Columbian Maya art, though, has been among the most affordable antiquities, competing in taste and craftsmanship with gold and textile material from South America, and with cultural material from Egypt, the Mediterranean, Asian, and African cultures.

The "golden age" of archaeological looting in the Maya area began in the 1950s, with a very pronounced peak in the 1960s and 1970s, followed by a sharp decline in the late 1990s.[3] Most of the artworks currently managed in private museums and collections were removed from Guatemala during the period of armed conflict. Even though a large mass of artworks were sacked during the 1960s–1980s, a considerable number of individual pieces continue to be looted and exported.[4] The first major scientific archaeological discoveries in Mesoamerica, and exhibitions of Pre-Columbian art, increased the demand for Pre-Columbian antiquities and escalated their prices, which also resulted in theft, counterfeiting, and destruction. The signing of international conventions[5] and the regulations for the trade of antiquities has, in part, diminished the "fashion" of possessing ancient cultural vestiges of this region. However, this activity continues mostly in the collecting of small and portable art (such as finely carved jade, bone, and shell), which are especially attractive for Asia and the Arab world. In contrast, anecdotally, private collectors in European countries continue to be attracted by elaborately painted ceramics and hieroglyphic monuments, even though sizable monuments that surfaced recently form only a small part of the trade in looted objects when compared with the much higher number of illegally traded portable objects such as polychrome ceramics (which is unsurprising considering the extraordinary efforts in logistics, manpower, and criminal energy needed to smuggle a massive stone monument). In Europe, a conspicuous amount of portable art, including recently acquired pieces, form part of private collections in France, Belgium, Italy, Germany, and Switzerland. Furthermore, numerous looted ceramics that entered the art market in the late 1960s and 1970s regularly reenter the market by means of galleries and auction houses in charge of reselling former private collections (due to the death of a collector, a partial transfer into another collection, or other reasons that led to a liquidation of individual pieces or complete lots).

Looting as a regional activity varies from country to country due to differences in political, historical, and socioeconomic backgrounds. Although it involves several levels of participation, the primary level of looting comprises mainly inhabitants of rural areas who sell their booty to intermediaries who in turn form a chain between looters, contractors, and collectors (Paredes Maury 1999). Guatemala is the country of origin of thousands of objects that are now part of museums and private collections around the world, foremost because they were very attractive to the art market. Among them are Classic Maya ceramic vessels, "Teotihuacan-style incense burners" from the Pacific coast, carved monuments with hieroglyphic inscriptions, and portable objects of smaller scale (e.g., greenstone, jewelry, royal paraphernalia) manufactured with splendid artistic techniques. Different regions of Guatemala have been destroyed for different reasons, resulting in the extraction of antiquities without archaeological control and their subsequent exodus to the national and international black market. Among the most affected areas are the Petén Lowlands, the "Ixil Triangle" in Quiché,[6] Kaminaljuyú in the Central Highlands (beneath Guatemala City), the peripheral lowlands of Eastern Guatemala (border with Honduras and El Salvador) and the Pacific piedmont (see fig. 4.1).

In the case of the Maya Biosphere Reserve (MBR), in the northern half of Petén (at Parallel 17°10'), nontimber extraction activities of products such as *chicle* (the base ingredient of chewing gum), *xate* (*Chamaedorea oblongata & elegans*),[7] and allspice (*Pimienta dioica*) allowed a large seasonal population into the forest and motivated a continuous traffic of people in otherwise unpopulated spaces. The department of Petén, in fact, has had two great colonizing periods, the first one promoted by the Spanish Crown with the reduction of native people in towns (Reducción de Pueblos de Indios) during the seventeenth century until the beginning of the nineteenth century. The second was under the Guatemalan State, whose government identified

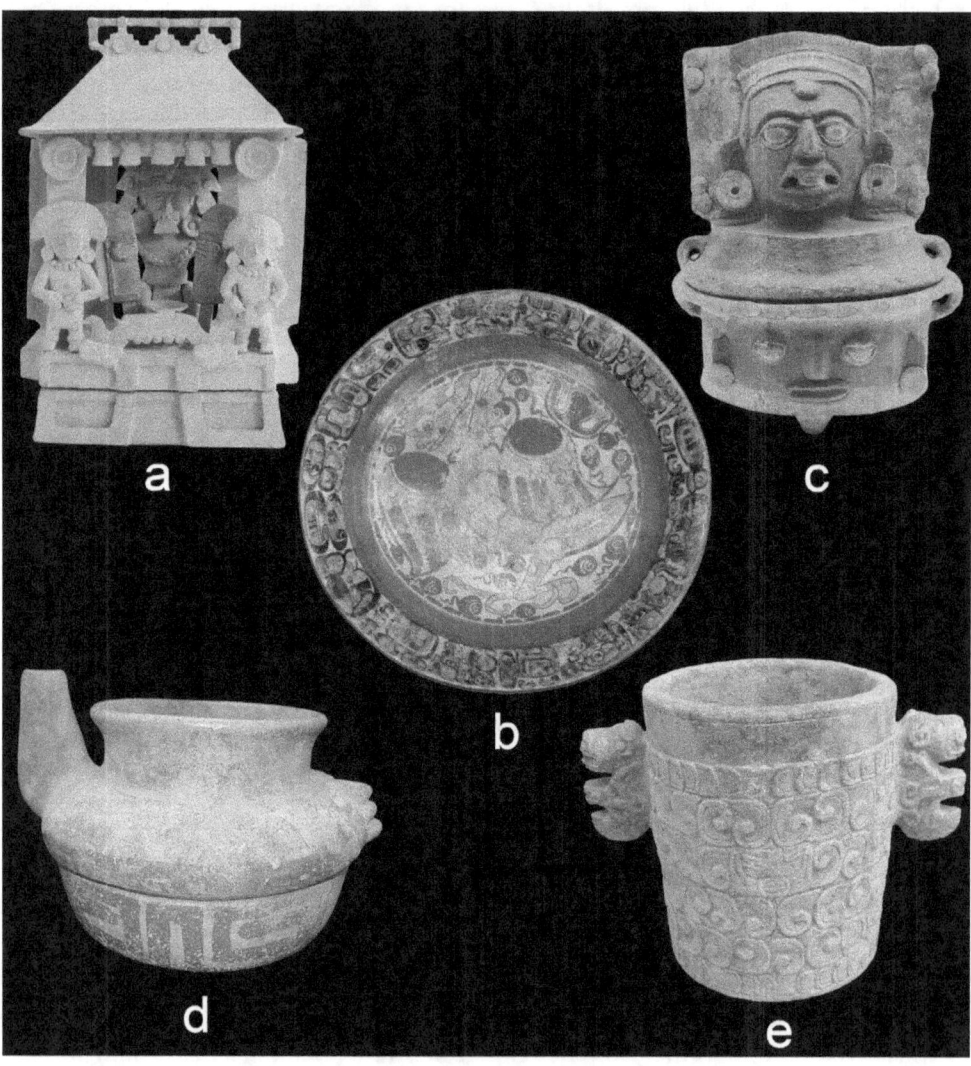

Figure 4.1. Selection of objects that illustrate the regions most affected by looting and destruction in Guatemala: (*a*) Teotihuacan-style urn, South Coast of Guatemala, Reg. No. 1.2.1.304; (*b*) ceramic plate with hieroglyphic writing from the Petén Lowlands, Reg. No. 1.2.159.194; (*c*) miniature ceramic urn from the "Ixil Triangle" in Quiché, Reg. No. 1.2.144.1343; (*d*) spouted ceramic vessel with red paint and human face from Kaminaljuyú, Reg. No. 1.2.144.1011; (*e*) vase carved in alabaster from eastern Guatemala, Reg. No. 1.2.159.43 (photos a, c, d, and e by La Ruta Maya Foundation; photo b courtesy of Camilo Alejandro Luín).

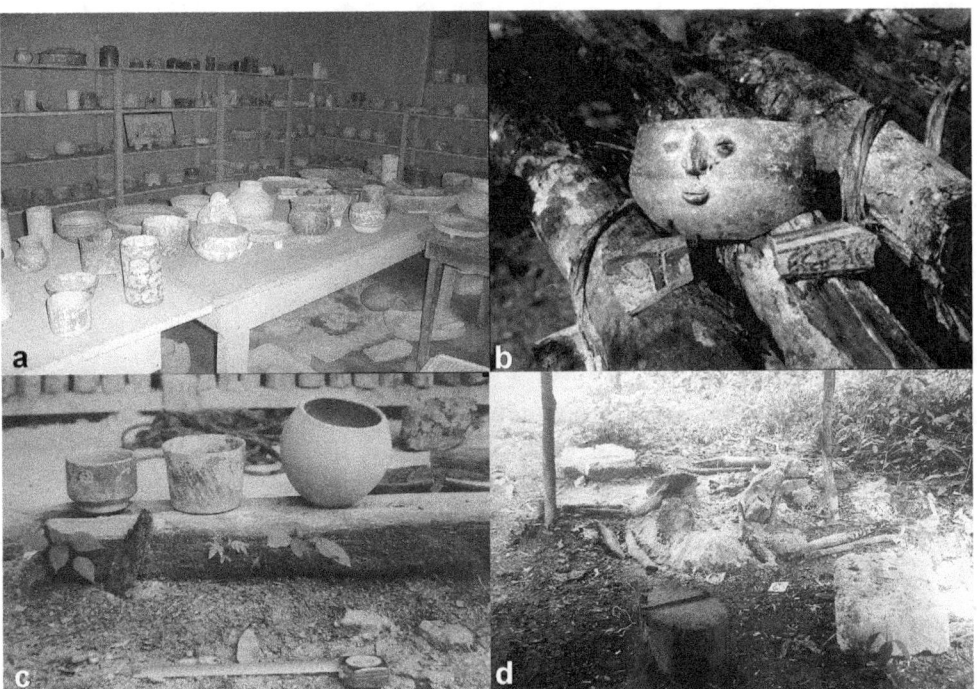

Figure 4.2. Use and reuse of abandoned archaeological material: (*a*) general view of the collection of the "Dr. Juan Antonio Valdés" Museum/ Herrera Collection, Uaxactún; (*b*) vessel with anthropomorphic face, abandoned in the camp in La Florida; (*c*) ceramic vessels kept in the warehouse of Biotopo Dos Lagunas with the intention of creating a small museum; (*d*) stela used to hold the pot to cook gum (Zacatal camp) because of its slab shape (photos a, c, and d by Sofía Paredes Maury; photo b by Lorena Castillo).

the territory as a land of colonization in the late 1950s. For that purpose, the government created by decree (Decree 1,286 of the Congress of the Republic of Guatemala) the Empresa Nacional de Fomento y Desarrollo Económico de Petén (FYDEP) (National Company for the Promotion and Economic Development of Petén-FYDEP) under the mandate of "colonizing the department and generating agricultural development," starting operations in 1959 (Secretaría de Planificación y Programación de la Presidencia—Segeplan 2013, 25). This action has perhaps been the most damaging resolution for the environmentally fragile territory. Besides logging activities (which have been partially controlled with the existence of "concessions" assigned to some local villages and companies), gum tapping, or *chiclería*, is a legendary activity intimately related to the modern history of Petén and by which locals identify their sociocultural background.

Because of its geographic location and its history, almost the entire population of Petén lives and works in places that were occupied in the Pre-Columbian period. This explains why, in addition to the professional looter, people working in the rainforest (*xate*-cutters, gum-tappers, hunters, and others) stumble upon archaeological sites and mounds in their daily walks, where everything—wood, medicinal plants, water, animals, stones, and even soil—is considered part of what the rainforest naturally provides. This situation sometimes even leads to the reuse of cultural heritage in other daily activities (see fig. 4.2).[8] In the illegal trade business, there are different categories of looters but also contractors who, depending on their capacity to pay human labor, can range from simple intermediaries to influential businessmen and women. One's logistics always serve the other as well. At present, the illicit trade in wildlife and drug trafficking intertwine with these networks (Paredes Maury 1999; Yates 2014).

Monuments and Objects in Private Hands: How Guatemala Copes with Local Collections and Their Management

According to the Law for the Protection of the Cultural Patrimony of the Nation (Decree 26–77, reformed by Decree No. 81–98), the term "cultural heritage" means "all goods and institutions that by ministry of law, or by declaration of authority, constitute and integrate any movable or immovable property, public and private, related to paleontology, archaeology, history, anthropology, art, science and technology, and culture in general, including intangible heritage, which contribute to the National identity" (Article 2—Cultural Heritage). In Guatemala, the cultural and geographical characteristics of the territory make it relatively easy for the population to gain access to archaeological features and objects.[9] Although this situation was not publicly and formally addressed until recently (Paredes Maury 2014a), the Guatemalan government has allowed the registration of cultural property since 1976.[10] Even though it is very difficult to enforce, the law also regulates and forbids the trade and exportation of antiquities.

There are several types and categories of cultural heritage in private hands, but perhaps most interesting are the community collections that have been inherited from one generation to the next. The patrimony of the *cofradías* (indigenous religious brotherhoods) and the *Aj'qijab* (Maya spiritual guides), for example, is usually not registered with the State as cultural property because of their traditional and ancestral nature. Indigenous leaders believe they are the caretakers or custodians of the objects left by their ancestors and "grandfathers";[11] therefore, their collections can be considered Pre-Columbian in nature or from the time of European contact.[12] Such collections can consist of ancient documents for ceremonial consultation (sometimes codices or handwritten manuscripts), archaeological objects (including sculptures, figurines, and musical instruments), and other objects for altars and ritual use. Artifacts like obsidian blades, jade beads, and objects made of quartz, for example, are used specifically for divination and their origin is explained through magical and cosmological events (Paredes Maury 2014b).

On the other hand, the best-known category is the "private collection." This term has caused mostly negative reactions in the archaeological field because of the prevailing idea that a "private collection" can be acquired by an individual only via direct plunder or purchase, in order to satisfy one's own pleasure of "possessing" high artistic quality material from past cultures. In Guatemala, any individual can register a collection but—due to the lack of proper information and thereby a lack of awareness—the collector usually thinks he or she is the owner of the objects, whereas factually, they are merely a custodian or depository under the law. The common denominator here is that most private collections are displayed only for personal view and enjoyment.

Another category includes "private museums," most of which were formed by individual collectors whose collections were registered or ceded in the name of a cultural association or institution. In such a case, the works of art are properly displayed for public visitation (by means of certain museum designs and standards) and can be accessible for research and publication, and usually an entrance fee is charged. The collections under the custody of foundations or associations could be included in the category of private museum, although some of them lack exhibition spaces or galleries and rely on external venues to organize their own exhibitions.[13] With the same functionalities as private museums, these collections can be accessible for research and publication, but no entrance fee is expected because of their nonprofit status. In all cases, either in a museum environment or in storage facilities, the collections are available for public display and research and are commonly the product of donations, gifts, or rescues.

A peculiar case in this category is a collection located in Uaxactún, Petén, registered as cultural heritage in the name of Neria Herrera and open to the public as "Dr. Juan Antonio Valdés Museum" (in honor of the Guatemalan archaeologist who directed excavations in Uaxactún from 1983 to 1986). This case is different from other cases of collecting, as it consists only of archaeological material that was plundered but abandoned by looters due to insufficient value to be profitable for sale (Paredes Maury 1999). Scattered in the forest, archaeological objects—mostly ceramic vessels broken into sherds—were collected by *chicleros* and stored in their seasonal camps before being given to Doña Neria, who had been the schoolteacher for the majority of the population of Uaxactún. Some material, though, was intended for illicit export, so she bartered for several objects in exchange for liquor. Afraid of sanctions by the authorities, she agreed to register her collection in 1996 and opened a small museum for public view and tourism.[14] Today, her collection consists of 565 objects that span the range from portable objects made from finely worked bone, shell, and stone (jade, obsidian, flint, and limestone) to a notable number of ceramic vessels, the latter ranging from simple monochrome decoration to highly elaborately painted and carved vessels.

One of the most outstanding cases is that of the Fundación La Ruta Maya in Guatemala City, the only private organization in the region that seeks—and aims to recover—archaeological objects that left the country illegally in past decades. La Ruta Maya is a collection of Pre-Columbian art that consists mainly of objects with a great artistic and/or archaeological value that have been recovered in foreign countries or obtained as donations from existing registered collections in Guatemala.[15] In this regard, La Ruta Maya is responsible for the custody and management of more than 3,000 Pre-Columbian objects, duly registered as National Cultural Heritage, with the objectives of custody, protection, conservation, research, and public exhibition for educational purposes. Its main activities are implemented through the following programs: (a) Recovery and repatriation of archaeological objects; (b) Registry and management of collections; (c) Exhibitions; (d) Education and research; and (e) Dissemination.

In the case of material located abroad, the process of repatriation follows the requirements established by both the Dirección General del Patrimonio Cultural y Natural (of the Ministry of Culture and Sports) and the Intendencia de *Aduanas* de la SAT (Customs Intendancy). Under this procedure, four repatriation processes were successfully completed in 2006, 2009, 2011, and 2017.[16] Locally, any object entering the collection usually comes from an already registered collection and its possession is transferred legally with the proper documentation.[17]

Recovering Artworks Inside the Country

Case Study 1: A Salvaged Masterpiece
of Unknown Provenance—The Vessel of Sak Mo'

In 2009, a resident of Uaxactún committed a severely damaged and fragmented polychrome ceramic vessel to the collection under the custody of Neria Herrera. It had reportedly been sacked from a looters' trench at a peripheral site in the Uaxactún region, and soon after the fragmented cylindrical vessel was glued together in an amateurish manner prior to display at the "Dr. Juan Antonio Valdés Museum." In the same year, the vessel was registered as Cultural Heritage of Guatemala. Soon after, the vessel began decomposing due to the tropical climate, the action of visitors (who were allowed to handle pieces during museum visits), the fragile reassemblage of the vase, and the way it was openly displayed.

While conducting fieldwork with the Uaxactún Regional Archaeological Project in 2012, Guido Krempel visited Doña Neria and inspected her collection. During this occasion, he noticed that one of the most significant pieces of the collection, here referred to as the Sak Mo' vessel, remained in an unfortunate state of conservation. Several sherds had completely broken off and there were many fractures throughout the object. Given that the piece was in such a critical state, Doña Neria was advised to store it in a separate box, preferably apart from the public display, until a professional could be commissioned to restore it and prevent further damage or even loss of fragments of this artwork. The vessel was evaluated and temporarily stored by the staff of the SAHI Uaxactún Regional Archaeological Project, until the team's restorer had the proper equipment readily available. The end of the field season was approaching, so the first attempt to safeguard the vessel had to be postponed until the return

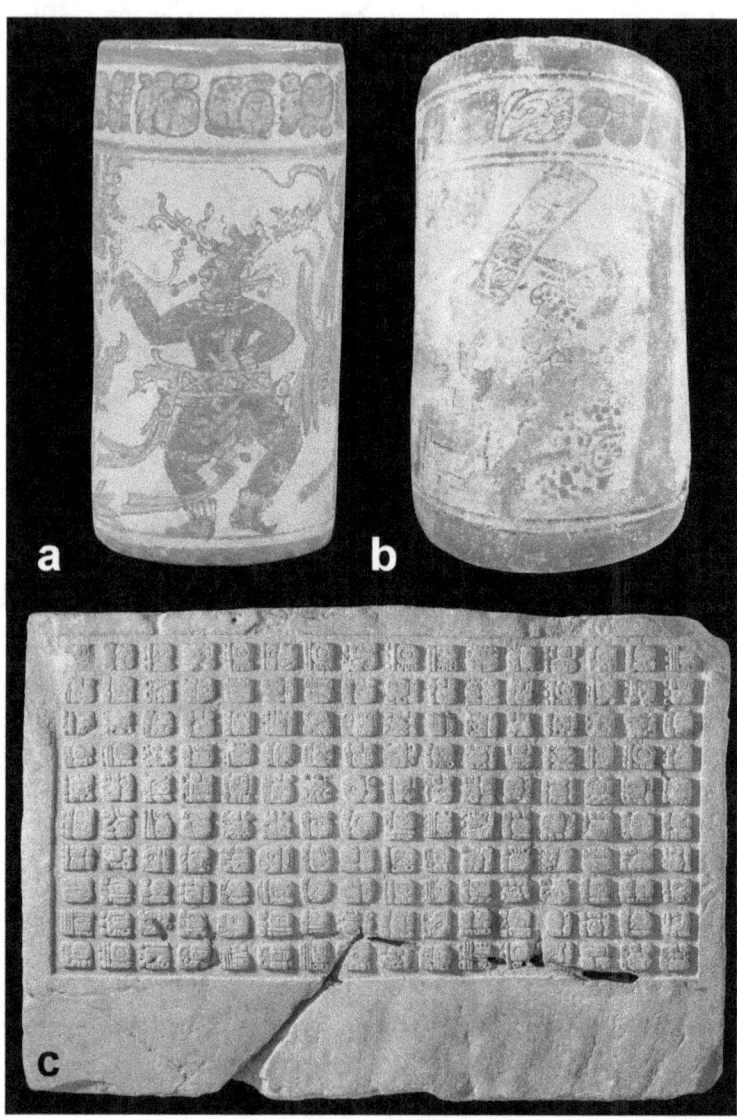

Figure 4.3. Extraordinary examples with hieroglyphic writing: (*a*) Maize Dancer vase in custody of La Ruta Maya Foundation, Reg. No. 1.2.179.7 (photo by La Ruta Maya Foundation); (*b*) Sak Mo' vessel in the custody of "Dr. Juan Antonio Valdés" Museum/Herrera Collection, Uaxactún, Reg. No. 17.2.1.543 (photo by Guido Krempel); (*c*) Cancuén Panel 1 in custody of La Ruta Maya Foundation, Reg. No. 1.2.144.244 (photo courtesy of Jorge Pérez de Lara).

of the staff for the 2015 field season. With a thought to making the vase available for loan for an international traveling exhibition to museums in Assen (Netherlands), Speyer (Germany), and Alicante (Spain), there was renewed motivation to treat the vase in a timely manner.

Since the fragile condition of the vessel made it impossible for travel, the archaeological project's conservator, Teresa Navarro Gómez, agreed to treat it (Navarro Gómez et al. 2015; Krempel 2016). Given the significantly different state of conservation since its registration in 2009, official permission from the Ministry of Culture and Sports had to be requested and the permit was issued shortly before the end of the field season in 2015. The restoration process (in which the vessel was disassembled, cleaned of its old adhesives, and professionally reassembled) was properly documented and included in a restoration report delivered to the Ministry, so that the vessel of Sak Mo' could finally be returned to the museum in a clean and stable condition.

The significance of this vessel—and with it the legitimization to safeguard it in a special way—not only lies in its aesthetic value as an elaborately painted artwork, but is further underpinned by epigraphic and iconographic analysis. In fact, it bears a rare dedicatory text which describes it to be a "vessel for his first creation/offering" (*y-uk'ib tu yax ch'ab*), meaning that this specimen was specifically manufactured for a certain initiation ritual (bloodletting) of a young man (Houston 2012, 2017). Apart from this vessel, there are few other known examples made for this specific purpose, which makes it an exceptional piece.

An even more intriguing piece of evidence underlining the importance of this vessel is the ending of its dedicatory text, which terminates in the sequence "it was stated by me, White Macaw" (*cheh'en sak mo'*). The latter is the signature of the scribe who wrote this dedicatory text, an individual named Sak Mo', whose scribal signature and individual painting style is attested to on only a few other ceramics of unknown provenance (all are representative of the most detailed and elaborate Late Classic Maya art). In the corpus of Classic Maya art known so far, there are only few examples that bear an individual's scribal signature, and much less a personal portrait of the scribe himself. The Sak Mo' vase, in fact, has the presence of a man writing a codex and wearing a white bird as a headdress, which leaves no doubt that Sak Mo' not only left his own signature in the dedicatory text but also depicted himself as a participant in the scene.

A sobering fact regarding the artworks of Sak Mo' is that none of them have been recovered from an archaeological context, resulting in an unsettled quest regarding their actual provenance and, in turn, a still unknown place of origin for their creator. In sum, the vessel of Sak Mo' is an important example of a historically significant Late Classic vessel of unknown provenance. Reportedly sacked from a site located within the periphery of Uaxactún, then transferred to a private collection, the vase has been safeguarded and conserved, and as a positive side effect, this conservation has enabled it to be exhibited in several international exhibitions where many visitors can see it.

Case Study 2: Polychrome Ceramics from the Xultún Region

Our second case study is likewise concerned with a looted cylindrical vessel of unknown provenance (Registry No. 1.2.179.7), which, contrary to the vessel of Sak Mo', bears sufficient calligraphic and stylistic evidence to enable us to trace its supposed place of origin (Matteo and Krempel, in press). Even though its precise place of origin remains unknown, the Maize Dancer vessel in custody of La Ruta Maya Foundation can be dubbed a fortunate case given that it was donated by the family of a man who had recently died and possessed a few archaeological objects and a small library of archaeology books. The care the vessel received allowed it to remain in relatively good condition, with enough details of the iconography and dedicatory text preserved to enable us to associate it with the name of Yax We'en Chan K'inich, and in turn, the painting schools/workshops of Xultún commissioned by this individual (Krempel and Matteo 2012, 2013).

Being a small cylindrical vessel, its outer surface is decorated with two dancing maize deities wearing a huge backrack (a motif known in the literature as Holmul or Maize Dancer theme). The vessel bears a standardized dedicatory text surrounding the rim, which is partially eroded but can be fully reconstructed thanks to several comparable ceramics supposedly originating from the same workshop (see e.g., Krempel and Matteo 2012, 2013; Matteo and Krempel 2011; Matteo and Krempel in press). The text states: "Here got consecrated the painted drinking vessel for Tzih of Yax We'en Chan K'inich, lord of Baax Witz, head of the land." In short, the text specifically mentions the intended generic purpose of the vessel (a drinking vessel for a certain beverage called *tzih*) and furthermore provides the personal name and titles of its owner/recipient. As fate had it, the name of Yax We'en Chan K'inich is attested on several other polychrome ceramics of unknown provenance. However, many comparable examples can be associated with the same individual, Yax We'en Chan K'inich, not the least by means of stylistic comparisons and similar calligraphic traits. Of the many examples today kept in private and institutional collections around the word, at least 14 vessels (the true figure is certainly much higher) bear the name of Yax We'en Chan K'inich. As evidenced by his titles, the aforementioned individual was a Late Classic ruler of Xultún (called Baax Witz "Hammerstone-Mountain"; see Prager et al. 2010), a huge site located in the Northeastern Petén that has been severely looted since at least the 1960s, and where archaeological excavations began in 2009.

Due to early illegal excavations, a tremendous number of valuable ceramics were removed from the site core and peripheral zones of Xultún. These ceramics were traded through the black market and finally landed in private collections; some stayed in Guatemala, but the majority passed through national borders and landed abroad. Such ceramics are now in collections in neighboring countries, several U.S. states, Australia, Asia, and European countries. Unlike the many objects that have passed through the Guatemalan border and will need additional efforts to enable their repatriation in the future, the Xultún vessel in the La Ruta Maya collection has—thanks to its donation—been made available for study. A recent analysis conducted by Dorie Reents-Budet (pers. comm.; Matteo and Krempel in press), for example, has revealed that its chemical ID matches with other pieces from private collections that can be associated with Xultún, either stylistically or by means of epigraphic analysis. Thus, these results independently support the results of epigraphic and stylistic approaches. In this regard, notwithstanding its unknown provenance, a thorough study of its dedicatory text—together with stylistic comparisons—plus an independent testing of its material composition, revealed that it was manufactured in Xultún and can be defined as Cultural Heritage of Guatemala. Of the many artworks bearing the name of Yax We'en Chan K'inich and contemporaneous individuals from Xultún, the vessel in custody of La Ruta Maya is one of only a few examples of clearly identified Xultún origin that remain within the national borders of Guatemala. Another looted vessel bearing the same name was confiscated in the Tikal National Park area and is displayed in the Sylvanus G. Morley Museum in Tikal. Unfortunately, most examples remain in private and institutional collections abroad. In sum, the Maize Dancer vessel in La Ruta Maya Foundation shows the significance of epigraphic, stylistic, and chemical analyses in reconstructing the place of origin of pieces lacking secure provenance.

Case Study 3. The Cancuén Panel

A major event in 2011 changed La Ruta Maya Foundation fundamentally: the closing of the "Museo Príncipe Maya" (formerly in Cobán, Alta Verapaz) and the transfer of the entire collection's possession rights to the Foundation. In this specific case, La Ruta Maya was the only organization able to receive this registered collection and keep the promise of making it available for display in public spaces. Important objects were transferred with the collection, including the famous Panel 1 of Cancuén (registered with the No. 16.2.5.244) which was, in the interim, traveling with an exhibition abroad and came directly to the Foundation's premises at the end of the show.[18]

In the case of Guatemala, the armed forces, local authorities, and paramilitary groups had an active role in the plunder of archaeological sites and wildlife trafficking, as a side-consequence of the internal armed conflict (which took place from 1960 to 1996). According to personal accounts by local men, the blocks of the hieroglyphic stairway of Cancuén, for example, were carefully cut and systematically removed and transported by military crews. Some blocks have been located in other countries such as the United States, Switzerland, and Australia. Panel 1 remained within national borders after it was looted, reportedly during the civil war (Guenter 2002; Kistler 2004; Mayer 1995a, 1995b; Yates 2012). Until 1994, when it surfaced for sale on the art market, its exact whereabouts had been unknown. The former owner of the Museo Príncipe Maya finally purchased it sometime after that, though it remained unregistered until April 22, 1999.[19] Today, as part of the collection in custody of La Ruta Maya Foundation, the panel has been openly studied, placed on public exhibition, and used as an education tool to teach the public the value of hieroglyphic texts and the disadvantages of looting.

Monuments and Objects Located Abroad

Case Studies in Repatriation Efforts by the Guatemalan
Government and the Role of the Private Sector

Currently the Guatemalan government has three options for the recovery of
archaeological heritage that left the country illegally. The first option is the
official claim to foreign governments and/or institutions. In this case, the
country depends on the statutes and processes established by the agreements
signed with one or more countries. The claiming country must provide proof
that the artifact was taken from within their territory, and that the piece has
been reported as stolen. Such documentation can include technical reports,
drawings, photographs, videos, and any other material (like epigraphic evaluations or stylistic analyses) that can provide information on the object's origin.
The requesting country must also hire legal services in the country where the
request is made in order to give follow-up in court. If a country fails to do
that, the case can be dismissed or take years to be resolved. Examples of such
scenarios include the recovery attempts for the famous jade mask from Río
Azul (Stuart 1999; Yates 2015) and several objects known to have been in the
possession of antiquities dealer Leonardo Augusto Patterson (Cascone 2015;
Mashberg 2015), who is being sought by Guatemalan authorities although he
is currently involved in ongoing criminal proceedings in Germany. Both cases
were failures as a result of technical and legal issues that Guatemala could not
fulfill in the foreign countries. Since then, Guatemala has been very careful
regarding international claims.

The second option is the voluntary return of material by a foreign entity.
Guatemala has received objects either confiscated by foreign authorities or
voluntarily returned by museums. Examples include the return of El Zotz
Lintel 1 in 1998; the 2004 return of a lot of 30 objects found inside a vault at
the destroyed World Trade Center in New York City in an event coordinated
by the U.S. Embassy in Guatemala and the Ministry of Foreign Affairs;[20]
and the return of Naranjo Stela 8 in 2015. The repatriation of El Zotz Lintel
1 was made as a voluntary return by the Denver Art Museum[21] in coordination with the Institute of Anthropology and History (IDAEH) of Guatemala,
while the repatriation of Naranjo Stela 8 was made as a voluntary return
by the St. Louis Museum of Art in Missouri with the coordination of the
Ministry of Culture and Sports of Guatemala.[22] Both are now housed in the

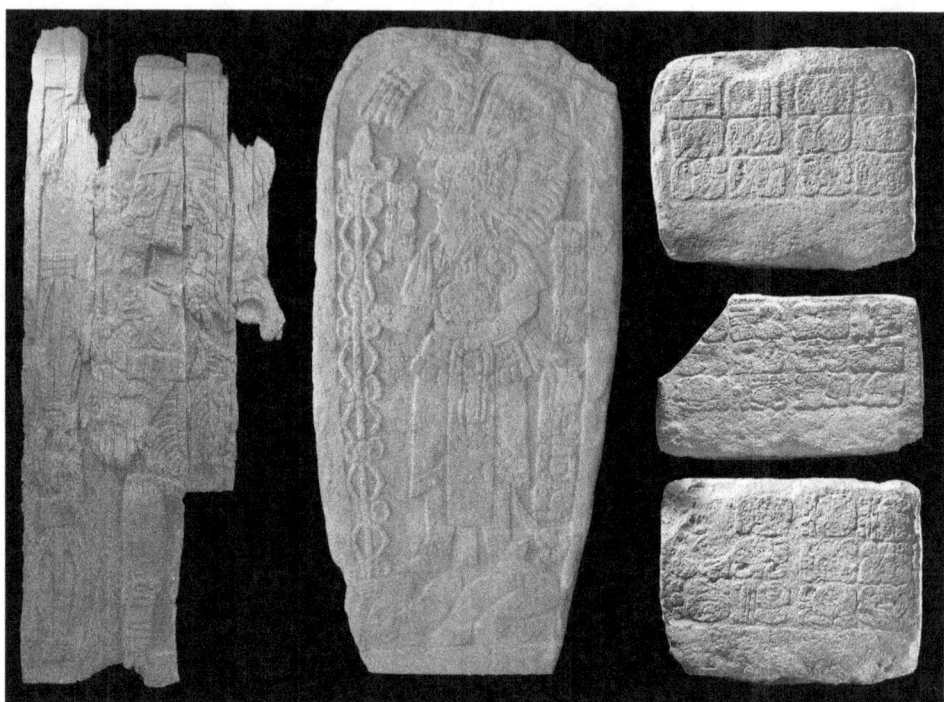

Figure 4.4. Sculptures that have been returned voluntarily to Guatemala and are currently exhibited in the National Museum of Archaeology and Ethnology of Guatemala: (*left*) Lintel 1 of El Zotz (photo by Guido Krempel); (*middle*) Stela 8 of Naranjo (located in the Museo Nacional de Arqueología y Etnología de Guatemala, photo courtesy of Proyecto Atlas Epigráfico de Petén, CEMYK); (*right*) the Corona Panels (K9126, K9128, and K9127, courtesy of Justin Kerr).

National Museum of Archaeology and Ethnology, on public display. In both cases, the negotiations were started by the foreign entities who wanted to return the pieces, with the assistance of the relevant embassies and Ministry of Foreign Affairs (see fig. 4.4).

A third option implemented only once—to date—with the hieroglyphic panels from La Corona, is the recovery and repatriation by the State with the support of a private entity, be it local or foreign. Unfortunately, there is no clear legislation or procedure for the repatriation of archaeological objects with no context in Guatemala, so the first repatriation under this model suffered several setbacks during the process. Internationally, though, there is legislation that can be taken into consideration for repatriation purposes.[23]

Case Study 4: The La Corona Blocks

On November 16, 2011, at 8:00 pm, three persons gathered on the airstrip next to the private hangars at the Aurora International Airport in Guatemala City: a representative of the Registry of Cultural Property, the director of La Ruta Maya Foundation (the institution assisting with the arrangements and paperwork for the import, packing, and transportation of the panels), and a Customs merchandise analyst of "Aduana Central de Aviación." They waited for the arrival of three elaborately carved limestone monuments originating from the hieroglyphic stairways of the archaeological site today known as La Corona (Petén, Guatemala). Almost an hour later, a small jet landed, and legal documents were immediately signed, endorsing the blocks to the Ministry of Culture and Sports (MCD) of Guatemala. The crate was moved to the main terminal, where the contents were photographed and checked under the supervision of Customs officials and the aforementioned representatives.

The monuments were placed in storage until the moment they were to be retrieved and transported to the National Museum of Archaeology and Ethnology of Guatemala (MUNAE) by the representatives of the legal department of the Ministry. After several setbacks, eight months later, the blocks finally arrived at the museum. Such a delay was caused by the authorities' lack of experience in proceeding with repatriations arranged, or coordinated, with nongovernmental actors. The monuments were presented to the public on September 11, 2012, during an event held at MUNAE by the Vice-Minister of Patrimony of the Ministry of Culture and Sports, the Director of MUNAE, the subdirector of the Regional Archaeological Project of La Corona, and the president of La Ruta Maya Foundation.[24]

The case of La Corona's sacked hieroglyphic stairway exemplifies the difficulties that a country faces when handling archaeological material that has been plundered and trafficked illegally. Guatemala's law establishes that all archaeological material is property of the State and therefore is classified as Cultural Heritage of the Nation. However, the context of looted art is often unknown or cannot be verified with certainty (usually because the historical information is missing or there is a lack of stylistic comparisons), which makes it difficult for the country to claim the return of objects following the procedures established in international agreements. In such cases, additional help by local or foreign institutions is needed. In this particular case, the three blocks were returned to the country after being located by members of the archaeological project and were imported with the assistance of a private organization filing the legal governmental permits.

Although details on the panels' route of acquisition are mostly unknown, the blocks were located in the United States in the hands of an individual who, in his own words, "made a sacrifice to catch these panels before they disappeared into the antiquities market." The directors of La Corona Regional Archaeological Project (PRALC, in Spanish) became aware of them and started a negotiation process that ended in the return of the hieroglyphic stones to their country of origin. According to Marcello Canuto and Tomás Barrientos, director and subdirector of PRALC, respectively, the three blocks "were precisely looted from La Corona and came to light about five years before they were repatriated, when their photographs circulated in the internet with the intention of being sold after the owner's death" (statement made at MUNAE press conference, 2012). Thanks to the initiative of Dr. Canuto, information was collected and the monuments were quickly incorporated into the list of looted monuments of the site. It is important to note that the identification of such material was made possible thanks to the collaboration of epigraphers around the world, who are on alert to identify sculptures in private collections.

In the case of these three blocks from La Corona, Dr. Canuto quickly reported their existence to the Guatemalan authorities. In addition, "it was established that these sculptures were part of a hieroglyphic staircase, of which four other blocks were already known." How was this proved? Thanks to the writing format, which consists of three rows and four columns of glyphs, the stylistic peculiarities of its carving, and the content of the hieroglyphic text. "While the process of repatriation was on its way, the excavations at La Corona uncovered another 14 blocks with the same format of glyphs, indicating that this stairway was large and with a significantly long text."[25]

In this case, thanks to epigraphic studies and the related correspondence among several scholars, it was proven that the three panels were part of the Hieroglyphic Stairway of La Corona, a site that was severely looted in the 1960s. The case of La Corona has been of great interest because its hieroglyphic panels, originally catalogued as being from "Site Q," were highly valued for their quality (for further information on Site Q, see Canuto and Barrientos 2013 and Stuart et al. 2015). According to scholars who have been able to track some of the panels, several glyphic panels from La Corona still remain in private collections spread around Europe, Australia, and the United States.

Concluding Remarks

In Guatemala specifically, looting and the illegal trade in cultural heritage is still a taboo subject. It is seldom addressed by academics, who often avoid talking openly about the issue.[26] Almost no efforts are being made by either the government or the private cultural sector (museums, foundations, and associations) to propose new "methods," strategies, or ideas for the recovery and management of what has been lost to plundering. Museums do what they are supposed to do, but in a very traditional way. New proposals should include, at the least, innovative projects such as the creation of a national program on dissemination and cultural education; a government strategy for the recovery and repatriation of archaeological artifacts and monuments located abroad; and the strengthening of the Registry of Cultural Property.[27] The above would also have to include a new relationship with cultural heritage in private custody and a comprehensive legislation shared by all.

As academics know, but the general public usually does not, the plunder of archaeological sites and the removal of their objects and monuments destroys all the information that could otherwise be provided for the social, environmental, historical, symbolic, and religious aspects of past communities. These circumstances leave decontextualized objects to be appreciated solely for their aesthetic attributes, and they can only be understood according to a variety of opinions about their function and use. For this reason, looted archaeological and historical vestiges have often been "tagged" as "black market material" lacking academic importance.[28]

On the other hand, the lack of resources and poor institutional strength of the government hinders the implementation of specific actions, such as mass dissemination, systematic training of officials on issues related to cultural heritage, and the creation of curriculum workshops for public school teachers. Legally, the administration of archaeological sites and national parks is shared by the Dirección General del Patrimonio Cultural y Natural (DIGEPAN) and the Consejo Nacional de Areas Protegidas (National Council of Protected Areas, CONAP),[29] due to the existence of several national parks, each containing natural reserves and numerous archaeological sites, as is the case regarding Parque Nacional Tikal, Parque Nacional Mirador-Río Azul, Parque Nacional Yaxhá, and Parque Nacional Laguna del Tigre.[30] All archaeological sites in the country that are outside the national parks have the protection only of DIGE-

PAN and perhaps local municipalities. Few have support from civic associations and committees.

The above would be enough justification to promote inter-institutional partnerships and joint public-private initiatives. In both cases, the results can be more effective because the resources are maximized and the capacities are strengthened. This does not release government institutions from their responsibility and reason for their very existence (that is, in order to safeguard Cultural Heritage), but rather serves as support to this cause. In this case, the private sector (hence the private depository of archaeological heritage of the Nation) should also become part of that responsible community.

Acknowledgments

For previous communications and sharing of their expertise, we would like to thank Dorie Reents-Budet, Karl Herbert Mayer, and Sebastián Matteo. Furthermore, we thank Justin Kerr, Jorge Pérez de Lara, Camilo Alejandro Luín, and Lorena Castillo for their kind permission to use their photographs for this chapter.

Notes

1. Studies by David Pendergast and Elizabeth Graham on Mexico, Belize, and Guatemala (1990); Ian Graham (2010), David Matsuda on Belize (1996); Sofía Paredes Maury on looting in the Maya Biosphere Reserve (1999), and reports on looters' trenches in structures by Julio Cotom Nimatuj (2012), among others.

2. The official Spanish title is *Ley para la Protección del Patrimonio Cultural de la Nación*.

3. Possible reasons for this could have been the reduction of demand for Pre-Columbian objects, the implementation of international treaties and agreements by other countries, the signing of the Peace Accords in Guatemala, and the establishment of drug trafficking as the primary illegal source of income in the region.

4. In these cases, either the objects that are appearing in the market have been hidden in Europe for some time or they have been hidden and accumulated in their countries of origin and exported later.

5. The most important international convention concerning antiquities today is the 1970 UNESCO Convention on the Means of Prohibiting and Preventing the Illicit Import, Export and Transfer of Ownership of Cultural Property. This seminal document gives member countries the right to recover stolen or illegally exported antiquities from other member countries, including the United States. U.S. legislation incorporated the UNESCO Convention in 1983

through the Convention on Cultural Property Implementation Act (CPIA), through which it has signed several bilateral agreements with countries of Mesoamerica, South America, Africa, Europe, and Asia. The United States has entered into bilateral selective agreements, for example, with Guatemala, El Salvador, and Peru since 1997.

6. This area includes three municipalities (Santa María de Nebaj, San Juan Cotzal, and San Gaspar Chajul) where large ceramic funerary urns with lids can be found, usually with jaguar, death, fire, and Earth Monster iconography.

7. *Chicle* is the latex or sap of the *chicozapote* tree (*Manilkara zapota*), while the *xate* is a palm leaf (of the Arecaceae family) used in flower arrangements in Europe, Japan, and the United States.

8. For additional information on the economy of the Petén region, see Dugelby, 1995.

9. Means by which the population can access archaeological objects include, but are not limited to, the following: destructive looting for illicit traffic; fortuitous finding by intensive, extensive, and plot agriculture; fortuitous finding by urban planning, construction and repair of infrastructure (public and domestic); findings by extraction of geological resources (mining); and exploration and outdoor sports and activities (hiking, diving, caving, among others) (Paredes Maury 2014a).

10. Regulations are explained in Article 23—Registration of cultural property; Article 24—Title of goods; Article 25—Declaration of property; Article 26—Legal effects; and Article 28—National Inventory of Heritage (Law for the Protection of the Cultural Patrimony of the Nation, Decree 26-77, Reformed by Decree No. 81-98).

11. The term "grandfathers" is a respectful word used to identify family or community ancestors. In Spanish, it is *los abuelos*.

12. The Alcaldía Indígena de Chichicastenango (Quiché), Guatemala) has started to work more closely with the Registry of Cultural Property since 2000 (Carlos Morán Alvizúres, Head of the Hispanic & Republican Sections of the Registry, pers. comm.)

13. Guatemala has two cases, Fundación La Ruta Maya and Asociación Tikal. A third one, FUNBA (Fundación para las Bellas Artes y la Cultura) is a private multiperiod art collection based in Antigua that plans to have its Pre-Columbian collection on view as soon as it builds its own private museum. Of the three, only La Ruta Maya organizes thematic shows each year and makes efforts to keep its collection circulating among researchers and the public.

14. In 1996, the Uaxactún collection was the first collection legally registered in Petén, but the authorities lacked the budget to travel and do the registration themselves. Therefore, a special mandate was given to Sofía Paredes Maury by the Registry of Cultural Property to do the registration in situ. At that time there was no road connecting the Petén to the rest of the country and most of the trips were done by plane.

15. See for example Matteo et al. 2014 for an example of one of the objects in the collection.

16. La Ruta Maya has repatriated 496 objects to date, from the United States. Three of them—the La Corona blocks—were given to the National Museum of Archaeology and Ethnology of Guatemala

17. With Form R-1 (Request for the Registry of Cultural Property) and Form R-5 (Request

for the Transfer of Portable Cultural Material) an organization or individual can request the registration of an object or group of objects, or request the transfer of custodianship, following what is established by the law.

18. Exhibition "The Fiery Pool, the Maya and the Mythic Sea." Fort Worth Museum of Art, Texas, USA. (August 2010 to January 2011).

19. The former owner of the "Museo Príncipe Maya" mentioned that the Panel was too hot to handle and after being kept in the garden of a military barracks and "buried" underground inside a "*costal*" or fiber sack in a shed for at least four years, it was finally bought by him and registered in 1999.

20. The 30 objects were delivered by the U.S. Ambassador in Guatemala City, John Hamilton. According to a statement from the U.S. government, "the Mayan objects of incalculable value were stored in a vault of the Customs service located in one of the two towers that fell. After the attack, the objects were found intact inside a vault located in the rubble." The pieces had been confiscated in Miami in 1998 when a couple attempted to illegally enter the United States with them. BBC Mundo.com Domingo, July 25, 2004: http://news.bbc.co.uk/hi/spanish/latin_america/newsid_3923000/3923673.stm.

21. Key facilitators for this return were Dr. Dorie Reents-Budet, curator of Pre-Columbian art at the Denver Art Museum (DAM); Dr. Lewis Sharpe, Director of DAM; and Dr. Juan Antonio Valdés, Director of the Institute of Anthropology and History of Guatemala (IDAEH).

22. A key facilitator for this return was Dr. Matthew Robb, former curator at the St. Louis Museum

23. The main legal articles can be found in the Political Constitution of the Republic of Guatemala (Title II. Human rights. Chapter II. Section Two. Culture); the Law for the Protection of the Cultural Heritage of the Nation (Decree 26–77, Reformed by Decree No. 81–98); CRIMINAL CODE. SECOND BOOK (TITLE VIII). About the crimes against the public faith and the national patrimony. CHAPTER IV. About the Plunder of National Heritage; Convention for the Protection of World Cultural and Natural Heritages; UNESCO 1970 Convention on the Means of Prohibiting and Preventing the Illicit Import, Export and Transfer of Ownership of Cultural Property; OAS Convention on the Defense of the Archaeological, Historical and Artistic Heritage of the American Nations, San Salvador Convention; Central American Convention for the Return and Restoration of Archaeological, Historical and Artistic Objects; UNIDROIT Convention on Stolen or Illegally Exported Cultural Property; Convention for the Protection and Restoration of Archaeological, Artistic and Historical Monuments between the Republic of Guatemala and the Estados Unidos Mexicanos; and the "Agreement between the Republic of Guatemala and Belize for the protection, conservation, recovery and return of cultural and natural property that has been stolen, imported, exported, and transferred illegally."

24. However, the museum's internal "non-official" policies ban the display of archaeological materials that have been privately recovered; therefore, the blocks are kept in the storage room, out of public view despite other objects returned voluntarily by foreign museums being on display.

25. Comunicado de Prensa. 2012. "Tres Bloques con Inscripciones Regresan a Guatemala;

Fragmentos de una escalinata jeroglífica de La Corona habían sido saqueados." Ministerio de Cultura y Deportes & Proyecto Arqueológico Regional La Corona, Guatemala.

26. See examples such as Reents-Budet (2014) for exceptions.

27. The Registry is under the Dirección General del Patrimonio Cultural y Natural (DG-PCYN) which in turn belongs to the Ministry of Culture and Sports and is the head of IDAEH (Institute of Anthropology and History). This Directorate also includes the Department of Pre-Hispanic and Colonial Monuments and the Unit against Illicit Traffic, among others.

28. John Dorfman (1998) addresses this situation.

29. To fulfill its aims and objectives, the National Council of Protected Areas is composed of representatives of the following entities: (a) Ministry of Environment and Natural Resources (MARN, previously the National Environment Commission, CONAMA); (b) Center for Conservationist Studies (CECON/USAC); (c) Institute of Anthropology and History (IDAEH); (d) A delegate of the nongovernmental organizations related to natural resources and the environment registered in CONAP; (e) The National Association of Municipalities (ANAM); (f) Guatemalan Tourism Institute (INGUAT); and (g) Ministry of Agriculture, Livestock and Food (MAGA).

30. Some of them include also biotopes (Biotopo Dos Lagunas and Biotopo Laguna del Tigre) under the administration of the Center for Conservationist Studies of San Carlos University (CECON) and the special case of Defensores de la Naturaleza Foundation, which has a co-management agreement with the government for the conservation and protection of Parque Nacional Laguna del Tigre and the magnificent sites within the park such as Piedras Negras, Tecolote, and others.

References Cited

Canuto, Marcello A. and Tomás Barrientos Q. 2013. "The Importance of La Corona." La Corona Notes 1 (1). *Mesoweb*. http://www.mesoweb.com/LaCorona/LaCoronaNotes01.pdf (accessed November 8, 2017).

Cascone, Sarah. 2015. "Infamous Antiquities Dealer Convicted of Smuggling and Forgery." *Artnet News*, December 9, 2015. https://news.artnet.com/topic/art-crime (accessed November 8, 2017).

Cotom Nimatuj, Julio Alberto. 2012. "El Registro Arqueológico en los Saqueos de los Sitios Prehispánicos del Sureste de la Cuenca Mirador." In *XXV Simposio de Investigaciones Arqueológicas en Guatemala*, edited by Bárbara Arroyo, Lorena Paiz Aragón, Adriana Linares Palma, and Ana Lucia Arroyave, 1191–1206. Guatemala City: Ministerio de Cultura y Deportes Instituto de Antropología e Historia.

Dorfman, John. 1998. "Getting Their Hands Dirty? Archaeologists and the Looting Trade." *Lingua Franca*, May/June 1998, 29–36. http://linguafranca.mirror.theinfo.org/9805/dorfman.html (accessed November 8, 2017).

Dugelby, Barbara L. 1995. "Chicle Latex Extraction in the Maya Biosphere Reserve: Behavioral, Institutional, and Ecological Factors Affecting Sustainability." PhD dissertation, Department of Environmental Studies, Duke University.

Guenter, Stanley. 2002. "A reading of the Cancuén Looted Panel." *Mesoweb*. http://www.mesoweb.com/features/cancuen/Panel.pdf (accessed November 8, 2017).

Graham, Ian. 2010. *The Road to Ruins*. Albuquerque: University of New Mexico Press.

Houston, Stephen. 2012. "A Liquid Passage to Manhood." *Maya Decipherment*, May 8, 2012. https://decipherment.wordpress.com/2012/05/08/a-liquid-passage-to-manhood/. (accessed November 8, 2017).

———. 2017. *The Gifted Passage: Young Men in Classic Maya Art and Text*. New Haven, Conn.: Yale University Press.

Kistler, S. Ashley. 2004. "The Search for Five-Flower Mountain: Re-evaluating the Cancuen Panel." *Mesoweb*. http://www.mesoweb.com/features/kistler/Cancuen.pdf (accessed November 8, 2017).

Krempel, Guido. 2016. "Análisis iconográfico y epigràfico de artefactos arqueológicos de Uaxactún y alrededores." In *Nuevas Excavaciones en Uaxactún VII Temporada 2015*, edited by Milan Kováč, Silvia Alvarado Najarro, Mauricio Díaz, and Tomáš Drápela, 262–404. Chronos, Bratislava: Center for Mesoamerican Studies. Comenius University.

Krempel, Guido, and Sebastián Matteo. 2012. "Painting Styles of the North-Eastern Peten from a Local Perspective: The Palace Schools of Yax We'en Chan K'inich, Lord of Xultun." *Contributions in New World Archaeology* 3: 135–172.

———. 2013. "A Maya Vessel dedicated to Yax We'en Chan K'inich Lord of Xultun, Guatemala." *Mexicon* 35 (1): 11–14.

Ley para la Protección del Patrimonio Cultural de la Nación (Decreto 26–77, Reformado por Decreto No. 81–98). Ministerio de Cultura y Deportes.

Mashberg, Tom. 2015. "Antiquities Dealer Leonardo Patterson Faces New Criminal Charges." *New York Times*, December 8, 2015. https://www.nytimes.com/2015/12/09/arts/design/antiquities-dealer-leonardo-patterson-faces-new-criminal-charges.html (accessed November 8, 2017).

Matsuda, David. 1996. "The Environmental Aspects of *Huaquerismo* (Artifact Looting) in Latin America." *ECO* Belize, Jul–Aug 1996, 14–15.

Matteo, Sebastián, and Guido M. Krempel. 2011. "La nobleza y el estilo cerámico de Xultun, Petén, Guatemala." In *XXIV Simposio de Investigaciones Arqueológicas de Guatemala*, edited by Bárbara Arroyo, Lorena Paiz Aragón, Adriana Linares Palma, and Ana Lucia Arroyave, 957–971. Guatemala City: Ministerio de Cultura y Deportes Instituto de Antropología e Historia.

———. In press. "A Maize Dancer vessel dedicated to Yax We'en Chan K'inich, Lord of Xultun." *Journal for Maya Studies*.

Matteo, Sebastián, Philip Galeev, Sergey Vepretskiy, and Camilo Luín. 2014. "Un Plato Asociado a un Gobernante de Piedras Negras, Guatemala, en las Colecciones de la Fundación Ruta Maya." *Mexicon* 36 (3): 80–84.

Mayer, Karl Herbert. 1995a. *Maya Monuments: Sculptures of Unknown Provenance*, Supplement 4. Graz: Academic Publishers.

———. 1995b. "A Unique Maya Glyphic Panel in Guatemala." *Mexicon* 17 (1): 3.

Navarro Gómez, Teresa, Enrique Pérez, and Lenca Horáková. 2016. "Restauración de Piezas Arqueológicas de Uaxactún y Sitios Periféricos." In *Nuevas Excavaciones en Uaxactùn VII Temporada 2015*, edited by Milan Kováč, Silvia Alvarado Najarro, Mauricio Díaz, and Tomáš Drápela, 256–361. Chronos, Bratislava: Center for Mesoamerican Studies. Comenius University.

Paredes Maury, Sofía. 1999. "Surviving in the Rainforest: The Realities of Looting in the Rural Villages of El Petén, Guatemala." Foundation for the Advancement of Mesoamerican Studies (FAMSI, Inc.). http://www.famsi.org/reports/95096/95096ParedesMaury01.pdf (accessed November 8, 2017).

———. 2014a. "Patrimonio Cultural en manos privadas: ¿qué hacer? Consideraciones y herramientas para una estrategia nacional de prevención del saqueo y el tráfico ilícito." In *XXVII Simposio de Investigaciones Arqueológicas en Guatemala 2013*, edited by Bárbara Arroyo, Luis Méndez Salinas, and Andrea Rojas, 171–180. Museo Nacional de Arqueología y Etnología, Guatemala.

———. 2014b. "Uso y Transformación del Patrimonio Arqueológico: Los Bienes Culturales y su Relación con la Población Actual." Paper presented at the VII Convención Mundial de la Arqueología Maya "Los Colapsos del Mundo Maya," June 13–15, 2014, Antigua Guatemala.

Pendergast, David and Elizabeth Graham. 1990. "The Battle for the Maya Past: The Effects of International Looting and Collecting in Belize." In *The Ethics of Collecting Cultural Property: Whose Culture? Whose Property?*, edited by Phyllis Mauch Messenger, 51–60. Albuquerque: University of New Mexico Press.

Prager, Christian, Elisabeth Wagner, Sebastián Matteo, and Guido Krempel. 2010. "A Reading of the Xultun Toponymic Title as B'aax (Tuun) Witz Ajaw 'Lord of the B'aax-(Stone) Hill.'" *Mexicon* 32 (4): 74–77.

Reents-Budet, Dorie. 2014. "Compañeros de curadores / huérfanos por académicos: el dilema de artefactos saqueados." In *XXVII Simposio de Investigaciones Arqueológicas en Guatemala 2013*, edited by Bárbara Arroyo, Luis Méndez Salinas, and Andrea Rojas, 137–141. Museo Nacional de Arqueología y Etnología, Guatemala.

Secretaría de Planificación y Programación de la Presidencia–Segeplan. 2013. *Plan de Desarrollo Integral de Petén*. Diagnóstico Territorial de Petén, Tomo 1, coordinated by Wagner Caal Morales. Guatemala.

Stuart, David, Marcello A. Canuto, and Tomás Barrientos Q. 2015. "The Nomenclature of La Corona Sculpture." La Corona Notes 1 (2). *Mesoweb*. http://www.mesoweb.com/LaCorona/LaCoronaNotes02.pdf (accessed November 8, 2017).

Stuart, George. 1999. "Conclusion: Working Together to Preserve Our Past." In *The Ethics of Collecting Cultural Property: Whose Culture? Whose Property?*, edited by Phyllis Mauch Messenger, 243–253. Albuquerque: University of New Mexico Press.

Tremain, Cara G. 2017. "Fifty Years of Collecting: The Sale of Ancient Maya Antiquities at Sotheby's." *International Journal of Cultural Property* 24 (2): 187–219.

Yates, Donna. 2012. "Cancuén Panel." *Trafficking Culture*, August 17, 2012. http://trafficking culture.org/encyclopedia/case-studies/cancuen-panel/ (accessed November 8, 2017).

————. 2014. "Displacement, Deforestation, and Drugs: Antiquities Trafficking and the Narcotics Support Economies of Guatemala." In *Cultural Property Crimes: An Overview and Analysis on Contemporary Perspectives and Trends*, edited by Joris Kila and Marc Balcells, 23–36. Leiden: Brill.

————. 2015. "The Río Azul Mask." *Trafficking Culture*. http://traffickingculture.org/encyclopedia/case-studies/rio-azul-mask-2/ (last modified June 14, 2015; accessed November 8, 2017).

5

The Odyssey of Piedras Negras Stela 5

JAMES A. DOYLE

Visitors to the gallery of Mesoamerican art at the Metropolitan Museum of Art in New York are faced with a large Maya work, lent by the Republic of Guatemala, titled *Commemorative Monument with Enthroned Ruler*. This monument is known as Stela 5 from the city of Piedras Negras, Guatemala, and was an important and unusual monument for its time. This chapter traces the compelling biography of this monument from when it stood overlooking a large Maya plaza in the eighth century to its current place at the Met. The history of Stela 5 intersects with the beginnings of scientific archaeology in Guatemala, the decipherment of Maya hieroglyphic writing, and the emergence of the art market for Maya sculpture in the United States and Europe. Continuing excavations and conservation of monuments at Piedras Negras today promise new avenues of collaborations between art museums like the Met and the local archaeologists and other protectors of the rich cultural patrimony of Guatemala.

Stela 5 and Antiquity

K'inich Yo'nal Ahk II (ca. AD 664–729), having taken his grandfather's regnal name, clearly wanted both to live up to the glory of his predecessors and to make a name for himself as the seventh ruler of Piedras Negras (Yokib, to its residents). He instructed the atelier of sculptors based in his royal court to create a row of stelae towering over a monumental circular altar right at the base of the city's massive palace acropolis. All visitors to the highest plaza would have seen the monuments from a distance. Special envoys would have been watched over by the limestone visages of Yo'nal Ahk II and his wife, Lady

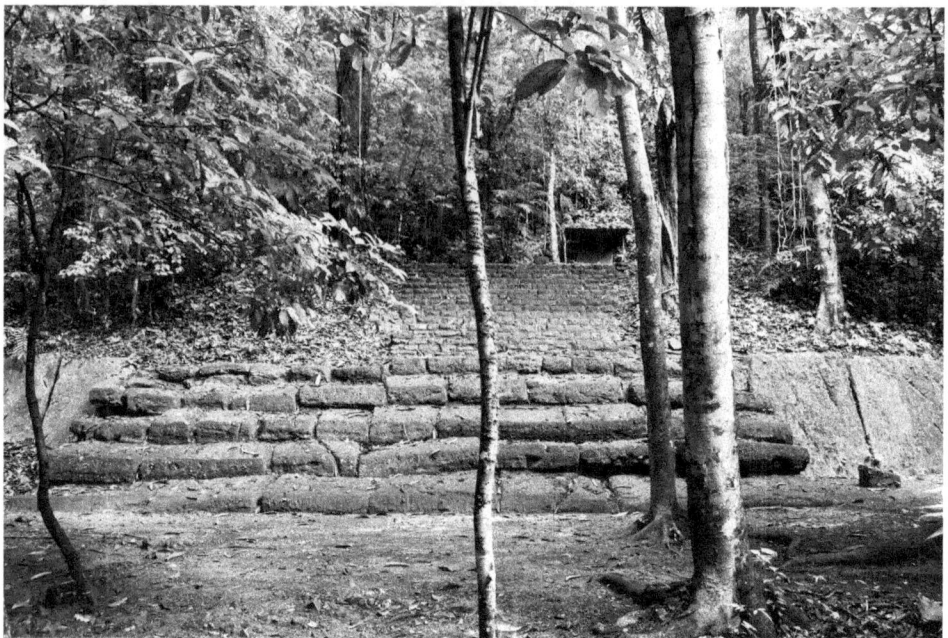

Figure 5.1. Entrance stairway to the Acropolis at Piedras Negras. Photograph by author.

K'atun Ajaw, as they tackled the megalithic staircase leading to the high patios overlooking the mighty Usumacinta River (fig. 5.1).

The ruler gave the artists creative license. One face of Stela 5 may have held a portrait of the ruler (or his family), similar to those found on monuments of his father and grandfather. Dedicated on November 2, AD 716 (9.14.5.0.0 12 Ajaw 8 K'ank'in), Stela 5 featured calendric dates on its sides that anchored the events in mortal time, likely followed by lists of Yo'nal Ahk II's accomplishments. The other face of the stela, possibly visible only to those granted access to the first tier of the royal compound, bears a striking departure from the traditional imagery of warriors and captives.

Many monuments at Piedras Negras show rulers sitting on perishable throne or scaffold platforms, such as Stela 33, commissioned by Yo'nal Ahk II's father, in which the ruler looks down upon his wife. On Stela 5, however, a *sajal*, or noble, stands to the left of the scene, wearing an elaborate jeweled headdress and crossing his arm over his chest in a gesture of submission to the seated lord. The volute projecting from the dignitary's forehead may indicate his role as a *ch'ajoom*, or one who burns incense at court (Scherer and Houston 2018). The seated Yo'nal Ahk II straddles the barrier between real time, represented by his loyal follower, and mythological time (fig. 5.2). The lord sits on a throne or palanquin, a tiered platform surmounted by a large bench adorned with a jaguar skin, its base decorated with motifs for water (see Clancy 2009, 93–99; García Juárez 2015). The empty eyes of the almost-skeletal feline stare out at the viewer, as if drawing us into this liminal space between the real and the mythical. It is not the lord's costume or feathered headdress that places him in a divine space; the jade bracelets, ear flares, pectoral, and long scepter represent real things that elite Maya people wore and used. The arching decoration over his head, however, departs from the images of mortal fealty, indicating the depiction of a myth or its reenactment (Scherer and Houston 2018).

The throne canopy on Piedras Negras Stela 5, upon further inspection, is the gaping maw of a *witz*, the Maya word for both mountain and pyramid, conceived of as a man-made mountain. The animate mountain is marked with the "grape-bunch" motif toward the top of the scene. Its scaly jaws—perhaps an oblique reference to the centipede jaws of the hieroglyph for cenote,[1] a deep sinkhole in limestone, a gigantic example of which sits on a hill above Piedras Negras—are crawling with supernatural creatures. A creepy skeletal figure, perhaps a monstrous firefly, smokes a cigar (itself often an indicator of nighttime, according to Maya artistic conventions) and reaches out toward the seated lord as if beckoning him to the darkness. A lively spider monkey above him gestures wildly as he presumably chatters away. A deity, possibly one known as the Jaguar Paddler God, paws his way out of the eye socket of the *witz*, his outstretched arms also seeming to say to the lord "join us." A large avian creature, perhaps a version of the being known as the Principal Bird Deity, perches atop the mountain and surveys the scene.

For the Maya of the Classic Period (ca. AD 250–900), especially in the region around Piedras Negras, mountains were the center of their cosmological world. From mountains, water flowed and animals emerged. Personified natural phenomena resided around the *witz*. Deities such as Chahk (the god of rain), the Principal Bird Deity (embodiment of riches and excess), nighttime lords of death, and trickster Monkey Scribes all populated the mountains of Maya minds. As if to underscore the mountainous theme of this palanquin, the sculptor of Stela 5 placed two stacked jawless *witz* heads in the lowest register, but the meaning of their upward-facing position is unclear.

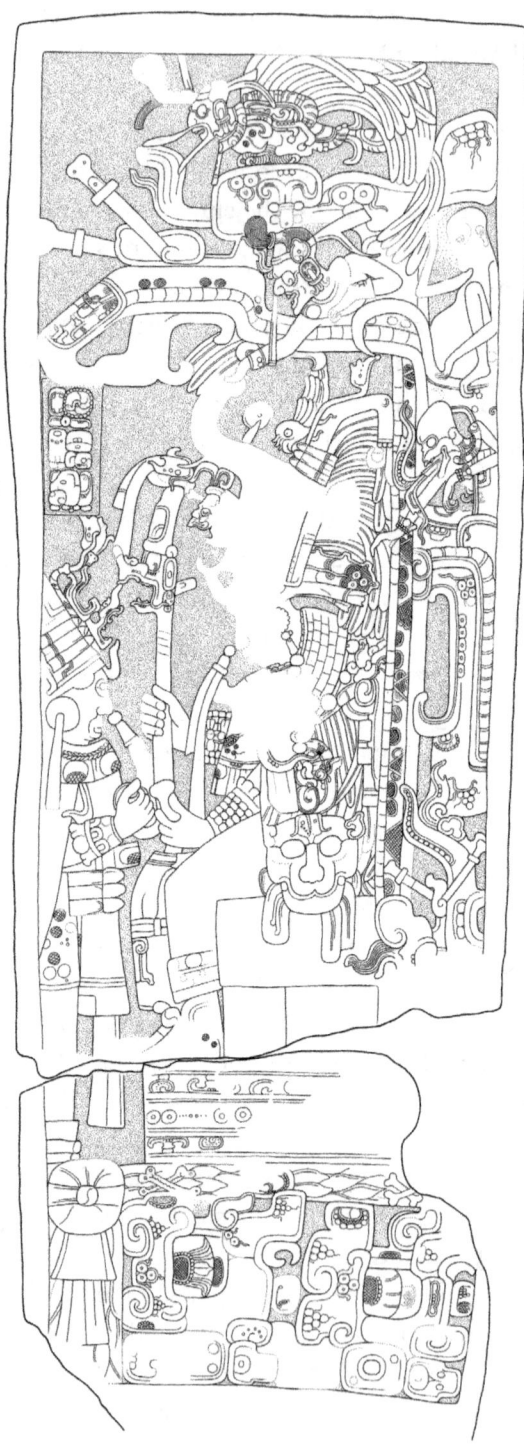

E
1
2
3

Figure 5.2. Stela 5. Drawing
by Ian Graham. Corpus
of Maya Hieroglyphic
Inscriptions © President
and Fellows of Harvard
College, Peabody Museum of
Archaeology and Ethnology,
PM# 2004.15.6.19.14.

Though the well-preserved scene is more or less easy to view, the imposing message of Stela 5 is still a bit lost to modern viewers. Subsequent to its dedication in ancient times, iconoclasts chipped away the face of the main figure, presumably Yo'nal Ahk II himself, rendering his stony gaze powerless over time. Though speculative, it is tempting to imagine raiders in the ninth century, presumably from the longtime rival polity of Yaxchilán, just upriver from Piedras Negras, toppling Stela 5 from its base along with the contemporaneous monuments lined up next to it (see Golden et al. 2016). Whether they were broken by nature or by human hands, they laid to be reclaimed by the rainforest vegetation for more than a millennium. In the centuries that followed, local indigenous Lacandon peoples periodically visited the ruins of the area and left offerings in reverence of the ancestral spaces.

Though the assumed outward-facing surface of Stela 5 was too eroded to read when encountered by Teobert Maler in the late nineteenth century, he was taken by the well-preserved surface of what he dubbed the reverse (fig. 5.3). He noted

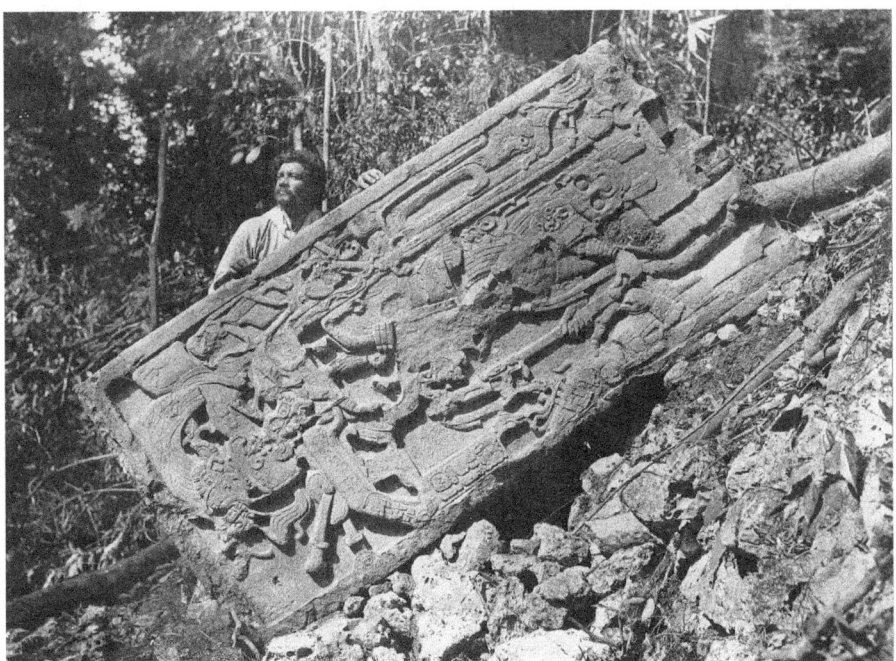

Figure 5.3. Teobert Maler and the top portion of Stela 5, Piedras Negras. Courtesy of the Peabody Museum of Archaeology and Ethnology, Harvard University, PM# 2004.29.7578.

the elaborate details of the ruler's costume, including the feathered headdress and "lance," upon which "the fantastic head of a monster has been impaled" (Maler 1901, 144). He noted "traces of dark-red color visible" on the stela, some of which is still visible today. Sylvanus Morley later recognized traces of green and blue paint as well as the overall significance of the stela, noting that it is "one of the most unusual at Piedras Negras" with such "superior" execution that "Stela 5 may be regarded as one of the finest monuments thus far encountered at Piedras Negras" (Morley 1938, 162–163).

As the archaeological project conducted by the University of Pennsylvania Museum of Archaeology and Anthropology got underway in the 1930s, excavations on the acropolis uncovered more carved monuments and a large tomb known as Burial 5. Located across the acropolis from Stela 5, the burial was likely the final resting place of Yo'nal Ahk II, the sculpture's patron. The lord was buried in an heirloom *Spondylus* shell tunic, and his teeth were inlaid with jade and pyrite (Coe 1959; Finamore and Houston 2010, cat. 34; Martin and Grube 2008, 145–147). Though the Penn project restored architecture during several seasons of successful excavations, the jungle soon reclaimed Piedras Negras for itself once again, leaving little trace of the expedition except for an abandoned tractor. Logging and collecting of *chicle* (tree sap used to produce chewing gum) brought people to the ruins from both sides of the Usumacinta River in the mid-twentieth century, ultimately leading to devastating looting and the illicit removal of Piedras Negras Stela 5 and several other monuments.

Stela 5 and the Midcentury Maya Market

The birth of the market for Maya art in the United States is difficult to pinpoint (see O'Neil 2017; O'Neil and Miller 2017). The earliest Maya objects purchased by collector Nelson A. Rockefeller, for example, may have been acquired in or around 1933 when a vacation to Mexico exposed him to Maya ruins. In fact, Rockefeller supported archaeologist Alberto Ruz Lhuillier's famous excavations at Palenque, in Chiapas, leading to the spectacular discovery of the tomb of K'inich Janaab Pakal in 1948. Grandson of the founder of Standard Oil and an avid art collector, Nelson and his mother developed an appreciation for indigenous arts of the Americas, in conjunction with their promotion of modern art. When Nelson was elected president of the board of the Museum of Modern Art in 1940, he supported the pioneering exhibition there, "Twenty Centuries of Mexican Art," which spanned the ancient to the modern (Pillsbury 2014, 18). His passion for art soon gave way to political ambition; he was elected as the governor of New York in 1959.

By the late 1950s, art collectors began to appreciate ancient Maya relief sculpture. Major discoveries at Tikal and Palenque fueled public interest, one the Maya world had not experienced since Stephens and Catherwood ignited interest in ruins in Mexico and Central America a century prior (see Stephens 1996 [1843]). Rockefeller and his advisors for the Museum of Primitive Art, which he founded in 1954 as the Museum of Indigenous Art, began to show interest in Maya sculpture as early as the mid-1950s. Some of the earliest Maya objects purchased by Rockefeller include ceramic figurines, acquired in 1956 from the Stendahl Gallery (1978.412.6; 1979.206.373); the head of a Rain God excavated by George Vaillant at Chichen Itza, presumably sold by Vaillant's widow through John Wise in 1957 (1978.412.24); and a fragment of Tortuguero Monument 6 with hieroglyphs from the Edward Primus Gallery in 1961 (1978.412.75). In 1962 alone, Rockefeller made transformative Maya acquisitions for the museum, including: a wooden Mirror-Bearer sculpture purchased from John Stokes (1979.206.1063); a modeled double-chambered ceramic vessel featuring the Principal Bird Deity (1978.412.90a, b) and a stone column featuring a Maya ruler (1978.412.88) from the Aaron Furman Gallery; and a low-relief sculpted lintel fragment covered in pigment from the Yaxchilán area, from the Everett Rassiga Gallery (1979.206.1047).

Though excavations at Piedras Negras had ceased decades prior, the site captured scholarly and public imagination again in the late 1950s. Tatiana Proskouriakoff, an artist and scholar who worked on architectural renderings of the buildings at Piedras Negras, succeeded in decoding the historical content of Classic Maya texts by studying patterns on the monuments. Her study of Piedras Negras inscriptions, published in 1960, was a pioneering contribution that formed a foundation for the later phonetic decipherments of Maya hieroglyphs (Proskouriakoff 1960). Unlike previous scholars, who maintained that Maya hieroglyphic inscriptions contained only astronomical and esoteric texts, Proskouriakoff's research revealed that Maya scribes recorded historical events, including births, deaths, and royal accessions. She noted that Stela 5, dated to her pivotal "Series 3"—a sequence of monuments that seemed to name the same individual as protagonist—was carved when the ruler featured on the most numerous monuments at the site, now identified as Yo'nal Ahk II, was in his 50s. It might have been his final depiction while alive, or even a posthumous portrait that showed him ruling from the realm of the afterlife.

Given the importance of Piedras Negras in burgeoning Maya scholarship, it was unsurprising that in 1963 Rockefeller's close advisor Rene d'Harnoncourt, then director of New York's Museum of Modern Art, gushed to him about the possibility of acquiring Piedras Negras Stela 5:

> Every now and then an object appears that is so rare that I feel I ought to write you regardless of the price because I want to be sure that if the object should be acquired by another institution you should at least have known of its availability. The Rassiga Gallery now has two pre-Columbian pieces which belong in this category. One is a Maya stela from Piedras Negras. This is certainly one of the highlights of Maya relief art. The piece is about nine feet high and over three feet wide. It is my understanding that it was taken out of Guatemala before Guatemala passed its law for the preservation of national monuments. To my knowledge there is no Maya stone carving of equal importance in this country. Some of the surface at the center of the stela has been chipped off. However, the profile of the priest can be very clearly seen in the original but is not as easily identified in the photograph. The stela is also missing a thin stone border that was still visible in a photograph which appeared in the *Peabody Museum Memoirs* of 1901.[2] It is almost impossible to give an estimate of value on either one of these pieces since nothing of this sort has come on the market as far as we can remember." (Letter from Rene d'Harnoncourt to Nelson Rockefeller, Nov. 15, 1963)

It is clear that Everett Rassiga, a savvy dealer, had led d'Harnoncourt to believe that the sculpture had left Guatemala before 1947, when the country passed its first cultural patrimony laws pertaining to illicit export of archaeological pieces.[3] On the contrary, Stela 5 had most likely been removed in the late 1950s or early 1960s along with many other fragments in the Usumacinta area, to feed the growing international demand for Maya sculpture (Luján Muñóz 1966, 19; Stuart and Graham 2003, 32). Rassiga also engaged in a common tactic of pitting his museum clients against one another. He told the Museum of Primitive Art that they were competing against the Cleveland Museum of Art, which itself had already begun acquiring a collection of Maya works, including a wall panel from the Piedras Negras region in the previous year (1962.32).

After negotiating with Rassiga to purchase the stela face (which had been cut off by looters and sawed into several pieces for ease of transport, presumably on mules) and another sculpture for a discount, the Museum of Primitive Art acquired Stela 5 and catalogued it as 63.163.

Rockefeller's museum was the first of its kind to display indigenous American art in the same manner as fine art from European and American traditions, that is, without comprehensive explanatory text, allowing the art to speak for itself. When Stela 5 arrived, conservation was a priority given its fragile state. The looters' action destroyed the texts on the sides, and the base of the stela was left at the site. After initial consolidation, the stela front went on view at the Museum of Primitive Art, across the street from the Museum of Modern Art, in midtown Manhattan. Despite the total de-contextualization of the monument, including the separation from the base of the sculpture and destruction of the texts on the sides that anchored it in the historic cycles of Maya time, one wonders if the stela accomplished a similar goal with visitors to Rockefeller's museum as it had with the original viewers (fig. 5.4). It invites a close look and full visual analysis of the characters portrayed. The mastery of low-relief sculpture was evident to ancient viewers and those in the 1960s, to be sure.

Soon, however, it became obvious that sites in Guatemala and Mexico were being destroyed at an alarming rate to feed the growing art market. The Museum of Primitive Art exhibited Stela 5 in "Masterpieces from the Americas" from May 20 to November 15, 1964, as number 19, "Stele. Guatemala, Piedras Negras: Maya. Ca. 600 A.D. 96" high. 63.163." At this exhibition, organized by curator Julie Jones, the renowned scholar of Maya hieroglyphs Heinrich Berlin recognized the stela and alerted authorities in Guatemala. The Institute of Anthropology and History of Guatemala officially declared the stela stolen on October 11, 1965. Guatemalan scholars also published reports citing various laws in an attempt to promote the legal reclamation of the sculpture. For example, it was noted that on April 24, 1931, Piedras Negras was declared a National Monument and on September 19, 1947, all monuments and historic, artistic, and archaeological objects were declared part of the national culture and falling under the authority of the state (Luján Muñóz 1966).

The alarm bell about looting in general, and about Stela 5 in particular, was soon rung among academics and museum professionals. The 38th International Congress of Americanists adopted a resolution in 1968 specifically asking the Museum of Primitive Art and the Brooklyn Museum, which had

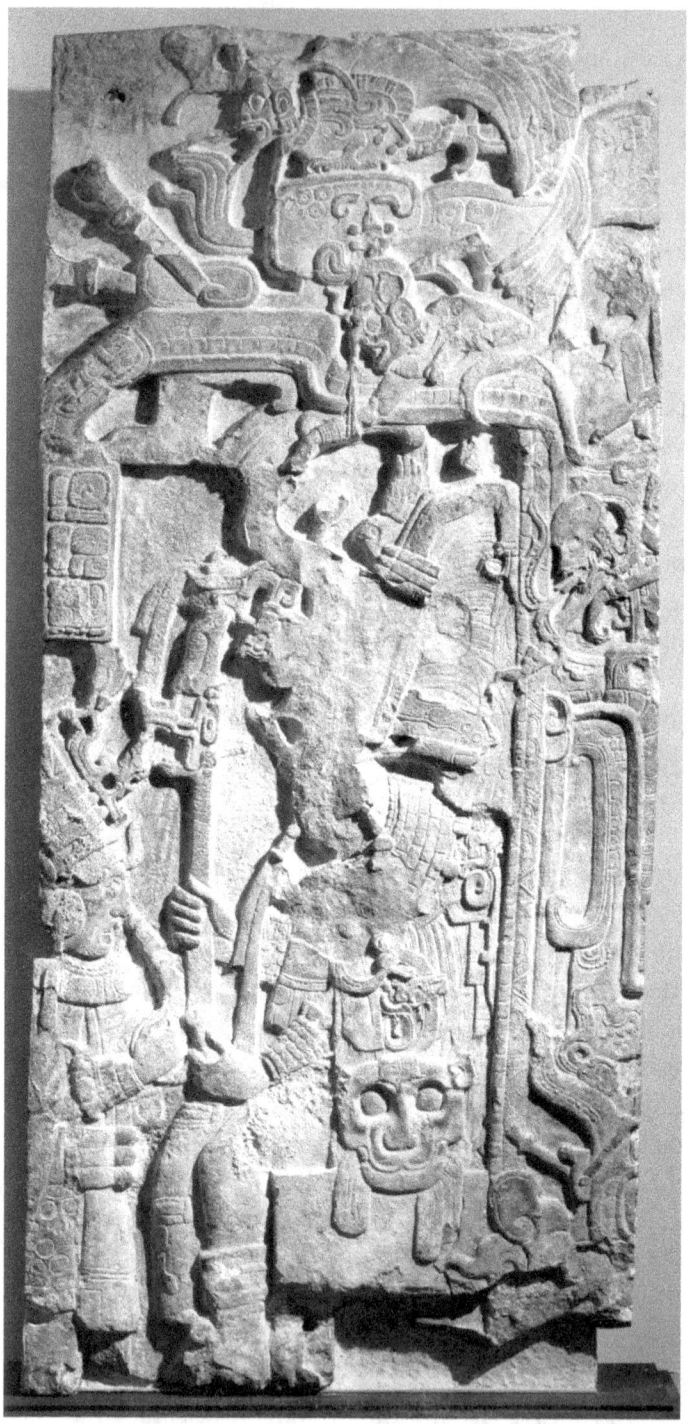

Figure 5.4. Top portion of Stela 5 as installed at the Museum of Primitive Art. Courtesy of The Metropolitan Museum of Art, New York.

purchased part of Piedras Negras Stela 3, to return both Piedras Negras stelae to Guatemala (O'Neil 2012, 204–205). In 1969, Clemency Coggins, then a doctoral candidate at Harvard, called out several more museums for fueling looting and destruction of cultural heritage (Coggins 1969). She championed the possibility that countries like Guatemala might promote the "legitimate sale of registered objects" or exchange arrangements. She also underscored that a collector, for the price of one stela, could have supported several seasons of archaeological fieldwork. One of the many "American Museums" she cited, of course, was the Museum of Primitive Art, which had exhibited Stela 5 a number of years earlier.

Coggins's article, published in autumn, also mentioned a stela from an unpublished, previously unknown Guatemalan site called El Zapote that had been photographed only by intrepid monument-recorder Ian Graham. The stela had been "apprehended as it was being transported into Campeche by two Mexicans" (Coggins 1969, 96). Earlier that year, in a letter from Elizabeth Easby[4] to Ian Graham, she had mentioned this very stela. Apparently the Easbys had been working with Mexico and Guatemala, perhaps to explore an opportunity to retrieve the El Zapote stela fragments after they had been recovered, conserve them, and exhibit them. To Graham, she wrote, "We have not yet received an answer to our request to borrow and restore it" (Letter from Mrs. D. T. Easby to Ian Graham, May 7, 1969).

Coggins also applauded an exchange arrangement underway in the late 1960s between the Metropolitan Museum of Art and Mexico. In his autobiographical *Making the Mummies Dance*, Thomas Hoving, then-director of the Met, describes the agreement with a more cynical tone than Coggins. He cites Dudley Easby as saying the agreement was "not totally altruistic," and mainly "to put a stop to what we all do and shouldn't do any longer—buy smuggled and stolen pre-Columbian goods" (Hoving 1994, 103). The Met was, however, making inroads with collaborative loan agreements, particularly in advance of the centennial exhibition "Before Cortés: Sculpture of Middle America," curated in part by Elizabeth Easby and featuring loans from the Museum of Primitive Art.

Across town, the Museum of Primitive Art (MPA) was also grappling with how to handle their recently acquired Maya relief sculptures. During this time, the MPA dramatically decreased its acquisitions of Maya art. The final Maya object they purchased was, in fact, in 1968: the so-called Metropolitan Vase (1978.412.206), one of the earliest "codex-style" vases to enter a museum collection in the United States (see Doyle 2016).

Stela 5 and the Metropolitan

In the late 1960s, Rockefeller began seeking out a long-term solution for where to house his collection of masterworks. The Met's Hoving decided to work with Rockefeller to acquire the collection of the Museum of Primitive Art, thereby cementing the Met as the country's premier encyclopedic museum. In 1969, Rockefeller announced the donation of his entire collection to the Met, celebrated by an exhibition of Museum of Primitive Art highlights, including Piedras Negras Stela 5 (fig. 5.5).

The Met itself had engaged with the art of the ancient Americas, and, indeed, Maya relief sculpture, since shortly after its founding in 1870. Its earliest acquisition was the gift of a Maya architectural fragment by the then-consul in Merida, Mexico, now recognized as the eyebrow of a monumental mosaic *witz* from the House of the Governor at the site of Uxmal. Though the Met acquired the large Petich collection of Mexican antiquities in 1900, the museum loaned

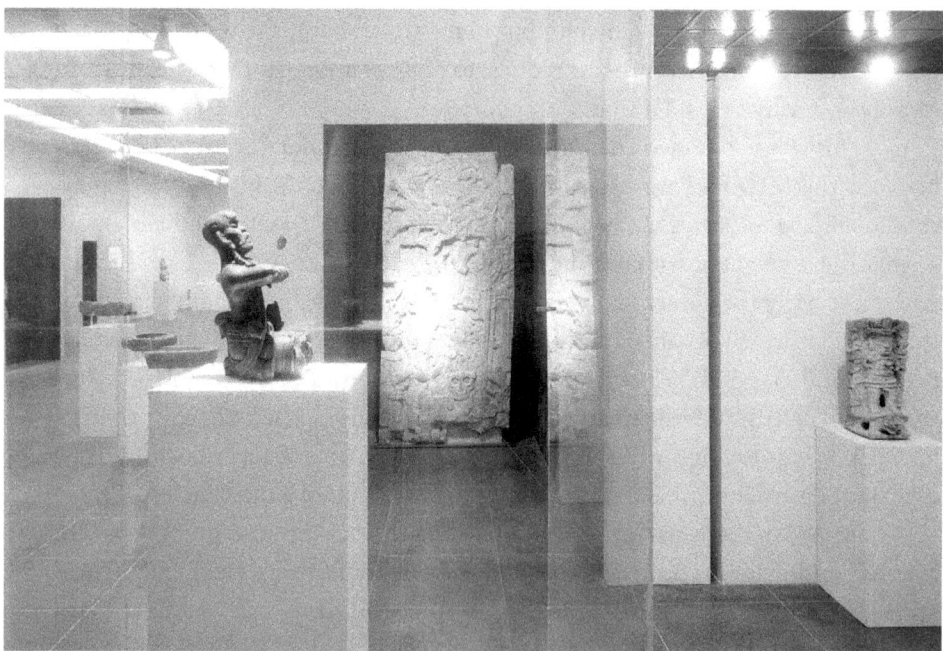

Figure 5.5. Stela 5 in "Art of Oceania, Africa, and the Americas from The Museum of Primitive Art" at The Metropolitan Museum of Art. Courtesy of The Metropolitan Museum of Art, New York.

most of these objects to the American Museum of Natural History (AMNH) in 1914, where some remain on view today. Other works were loaned to the Brooklyn Museum in the 1930s. In a May 1969 memo, presumably requested during the plans for Rockefeller's announcement, Elizabeth Easby noted that pre-Columbian art was the only field of "Primitive" art at the Met at that time. She attached to that memo a report she completed back in 1952, outlining the possibilities for a renewed focus on Art of the Ancient Americas at the Met.

Met files show that Dudley Easby, during the 1960s, used his position as secretary to influence the purchase of notable Mesoamerican sculptures that were appearing on the U.S. art market. This included the 1962 purchase of the Standard Bearer in a provincial Aztec style (62.47) from dealer John Wise, who also dealt extensively with Rockefeller and other collectors. Additionally, a monumental figure of the Maya Rain God (66.181), purchased by the Met in 1966 from Stendahl Galleries, was at the time said to have been from Campeche or Tabasco on the Yucatán peninsula. Both the Standard Bearer and the Maya Rain God were included in "Before Cortés."

Between the opening of the exhibition of Rockefeller's collection at the Met on May 10, 1969, including Stela 5, and the opening of "Before Cortés" in September of 1970, however, Nelson Rockefeller decided to return Stela 5 to Guatemala. Writing to Ambassador Dr. Francisco Linares Aranda on March 9, 1970:

> As revealed by the enclosed letter to your President, which I hope you will do me the honor of transmitting, I have given much thought to the problem of the fragment of the Mayan Stela which you brought to my attention.

He enclosed a long letter, dated March 16, 1970, to the sitting president, Julio César Méndez Montenegro:

> Before you leave office, it is my pleasure to state that since the visit of your Ambassador, our mutual friend His Excellency Dr. Francisco Linares Aranda, I have been able to work out with both the Metropolitan Museum and the Museum of Primitive Art an arrangement whereby I am now at liberty to give to your country the portion of the Mayan Stela which I purchased in New York a number of years

ago. This is a magnificent evidence of the high cultural achievement of the art of the Mayan civilization, which I acquired without the knowledge that it had been taken from one of that civilization's temples.

Ever since this problem came to my attention I have been torn between the chagrin that I acquired a piece which had been so rudely removed from one of the great historical Mayan sites and my pleasure in knowing that it would be admired by so many people here in New York.

Because I do not believe that we can or should condone the destruction of great historical monuments for the purposes of trade, I regard this as a very special case. Accordingly, I hereby give back to your country this portion of a Stela. Since it can now not be restored to its original state and since as a fragment it is such a beautiful example of your country's cultural heritage, it is my hope that you will agree with the Metropolitan Museum to loan it to them for an extended period so that it may there be enjoyed and admired. It would also be my hope that at such time that your government should wish to repatriate it, it will loan from time to time other pieces of comparable artistic merit so that Guatemala may continue to have honored representation in the Museum's collection.

In other words, perhaps this unfortunate occurrence can be turned into a positive gain for both our countries by entering into a period of closer cultural cooperation and exchange.

To the Ambassador, he added:

> In addition to the personal action referred to in this letter, my representatives ever since our conversations have been working with representatives of the Department of State and various museums throughout the country looking towards more effective intergovernmental cooperation to prevent in the future this kind of defacement of historical edifices. I hope that this experience may lead to more effective and understanding cooperation between our governments and a wider appreciation in this country and throughout the world of the cultural heritage of Guatemala.

The response from Guatemala was favorable. President Méndez Montenegro responded on May 5, 1970, less than two months before he left office:

> Your generous gesture to return to Guatemala the Mayan stela you acquired some years ago through purchase in New York is a handsome attitude which honors you and which places you among the true friends of my country. Please accept my warmest thanks. With regard to the suggestion that the stele be shown for an additional time at the Metropolitan Museum, I am pleased to tell you that I am entirely in agreement with this and consequently you are at liberty to decide whatever is appropriate.[5]

The Stela fragment was exhibited again at the Met in "Masterpieces of Fifty Centuries" (SL 70.333) from November 14, 1970, to June 1, 1971. It has been on loan at the Metropolitan Museum of Art since the deinstallation of that exhibition. Numbered L.1970.78, it remains on view today in Gallery 358 (fig. 5.6).

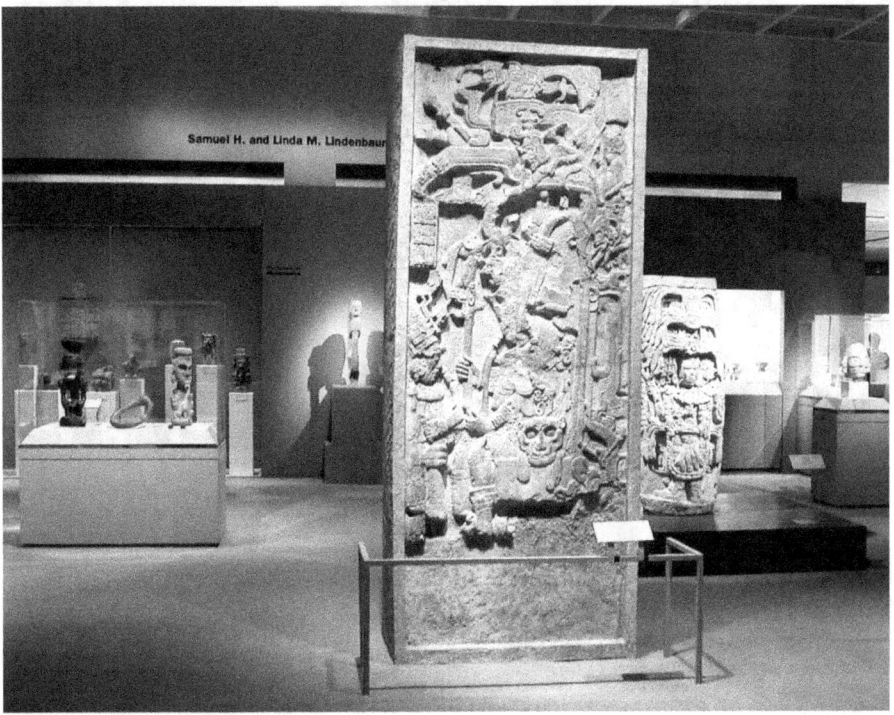

Figure 5.6. Stela 5, on loan from Guatemala to The Metropolitan Museum of Art. Courtesy of The Metropolitan Museum of Art, New York.

Stela 5 and a Thwarted "Rescue"

A previously unknown chapter in the biography of Stela 5 emerges from the
Metropolitan's archives, specifically pertaining to the lower portion of the stela
that remained at the site after the face of the upper portion was carted away
(fig. 5.7). Before the upper fragment of Stela 5 went on view at the Met in the
newly built Michael C. Rockefeller Wing in 1982, Ian Graham of the Peabody
Museum had reached out to Julie Jones. In 1977, she became the curator for Art
of the Ancient Americas in the Met's newly founded department of Primitive
Art, after having served as assistant curator at Rockefeller's museum. Graham,
in his efforts to record monuments along the Usumacinta, had heard in 1970
at Yaxchilán, Mexico, that panels from the Guatemalan side of the river were
being moved out in groups by mules and boats (Graham 2010, 453). He must

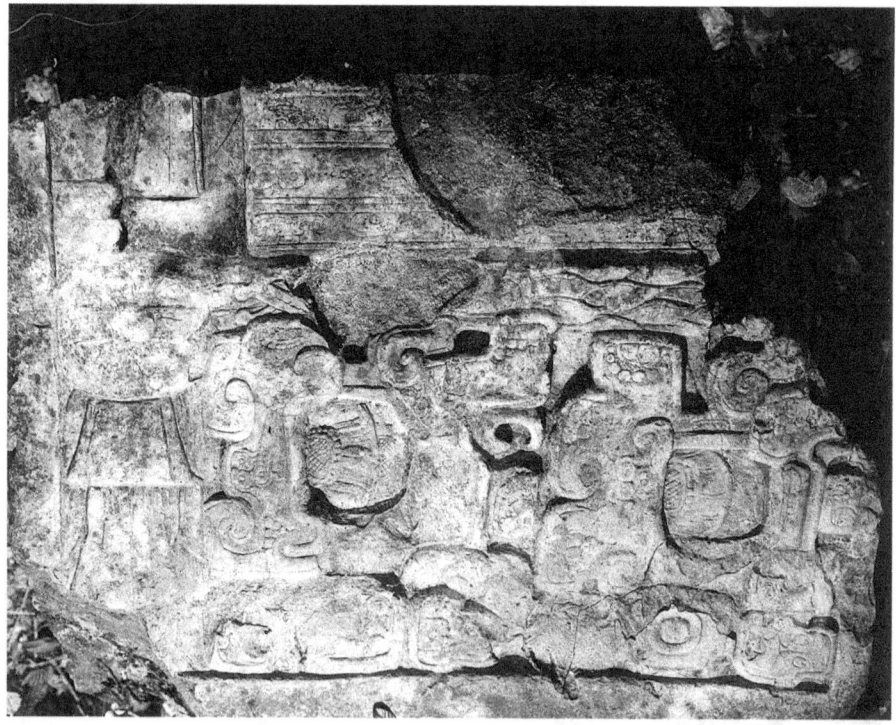

Figure 5.7. Bottom portion of Piedras Negras Stela 5, June 1978. Photograph by Jeffrey Miller
and Allison Krebs. The Metropolitan Museum of Art, Photo Study Collection. Courtesy of The
Metropolitan Museum of Art, New York.

have been worried that further depredation was taking place at Piedras Negras by the mid-1970s.

In September of 1977, Jones wrote to Graham to follow up on a previous conversation about rescuing the bottom portion of Stela 5, which had remained at Piedras Negras since the original destruction of the monument in the end of the Classic Maya era and through the looting of the stela's carved face. Jones wanted to reunite the two main fragments of the monument in the new Metropolitan wing. Unfortunately, Graham wrote on October 7, 1977:

> My rescue plans for Piedras Negras came to naught. The Instituto[6] was in favor of it, and I thought I had persuaded the Vice-Minister of Defense to send a helicopter, but then, having prepared the landing ground, I waited . . . and waited. Back in Guatemala City I learnt that the steep rise in the price of fuel had made them change their minds: I could still have the helicopter, but I'd have to pay for the fuel, and that would come to about $3000.

By December, Jones had convinced the Met to consider helping with Graham's rescue effort. She also asked Graham to "see if there was any conceivable way of finding the sides and back (however deteriorated)" so that the stela could be pieced back together in New York, echoing the unrealized plan Elizabeth Easby had for the El Zapote stela at the Met almost a decade prior.

Graham produced new photos of the lower portion for review by the Metropolitan but was unable to find any further fragments from the upper portion. "You would imagine that the parts cut off from the stela would still be around," he wrote on January 5, 1978, "as they could not have had the slightest market value, but I couldn't see them anywhere." Thinking that the helicopter would still not materialize, Graham was worried that the alternative, namely hauling it along a lumber road opening up in the nearby area, would attract the wrong kind of attention to Piedras Negras. "In which case one ought to look sharp, else some other gentlemen, viz. the lumbermen themselves, may help themselves to the goodies, such as they are. Because there *are* several pieces worth taking out, still."

A week later, Jones then proposed that, pending approval from Guatemala, the Met would pay not only for the piece to get out by helicopter, but also for packing and freight expenses from Guatemala City to New York. Though she was disappointed that the back and sides were not located, she would propose that the Met's Conservation team reconstruct the missing parts "so the stela will have some semblance of its original form." Unfortunately, it seems that Graham was unable to get support for the rescue plan. On October 9, 1979, Jones followed up with Graham given that the Rockefeller Wing was set to open, noting that the museum was still interested in reuniting the fragments.

For the top portion, Met conservators constructed a fiberglass structure around the mount. Though roughly approximating the original dimensions of the stela without the bottom portion, the fiberglass could be criticized for perhaps distracting from the original sculptors' work and misleading visitors about the wholeness of what was once an imposing monument. Nevertheless, when the *New York Times* reviewed the opening of the Michael C. Rockefeller Wing on January 24, 1982, it noted "a large, elaborately carved stone panel from an eighth-century stele found in the Piedras Negras area of Guatemala," as one of the highlights.

Stela 5 and the Twenty-First Century

While Stela 5 was on view at the Met, excavations in the late 1990s and early 2000s by Brigham Young University and Guatemalan authorities refined the chronology of the site and recovered unknown monuments. Investigations were conducted by Stephen Houston and Ernesto Arredondo in the temple identified as Structure J-4, known by Maler as the "Temple of the Eight Stelae," which towered over Stela 5's original location (Houston and Arredondo Leiva 2001). This renewed phase of archaeological study at Piedras Negras underscored the importance of K'inich Yo'nal Ahk II, who clearly led a resurgence of the city's dynasty at the end of the seventh century. The royal court of Piedras Negras hosted one of the most prestigious sculptural workshops in the ancient Americas, which developed its own distinct style of representing rituals and triumphs in an enduring lithic medium. So celebrated were these sculptors that at least 42 of them from the seventh to ninth centuries signed their works (Houston 2016).

Building upon the long-term loan of Stela 5, and to initiate a new phase of involvement between the Met and Piedras Negras, I undertook a visit to the site in 2016 with the support of the Fondazione Ligabue. There I observed excavations and conservation efforts conducted by an international project under the auspices of the Guatemalan Ministry of Culture and Sports and the Institute of Anthropology and History (Pérez Robles, Scherer, and Golden 2017). As the jungle has once again taken over the center of the city, it is difficult to get a sense of the grandeur of the wide spaces that K'inich Yo'nal Ahk II and his family created. Nothing is more impressive, however, than the massive acropolis, a terraced hillside that creates a maze of passageways, courtyards, and palace rooms, in front of which Stela 5 once stood.

There are dozens of stelae and altars still in situ, most having been broken in antiquity, some bearing the scars of modern looting. The conservation efforts of the in situ monuments, led by Guatemalan conservator Griselda Pérez Robles in June 2016, consisted of a pilot project to consolidate and protect them by rehousing them on new platforms under translucent roofs of fiberglass (Pérez Robles et al. 2017). A team from the Department of Pre-Hispanic Monuments oversaw the construction of the new platforms, custom designed to shelter the aging limestone stelae and altars, consisting of powdered lime, sand, and stones from the site. Given that the chemical reactivity of local materials closely matches that of the monuments, these methods are in line with best practices at other archaeological sites in Guatemala. They then used a system of pulleys to consolidate fragmented monuments and fit them together as best as possible.

A custom shelter consisting of dense wood was then constructed and covered with a translucent fiberglass corrugated roof to protect the monuments from rainfall. Translucence was selected by the conservation team in order to allow some sunlight on the monuments as a preventive measure against the growth of mosses and other biological agents. Prior shelters had been constructed using local tree wood and palm-thatch roofs. Over time, however, such covers created a humid and darker environment, allowing molds, lichens, and mosses to flourish on the surface of the monuments. Using local saplings as supports for the roofs was also problematic as they were susceptible to invasion by wood-consuming insects. Pérez Robles designed supports of a specific local hardwood known as *pucte* that has been shown to be especially resistant to moisture and termites, with an estimated use-life of 20 years.

In 2017 I participated in the second field season at Piedras Negras, with support from the Met's Adelaide Milton de Groot fund for archaeological projects. One month of fieldwork, directed by Andrew Scherer of Brown University, Charles Golden of Brandeis University, and Mónica Urquizú of the Guatemalan Institute of Anthropology and History, included conservation

efforts focusing on the monuments at the site, in collaboration with Guatemalan conservator Edwin Pérez Robles.

It was clear one year later that the pilot project implemented for the construction of the roofs to protect the monuments from precipitation was very
successful. The opacity of the panels allowed sufficient light and heat to impede the growth of algae, lichens, and other organisms. The supporters of the
conservation, the Harvard University Peabody Museum and Santander Bank
Foundation, provided additional funds for environmental monitoring systems
to be placed in 2017. They will collect data on the effectiveness of the new roof
system with respect to temperature and relative humidity over time. In order
to provide some preliminary analysis of the effectiveness of the system, I took
photos of rehoused monuments, including Altar 1 (fig. 5.8) which originally
stood near Stela 5, in order to create three-dimensional photogrammetric
models to compare with those created in 2016.

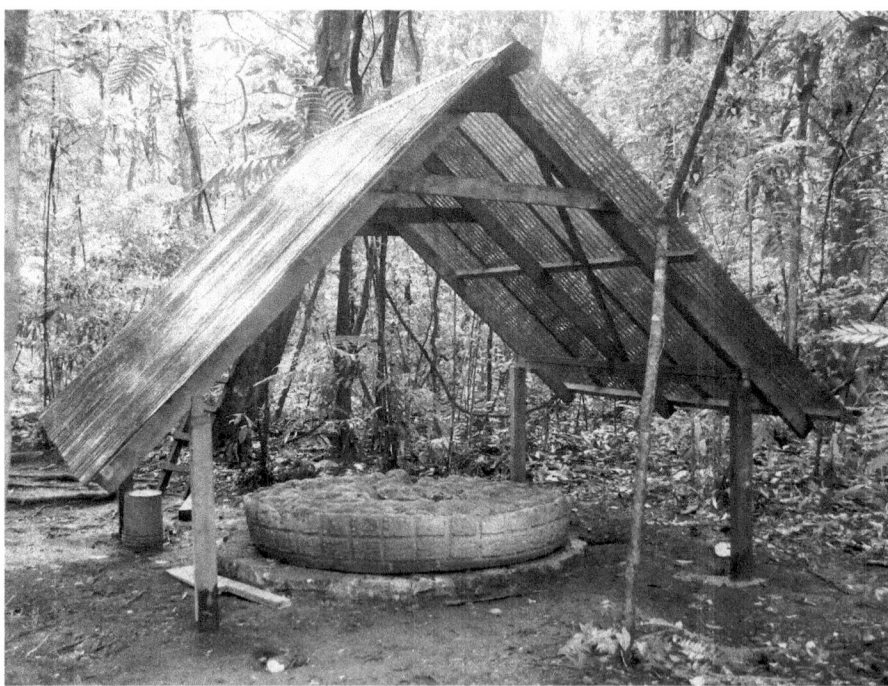

Figure 5.8. Piedras Negras Altar 1, under new translucent conservation shelter, 2016. Photograph
by author.

Other major monuments are slated to receive roofs, including one of the most recognizable monuments in the corpus of Maya sculpture, Piedras Negras Altar 4 (fig. 5.9). Encountered in situ by early explorers such as Teobert Maler, the megalithic sculpture takes the form of the oversized paw of a jaguar, which was originally rimmed with a double row of hieroglyphic texts. The paw was placed atop four supports that depict deity heads; three are currently in the National Museum of Archaeology and Ethnology in Guatemala City, the other is on loan from Guatemala to the University of Pennsylvania (see Stuart 2004). Having been broken into two large pieces by ancient iconoclastic events, the altar was at risk of deterioration because it was placed on the jungle floor when the supports were removed. Edwin Pérez Robles led the construction of a new stone platform supported by lime and sand, and the two fragments were moved and reunited atop this intervening surface.

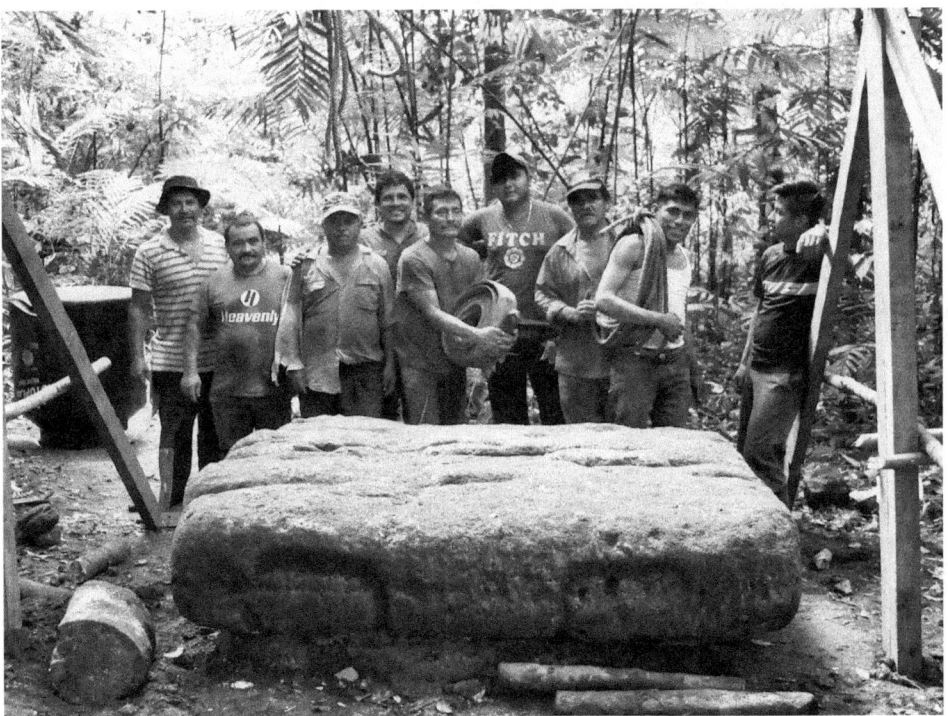

Figure 5.9. Altar 4 with members of the monument conservation team, Proyecto Paisaje Piedras Negras-Yaxchilan, 2017. Photograph by author.

Conclusions

The placement of Stela 5 in a row of monuments commemorating the achievements and family of K'inich Yo'nal Ahk II ensured that the lord lived on in the cyclical narratives of Piedras Negras in a royal court for divine rulers. This lasted for a while, surely, but iconoclasm by rivals removed the dynast's face from the otherworldly scene, presumably before toppling the top half of the monument with that face down and sliding it down the acropolis terrace. Lying undisturbed and exposed to the elements until Maler and Morley recorded the eroded sides and opposite face, it attracted the attention of opportunistic middlemen who ferried the well-preserved surface to the art market. After Nelson Rockefeller decided to return it to the Republic of Guatemala, Stela 5 has been seen by millions of visitors in the Metropolitan Museum of Art since the Mesoamerica gallery opened in 1982 under the terms of the long-term loan authorized by the country's president. The current label explicitly acknowledges its rough journey: "The sides, inscribed with hieroglyphs in two vertical rows, were lost when the sculpture was illegally cut apart."

Technology opens new possibilities for the next phase of research and outreach with Stela 5, one of the earliest examples of a successful repatriation and long-term loan collaboration between a U.S. art museum and an archaeologically rich source country. Monument conservation at the site could lead to better laboratory techniques on stone from this specific area for future treatments by the Met or by Guatemala. A high-resolution three-dimensional scan performed in New York could be used to improve didactic material online, at the National Museum of Archaeology and Ethnology in Guatemala City, or eventually at the site of Piedras Negras itself. The city will undoubtedly live on in Maya archaeology and art history as a crucible of artistic choices highlighting the practice of ancient Maya sculptors and indigenous genius of the Americas.

Acknowledgments

Many thanks to Stephen Houston, Charles Golden, Andrew Scherer, and Caitlin Earley for insightful comments on the various stages of the life story of Piedras Negras Stela 5. The Proyecto Paisaje Piedras Negras-Yaxchilan relies on long-term collaborations with the members of the communities of Santa Rita and the Cooperativa La Técnica Agropecuaria, both in Petén, as well as the staff of the Defensores de la Naturaleza and the Consejo Nacional de Áreas Protegidas that administer the Sierra del Lacandón National Park. The Fundación del Banco Santander and the Corpus of Maya Hieroglyphic Inscriptions at the Peabody Museum of Archaeology and Ethnology at Harvard University provided funds for the pilot project of monument conservation. The project is also supported by permits from the Guatemalan Institute of Anthropology and History. Other funding sources include the U.S. National Science Foundation (BCS 1505483, 1505483, 1505399), the Alphawood Foundation, Brown University, Brandeis University, The Metropolitan Museum of Art, New York, and McMaster University, Canada

Notes

1. Or, perhaps, a metaphor for *chan*, the celestial serpent (Stephen Houston, pers. comm. 2017)

2. Maler 1901, plate 15, fig. 2.

3. Decreto 425: "Ley sobre protección y conservación de los monumentos, objetos arqueológicos, históricos y típicos"

4. Curator and wife of Dudley Easby, the longtime secretary of the Metropolitan Museum of Art who was named the first chair of the Department of Primitive Art.

5. Translated from: "Su generoso gesto que retorne a Guatemala la estela maya que usted adquiriera hace algunos años por compra en New York, es una hermosa actitud que mucho lo honra y que lo sitúa entre los verdaderos amigos de mi patria. Le ruego se sirva aceptar mis más cumplidos agradecimientos. En relación a la sugerencia que sea exhibida por tiempo adicional en el Museo Metropolitano, me complace expresarle que estoy enteramente de acuerdo en que así sea, por lo que queda usted en libertad de resolver lo pertinente."

6. Instituto de Antropología e Historia (IDAEH), the body within the Guatemalan Ministry of Culture and Sports charged with management of archaeological sites, objects, and excavations.

References Cited

Clancy, Flora. 2009. *The Monuments of Piedras Negras, an Ancient Maya City*. Albuquerque: University of New Mexico Press.

Coe, William R. 1959. *Piedras Negras Archaeology: Artifacts, Caches, and Burials*. University Museum Monographs 18. Museum of Archaeology and Anthropology, University of Pennsylvania.

Coggins, Clemency. 1969. "Illicit Traffic of Pre-Columbian Antiquities." *Art Journal* 29 (1): 94–114.

Doyle, James A. 2016. "Creation Narratives on Ancient Maya Codex-Style Ceramics in the Met's Collections." *Metropolitan Museum Journal* 51: 42–63.

Finamore, Daniel, and Stephen Houston. 2010. *Fiery Pool: The Maya and the Mythic Sea.* Salem, Mass.: Peabody Essex Museum.

García Juárez, Sara Isabel. 2015. La historia de Piedras Negras a través de sus inscripciones jeroglíficas: Auge y ocaso del linaje de las tortugas. Unpublished Licenciado Thesis, Universidad Nacional Autónoma de México.

Golden, Charles, Andrew K. Scherer, Melanie Kingsley, Stephen D. Houston, and Héctor Escobedo. 2016. "The Life and Afterlife of the Classic Period Piedras Negras Kingdom." In *Ritual, Violence, and the Fall of Classic Maya Kings*, edited by Gyles Iannone, Brett A. Houk, and Sonja A. Schwake, 108–133. Gainesville: University of Florida Press.

Graham, Ian. 2010. *The Road to Ruins.* Albuquerque: University of New Mexico Press.

Houston, Stephen D. 2016. "Crafting Credit: Authorship among Classic Maya Painters and Sculptors." In *Making Value, Making Meaning: Techné in the Pre-Columbian World*, edited by Cathy Lynne Costin, 391–431. Washington, D.C.: Dumbarton Oaks Research Library and Collection.

Houston, Stephen D., and Ernesto Arredondo Leiva. 2001. "PN 48: Excavaciones en la Estructura J-4 en la Plataforma J-1." In *Proyecto Arqueológico Piedras Negras, Informe Preliminar No. 4, Cuarta Temporada, 2000*, edited by Héctor L. Escobedo and Stephen D. Houston, 217–226. Report submitted to the Instituto de Antropología e Historia de Guatemala.

Hoving, Thomas. 1994. *Making the Mummies Dance: Inside The Metropolitan Museum of Art.* New York: Touchstone.

Luján Muñóz, Jorge. 1966. *Dos estelas mayas sustraída de Guatemala: Su presencia en Nueva York.* Guatemala City: Universidad de San Carlos.

Maler, Teobert. 1901. *Researches in the Central Portion of the Usumatsintla Valley: Report of Explorations for the Museum, 1889–1900.* Memoirs of the Peabody Museum of American Archaeology and Ethnology, vol. II, no. 1. Cambridge: Harvard University.

Martin, Simon, and Nikolai Grube. 2008. *Chronicle of the Maya Kings and Queens.* London: Thames & Hudson.

Morley, Sylvanus G. 1938. *The Inscriptions of Petén*, Vol. III. Publication no. 437. Washington D.C.: Carnegie Institute of Washington.

O'Neil, Megan E. 2012. *Engaging Ancient Maya Sculpture at Piedras Negras, Guatemala.* Norman: University of Oklahoma Press.

———. 2017. "Collecting Pre-Hispanic Art in Los Angeles." In *Found in Translation: Design in California and Mexico, 1915–1985*, edited by Wendy Kaplan, 176–177. Los Angeles: LACMA and Prestel.

O'Neil, Megan E., and Mary Ellen Miller. 2017. "An Artistic Discovery of America: Exhibiting and Collecting Mexican Pre-Hispanic Art in Los Angeles from 1940 to the 1960s." In *Found in Translation: Design in California and Mexico, 1915–1985*, edited by Wendy Kaplan, 162–167: Los Angeles, LACMA and Prestel.

Pérez Robles, Griselda, Juan Carlos Pérez, Edwin Pérez, Efrain Peralta, and Rony Piedrasanta. 2017. "La conservación de los monumentos de Piedras Negras." In *Proyecto Paisaje Piedras Negras-Yaxchilan, 2016, Informe de la primera temporada de investigación, Presentado a la Dirección General del Patrimonio Cultural y Natural*, edited by Griselda Pérez Robles, Andrew K. Scherer, and Charles Golden, 130–154. Guatemala City: Guatemala.

Pérez Robles, Griselda, Andrew K. Scherer, and Charles Golden. 2017. *Proyecto Paisaje Piedras Negras-Yaxchilan, 2016, Informe de la primera temporada de investigación, Presentado a la Dirección General del Patrimonio Cultural y Natural*. Guatemala City: Guatemala.

Pillsbury, Joanne. 2014. "The Pan-American: Nelson Rockefeller and the Arts of Ancient Latin America." In *The Nelson A. Rockefeller Vision: Arts of Africa, Oceania, and the Americas.* The Metropolitan Museum of Art Bulletin, Summer 2014: 18–27.

Proskouriakoff, Tatiana. 1960. "Historical Implications of a Pattern of Dates at Piedras Negras, Guatemala." *American Antiquity* 25 (4): 454–475.

Scherer, Andrew K., and Stephen Houston. 2018. "Blood, Fire, Death: Covenants and Crises among the Classic Maya." In *Smoke, Flames, and the Human Body in Mesoamerican Ritual Practice*, edited by Andrew K. Scherer and Vera Tiesler, 109–150. Washington, D.C.: Dumbarton Oaks.

Stephens, John Lloyd. 1996 [1843]. *Incidents of Travel in Yucatan*. Abridged by Karl Ackerman. Washington, D.C.: Smithsonian Institution Press.

Stuart, David. 2004. "The Paw Stone: The Place Name of Piedras Negras, Guatemala." *PARI Journal* 4 (3): 1–6.

Stuart, David, and Ian Graham. 2003. "Piedras Negras." *Corpus of Maya Hieroglyphic Inscriptions*, vol. 9.1. Cambridge: Peabody Museum of Archaeology and Ethnology, Harvard University.

6

"From a Cave near Tehuacán"

An Attempt to Reassemble Post-Classic Mesoamerican Ritual Deposits Separated by the Art Market

MARTIN BERGER

The mid-twentieth-century market for pre-Columbian antiquities is notoriously opaque. Riddled as this moment in the market is with stories of looting, forgery, and deceit, the period between roughly 1950 and 1990 is also the era in which significant parts of today's best-known museum collections of pre-Columbian art were formed. This holds especially true for Maya pieces that started to come onto the market in large numbers in the 1960s, when looters began commercially exploiting Maya sites on a large scale (Coe 1993; Coggins 1969). As a result of the advent of New Archaeology, the 1960s also marked the moment in which archaeologists started to lose interest in studying museum collections without a secure provenience (i.e., those from the art market). Since these artifacts lacked a secure context, their value as archaeological objects of study was considered seriously limited (Boone 1993, 330). As a result, museum collections moved out of the realm of study of many archaeologists—indeed, some journals prefer not to publish pieces not obtained through professional field research—while at the same time, art historians started to take an interest in these pieces (Chase et al. 1988).

Even though hesitancy to publish looted material that journals and professional organizations promote is entirely understandable and justified, one can wonder whether, in the longer term, this is the most productive strategy when attempting to right historical wrongs. After all, a source country or community cannot ask for repatriation of material if the existence of these objects is not known outside the museum where they reside.[1] At the same time, because of the nature of the art market, many pieces that once formed part of the same original deposit are now scattered all over the globe. Any possible information on the provenance and provenience of these clusters of objects can only be found hidden away in the archives of the institutions that hold them, and they are often fragmentary and difficult to access. Hence, the only way to bring these pieces back together (if only virtually) and partially recontextualize them is through the publication of objects and, especially, object biographies.

The study of biographies of pieces and the networks that moved them is relatively well developed for those pre-Columbian pieces that entered European collections before 1900 (e.g., Caygill 2012; Domenici 2017; Feest 1990). In contrast, the study of those networks in the twentieth-century art market is still in its early stages. Quite a few studies exist on the activity of looting Mesoamerican cultural heritage (e.g., Coggins 1969, Graham 2011), as well as on forgeries and faking in Mesoamerica (e.g., Ekholm 1964; Bruhns and Kelker 2010; Taylor 1982). Quantitative studies of the market for pre-Columbian art have started to appear more recently (e.g., Levine and Martínez de Luna 2013; Tremain 2017). However, relatively few studies exist that attempt to do what Levine and Martínez de Luna (2013, 264) have termed "museum salvage," that is, the study of cultural material in museum collections that lacks any kind of information on its provenience.

Despite the lack of an archaeological context, many pieces without a secure provenience can hold a wealth of information, especially in the light of the ever-increasing possibilities provided by new hard-science techniques to tease out secrets from otherwise mute archaeological material. I find myself in agreement with the aforementioned authors when they say that ignoring museum objects without a secure provenience amounts to a "double-loss" (Levine and Martínez de Luna 2013, 264), in which we not only have lost the original context of the deposit, but also, by not studying and publishing these objects, deny ourselves the possibility to learn more from this material.

As Michael Coe has suggested, museum and private collections can be examined in a way similar to that of archaeologists studying archaeological assemblages. In Coe's (1993, 272) words, "Archaeological questions can be asked about these artifacts: what is their origin, who made them and when? How did they get into the site? How are they distributed there? And what happens to them once they are deposited? For our purposes, perhaps the most significant question would be what kind of socio-economic system has operated to bring such objects from their place of origin to the site?" In this chapter, I trace the history of a corpus of Post-Classic Mesoamerican turquoise pieces that appeared on the market between roughly 1950 and 1980. Through this provenance study, I try to find answers to the questions outlined by Coe. The entire corpus lacks secure information on its provenience but can be relatively securely linked to specific localities or regions through a combination of stylistic, archaeological, and archival research. I hope to show not only that the way this material was distributed around the world is characteristic of the way the pre-Columbian art market functioned in the mid-twentieth century, but also that the study of this material can further archaeological knowledge, despite its unprovenienced state.

In this chapter, I treat collections currently in museums in the same way as those pieces that surfaced at auction and are now quite probably in private hands. While I recognize that there is a significant difference between museum collections and private collections, and that one should be careful about conflating them, I feel that for the purposes of this article the combination of both is inevitable, for several reasons. First, the combined discussion of museum and auction/private collections requires us to acknowledge that all these pieces derive from looting practices and that, at the time they were looted, no distinction was made between pieces for collectors and pieces for museums. Second, I feel that in the period when most of these pieces were probably unearthed (1950–1970), museums, art dealers, and private collectors were in more frequent contact than they are today and worked more closely together. Art dealers were welcome guests in many museums and they often maintained close personal relationships with museum staff. Exchanges, donations, and acquisitions took place among museums, dealers, and collectors. While many museum academics and archaeologists acknowledged the problematic nature of this relationship, it should not be forgotten that the ICOM Code of Ethics was only introduced in 1986. Finally, in trying to reconstruct an original corpus, it does not necessarily matter where the pieces are located today. The aim of this research is to see whether it is possible to come to an understanding of the original context and the possible provenience of these pieces. In this context their current location is of relatively minor importance.

Defining the Corpus and Its Possible Archaeological Context

Some of the most quintessential pieces of Post-Classic Mesoamerican art are turquoise mosaics. These include masks, shields, and figurative pieces, the most famous of which reside in museum collections in Europe and the United States. Many of the best-known European pieces probably left Mexico relatively early after the Spanish invasion and made their way into *Kunstkammern* and other collections, eventually ending up in the national ethnographic museum collections of which they now form a part.[2] It seems pertinent to note here that, despite all the scholarly study that has gone into tracing the history of these pieces, they were not unearthed or collected during a documented scientific endeavor and they lack secure information about their provenience.

Apart from these very early pieces that were probably traded with or seized by Europeans in the early Colonial period, rather than excavated, quite a few turquoise mosaic pieces exist that were found during professional archaeological undertakings. Many of these were found in the modern-day states of Oaxaca and Puebla (e.g., Gallegos 1963; Steele and Snavely 1997; Vargas 1989). Despite the fact that this material was found in context, relatively few of the pieces from this corpus have gained the notoriety of some of the sixteenth-century artifacts—especially those of the British Museum. All this material is now in Mexico in several regional and national museums. While some of these pieces have been researched quite thoroughly and widely published, many others remain little known.

A last category of turquoise mosaic objects is that of artifacts unearthed during undocumented/illicit excavations in the twentieth century, and that made their way into private and museum collections through acquisitions by art and antiquities dealers. The earliest of these collections is the one amassed by Carl A. Purpus in the beginning of the twentieth century, which was sold to George Heye in the early 1920s (Saville 1922). While this collection is very important as reference material for the corpus of mosaic masks and shields that I will discuss more at length, I will not address it in detail because it was acquired directly from the collector by Heye and made its way into the museum before the 1950s–1960s—the period of main concern in this chapter.

The corpus on which I focus consists mainly of two types of artifacts: wooden mosaic masks and shields, and the nonmosaic material that accompanies these pieces in offerings. This research started out with an attempt to locate in museum collections specific types of Post-Classic wooden masks from the border region of the modern-day states of Puebla and Oaxaca, primarily the Tehuacán Valley, the Cuicatlán Cañada, and the Coixtlahuaca Basin. The distinctive style of these masks and their relatively restricted regional distribution allow them to be easily recognized in databases and catalogues. Because of the clear association of these masks—which may or may not be decorated with turquoise—with disks or shields decorated with mosaics, these were also included in this corpus. These two types of artifacts form the primary basis of this research (figs. 6.1 and 6.2). At the same time, because these masks and shields are often accompanied by other types of artifacts—such as *amate* paper,

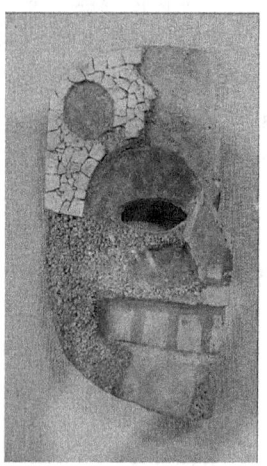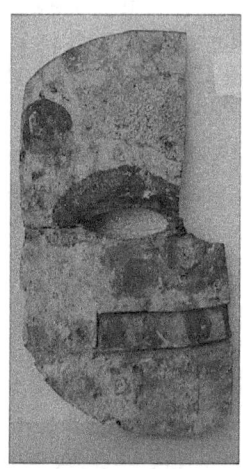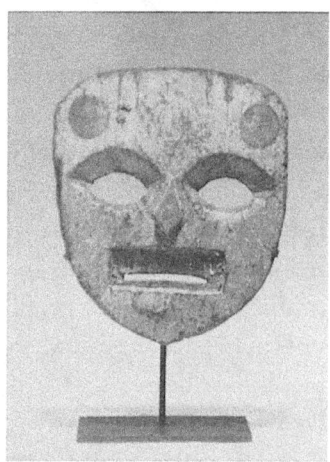

Figure 6.1. Comparison between a mask from the collection of the Ethnologisches Museum, Berlin; the National Museum of the American Indian/Smithsonian; and the Saint Louis Art Museum. Image by the author.

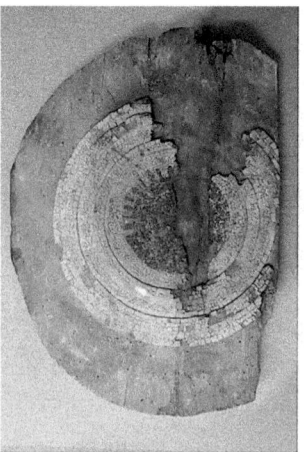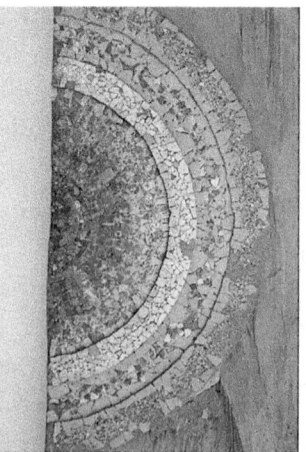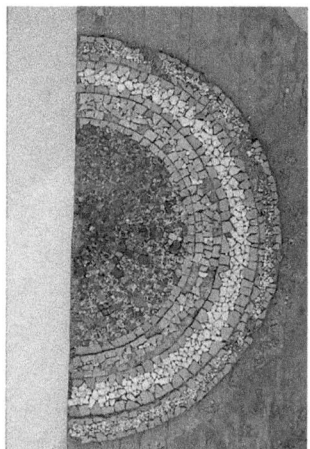

Figure 6.2. A comparison of a shield (IV Ca 46940) from the Ethnologisches Museum, Berlin (*left*), and two shields from the collection of the NMAI/Smithsonian Institution (*middle, right*). Image by the author.

reed bundles, mosaic frogs, ear plugs, and jaguars—the corpus was expanded to also include these other materials.

Most of the material in this corpus is said to come from the Oaxaca-Puebla border region, though the vast majority was looted and sold through the art market. All the material was likely recovered from either caves or tombs. The only documented recovery of material of this type is from a cave near Santa Ana Teloxtoc, Puebla (Vargas 1989). Even though the pieces from this cave were removed by professional archaeologists, it should be noted that no excavations took place and many of the masks had already been removed from the site by the speleologists who discovered them prior to the arrival of the archaeological team. As a result, hardly any specimens have been retrieved from undisturbed primary contexts that were professionally excavated.

With the exception of the Coixtlahuaca mask (Bernal 1949), the only similar material that has been found in documented excavation comes from well outside this area (Bernal 1951; Gallegos 1963). In the region itself, many archaeological sites have been located that were looted before archaeologists got to them. At many of these sites, material was found that may well have once formed part of turquoise mosaics, but it was likely left behind by looters because it was no longer intact and therefore did not represent any monetary value on the art market (Steele 2005; Martínez Tuñón and Robles Garcia 2010; Rincón Mautner 2005; Moser 1975; Steele and Snavely 1997; Urcid 2004). Indeed, two sites explored by archaeologists have turned up material that was found in looters' debris (Moser 1975; Steele and Snavely 1997). In the following section, I will attempt to tentatively reconstruct those deposits that may have once belonged together but were later looted and separated by the art market.

"Found in a Cave near Tehuacán"

In February 1968 the Royal Museums of Art and History (KMKG/MRAH) in Brussels acquired a large collection of Post-Classic Mesoamerican material from Emile Deletaille, an antiquities dealer with a renowned gallery in the center of Brussels who specialized in pre-Columbian material. The collection consisted of what was thought to be the complete contents of two tombs or funerary caves, referred to as "Tomb 1" and "Tomb known as Cave of the Tigre" by Deletaille (Serge Lemaître, pers. comm. 2016). The diversity of material is large, ranging from ceramic vessels and figurines, woven textiles and fiber baskets to jade beads and even wooden disks and masks decorated with turquoise (see Montoya 2016 for the full corpus). The tombs or caves in which the material was found were said to be located in the "region around Tehuacán." Around the same time as the Brussels acquisition, a large number of similar pieces came onto the market (see table 6.1). A closer look at this corpus not only gives more insight into how individual antiquities dealers and the networks in which they moved have dispersed objects around the globe, but can also aid in the reconstruction of the possible contents of looted sites that can no longer be studied in documented excavation.

Following the methodology that Coe (1993) has proposed for studying museum and private collections, I will consider the origin, trajectory, distribution, and postdepositional life of this corpus, starting with the question of distribution. Since the focus of this chapter is on the pre-Columbian art market and the way that (networks of) dealers have distributed artifacts, rather than on the meaning of these pieces for the people who made them, I will concern myself only with where these pieces are and how they got there, rather than with their cultural interpretation (see Domenici 2016 for an interpretation of the cultural significance of these pieces).

Table 6.1. An overview of pieces identified, sorted by date of acquisition

Museum/Auction	Acquired/Sold	From (Dealer)	Material
San Antonio Museum of Art	1951 (by Robert Woods Bliss/ Dumbarton Oaks)	Helmut de Terra	One (high-quality) mask, heavily restored
Nelson-Atkins	1966, excavated 1965/66	Everett Rassiga	Collection of mosaics, ceramics, fiber fragments
Textile Museum, Washington, D.C.	1966	Everett Rassiga	Textile and fiber materials
KMKG/RMAH, Brussels, Belgium	1968	Emile Deletaille	Contents of "Tomb 1" (ca. 100 pieces) and "Tomb/Cave of the Tiger" (ca. 50 pieces)
Saint Louis Art Museum	1968	Everett Rassiga	Stone *ñuhu* mask

Museum/Auction	Acquired/Sold	From (Dealer)	Material
Saint Louis Art Museum	1969	Everett Rassiga	Turquoise jaguar
Israel Museum, Jerusalem	Late 1960s	Merrin Gallery (1966)	One mask
National Museum of the American Indian	First offered November 1970, excavated early 1967/68	Robert Stolper (Socorro Navarrete)	Two separate sets of masks and shields, around 75 in total
Saint Louis Art Museum	1970 (collected by George Pepper between 1951 and 1968)	Everett Rassiga	Collection of mask, shield, and ear plug fragments
Etnologisches Museum, Berlin	1971	Emile Deletaille	1 mask, 6 shields, earplugs
Museum of Ethnology, Budapest	1971	Everett Rassiga	One (high-quality) mask
Israel Museum, Jerusalem	1980s	Ex-William Palmer III collection	One jaguar
Parke-Bernet	26.04.1968	?	Two fragmentary masks
Sotheby's	25.02.1981	?	One mask
Sotheby's	13.5.1983	Ex-Jay C. Leff collection, sold 1970, again by Merrin around 2016	One mask
Sotheby's	27.11.1984	? Ex-William Palmer III collection	Ear Ornament Frog
Sotheby's	18.11.1987	?	One (high-quality) mask
Sotheby's	23.11.1998	?	One mask
Collection Veranneman, Belgium	?	? 5.1.1972 Andre Emmerich Catalogue	One (high-quality) mask
Ed Merrin	?	Ex-collection William Palmer III (collected in 1950s or 60s), Ex Collection Gilbert, Ex-collection New York Private.	Mosaic plaque

Distribution—Where Are They?

"Distribution" refers to the different museums and private collections in which pieces from this corpus are present, that is, their distribution around the world as a result of sales through the international art market. Table 6.1 gives an overview of those artifacts in museums or from auction catalogues that were identified as part of this research. Clearly, this list is not exhaustive and more artifacts from this corpus may be held in collections around the globe. The material presented here was identified through a study of exhibition catalogues, museum collections (online databases), and auction catalogues. Because many of the pieces that are part of this corpus are fragmentary, most of them have rarely or never been exhibited or published. The material that makes up this corpus is part of museum collections on three different continents. Since much of it has neither been exhibited nor published, the obvious similarities that exist between the pieces has largely gone unnoticed (but see Domenici 2016, Thibodeau et al. 2018). A closer look at the provenance of this material, and the networks involved in bringing these pieces to the market, reveals possible scenarios of how these pieces might be interrelated and raises the possibility that at least some of them were once part of the same original deposit or deposits.

Origins—Where Do They Come From?

In the context of this research, the origin of a corpus or artifact can be understood as two rather different things. On one hand, the origin of an artifact or collection can be the place of excavation, be it legally or illegally, at which an object was first unearthed. On the other, considering the lack of provenience of most pieces on the art market, we could also say that an object starts a second life once it is removed from its original context and becomes "a work of art" or "an antiquity." In this case, the origin of the piece would be the place in which it first surfaces on the market—most likely in the hands of a dealer. In most cases the dealer will not be the same person as the one who looted the piece (Coe 1993). However, because of the nature of the art market, reconstructing the trajectory of a piece from looter to dealer is extremely difficult, if not impossible. It is in this in-between grey area that one origin of the piece is often lost and a new one is created.

The origins, in the first meaning of the word, of this entire corpus are remarkably similar. The provenience supplied by Deletaille to the Brussels museum is relatively precise: Tomb 1 and the Tomb known as Cave of the Tiger, in the region around Tehuacán. While a location for these caves/tombs is not provided, places are named that could hypothetically be located with the help of Tehuacán Valley locals. The material at the Nelson-Atkins Museum in Kansas City also has a relatively secure provenience. Part of the collection is accompanied by an inventory card that identifies the pieces as coming from "La Tambour Cave," although La Tambour seems an unlikely name for a location in Mexico. It is more probable that a cave with the name El Tambor is meant. For the other pieces in this corpus, the origin provided is less exact. The provenience provided in auction catalogues is by far the least precise. One of them mentions Tehuacán (Sotheby's 1981), others say southern Puebla (Merrin Galleries 1966) or Puebla (Sotheby's 1983). Most, however, only name the cultural affiliation as Mixtec (Parke-Bernet 1966) or even Mixtec/Aztec (Sotheby's 1987), providing a geographic location by association. The mask auctioned at Sotheby's in 1983 has only Puebla named as its provenience, while it was actually accompanied by a slightly more precise location—southern Puebla—when the same artifact was exhibited at the Brooklyn Museum as part of the Jay C. Leff collection in 1966/67.

Naturally, museums are more preoccupied with understanding the correct provenience of a piece. As a result, most museums have a marginally better understanding of the overall geographic provenience of their material. Still, many do not have a clear view of where their collections come from. Apart from the aforementioned Nelson-Atkins material, the rest of the museum objects (Saint Louis Art Museum [SLAM], Berlin, Textile Museum, National Museum of the American Indian [NMAI]) are all catalogued as coming from "a cave near Tehuacán." The NMAI archives are most specific in this regard. The correspondence between Robert Stolper, the dealer who donated the collection to the museum, and Frederick Dockstader, the director at the time, provides some background to their origin. On November 4, 1970, Robert Stolper writes to Dockstader "I have a collection of more than a hundred fragments of Mixtec wood masks of all shapes and sizes. All found together but actual site unknown" (Stolper 1970). When Dockstader enquires about a more precise location for the find, Stolper says, "The wood masks come from a cave just outside of the city of TEHUACAN [sic] in the State of Puebla. While I do not have the name of the cave, it was one which was persued [sic] by MacNeish & Fred Petersen, but they evidently did not go deep enough for these were found [. . .] in early 1967 [and] in early 1968. Of those found in 1968 there were [sic] one which was absolutely complete including the inlays of crude size and se-cion [*sic*] and sold for a huge price" (Stolper 1971a). Since the Tehuacán Project explored dozens of caves, it is hard to say from which of these this material may have come, but, like the named tombs of Deletaille, this information does at least provide a starting point for their identification.

Clearly, all the material in this corpus has a "narrative provenience" from the area around Tehuacán. Similar material has been found in (more or less) secure archaeological contexts in the vicinity of Tehuacán and in northern Oaxaca (Moser 1975; Steele and Snavely 1997; Vargas 1989). Since this is a relatively well-circumscribed area, it seems probable that the pieces lacking provenience also derive from this general region (though, clearly, there is no unequivocal evidence to support this).

Trajectory—How Did They Get There?

Having a relatively clear idea of where much of this material is today and where it originally may have originated, the question arises: how did it get to its cur-rent location? This is where the pre-Columbian art market comes into play. As mentioned, it is difficult, if not impossible, to reconstruct exactly when, where, and by whom these pieces were looted. Likewise, documentation is lacking on how many steps it took for this material to get from the hands of the looter into the hands of the dealer or collector who brought these pieces into public view. The NMAI material is an exception, since Robert Stolper explains that "the cache of mask fragments is complete with the exception of two masks, so I heard, which were each sold for $4,000.00. . . . I purchased them in two groups from Navarette [*sic*] (his wife Socorrita to be more precise) and then felt they should all remain together" (Stolper 1971b). This shows that Stolper himself got the material from Veracruz-based Mexican collector/dealer Socorro Navarrete (Andrew Turner, pers. comm. 2017), taking the provenance at least one step further back. For all the museum material in the corpus, we know from which dealers they were acquired. Looking more closely at who owned these pieces before they came to the museums can give us an indication of which pieces may have once been part of the same deposit.

Only a few dealers seem to have been involved in bringing this material to the market. These were Everett Rassiga, Robert Stolper, Emile Deletaille, Ed Merrin, and Andre Emmerich. The person who sold most of the pieces was Everett Rassiga, an unscrupulous New York–based dealer who sold pieces from this corpus to at least four different museums. All of these may have come from the same original context. For example, in 1966 Rassiga sold a piece of a cotton weaving and some woven fiber material to the Textile Museum in Washington, D.C. that were said to have come from a cave in southern Puebla (King 1979; Montoya 2016). In the same year, the Nelson-Atkins Museum in Kansas City acquired a large collection of turquoise fragments, ceramics, organic material, and human remains from Rassiga. According to Rassiga, the Nelson-Atkins collection represented the entirety of the contents of a Mixtec tomb in southern Puebla (Jennifer Byers, pers. comm. 2017). From the few pieces found in context in caves in Tehuacán (Moser 1975; Vargas 1989), we know that offerings of masks, shields, and textile and fiber material invariably are found together. Since the Textile Museum collection and the Nelson-Atkins collection were sold in the same year, by the same dealer, and both are said to have come from a cave in southern Puebla, it seems probable that Rassiga chose to split up the contents of one deposit. It is likely that he sold all the nontextile material to the Nelson-Atkins and the textile and fiber material from the same original context to the Textile Museum. Quite probably the Textile Museum was prepared to pay more for the few pieces of material in which they specialized than the Nelson-Atkins would have for textiles sold as part of a larger lot.

Rassiga's connections to this material do not stop there, however. In 1971 he traded material with the Museum of Ethnology in Budapest (Gyármati 2008). Part of this trade was a turquoise mask that is clearly part of this corpus, though of significantly higher quality (fig. 6.3). There is no way of knowing whether this mask was part of the same corpus Rassiga sold five years earlier to the Nelson-Atkins and the Textile Museum; however, knowing that he separated material for sale to different museums, it is possible. Another intriguing possibility arises from the aforementioned Dockstader-Stolper correspondence, in which Stolper mentions that during the 1968 find of the NMAI masks "there were were [sic] one which was absolutely complete including the inlays of crude size and secion [sic] and sold for a huge price" (Stolper 1971a). Again, there is no way to prove that the mask mentioned by Stolper is the same one that Rassiga traded to the Museum of Ethnology, but the circumstantial evidence suggests it might be, as it is the only complete mask to have surfaced in the past 50 years.

Two other high-end pieces that went through Rassiga's hands are housed at the Saint Louis Art Museum (SLAM). One of them is a mosaic-decorated zoomorphic figure that has often been described as a jaguar,[3] the other a stone

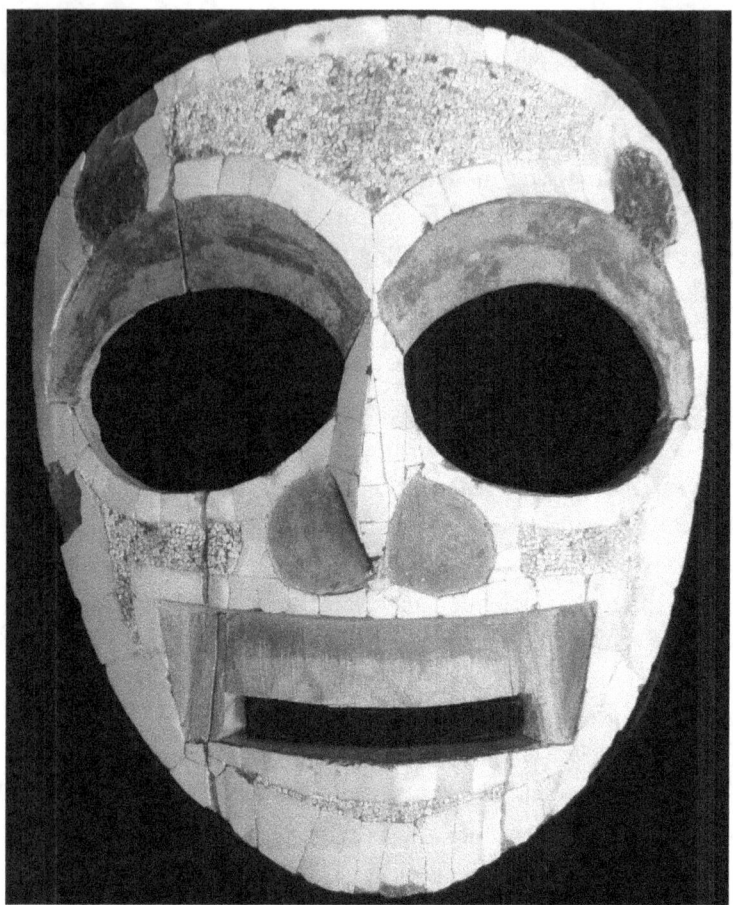

Figure 6.3. A mask acquired by the Museum of Ethnography, Budapest, in 1971 in a trade with Everett Rassiga. Image Credit: Museum of Ethnography/Neprajzi Museum.

decorated with a mosaic of a face that has been interpreted as a *ñuhu* figure (Parsons 1980). While it is unclear from what kind of context the *ñuhu* figure derives—though it may have been part of a sacred bundle accompanied by objects from this corpus (see Domenici 2016)—the jaguar clearly falls within the scope of this research. Companion pieces for the jaguar are in the KMKG/RMAH Brussels collection, which holds one complete jaguar and fragments of several others (Montoya 2016), and in the Israel Museum in Jerusalem. Also at the SLAM is a collection of masks and ear plugs, most of them fragmentary, which are part of the material collected by George Pepper in Mexico between 1951 and 1969. After Pepper's death in 1969, his widow sold his collections to Rassiga, the bulk of which was acquired by Morton D. May, who donated it to the SLAM (Amy Clark, pers. comm. 2015).

Apart from the Budapest mask that came from Rassiga, the other pieces in European museums were sold by Belgian dealer Emile Deletaille. I have already briefly described the collection at the KMKG/MRAH in Brussels, and another collection is located at the Etnologisches Museum in Berlin. There is no way of knowing the exact relationship between the pieces Deletaille sold to Brussels and those he sold to Berlin. It is remarkable that the so-called Tomb 1 collection in Brussels only holds a few very low-quality masks and no shields, which is an anomaly compared with the other collections in this corpus. The Berlin collection, in contrast, consists of masks and shields but no associated material. This raises the possibility, but again this is highly speculative and cannot be proven at this point, that Deletaille separated some of the material from the Brussels collection for sale to Berlin, in the same way Rassiga seems to have done for the Textile Museum and the Nelson-Atkins Museum.

In comparison to Deletaille and Rassiga, Robert Stolper had a relatively minor involvement in the trade of this "Tehuacán material"—in contrast to his involvement in the sale of several turquoise mosaic-decorated skulls that appeared on the market around the same time (Berger 2013; Urcid 2010). In correspondence with Dockstader, Stolper makes it clear that, prior to the acquisition by the NMAI, he attempted to have some of the fragments of the masks restored and put together. He writes: "I had them since 1967 & 1968 with Herr Falk of the Rautenstrauch-Joest-Museum [in Cologne, Germany] to try to put together . . . but he did not have the time to work on these. I thought that when I bought ALL THE FRAGMENTS [sic] that they could possibly be put together, but simply do not know and felt that the cost of experimenting too prohibitive" (Stolper 1971a). One might wonder whether the pieces would have been sold separately if they could have been fitted together, as all the masks that have appeared in public auctions are complete, many having been restored.

For those materials that were sold in public auction, it is much more difficult to reconstruct their trajectory (see fig. 6.4 for an example of a mask sold at auction). While some masks appear on the market multiple times, some appear only once and do not resurface. Still, even for these pieces, it is sometimes possible to reassemble collections that have been dispersed. This is the case, for example, for those artifacts once in the possession of William P. Palmer III, a collector of pre-Columbian material who bequeathed his collection to the Hudson Museum of the University of Maine. Between 1965 and 1970 Palmer acquired a renowned collection, primarily from Larry Borenstein, Edward Merrin, and the Stendahl Galleries. Several turquoise pieces listed in table 6.1 appeared separately in public auction after Palmer's death in 1982, while two others were sold at the Edward Merrin Gallery.

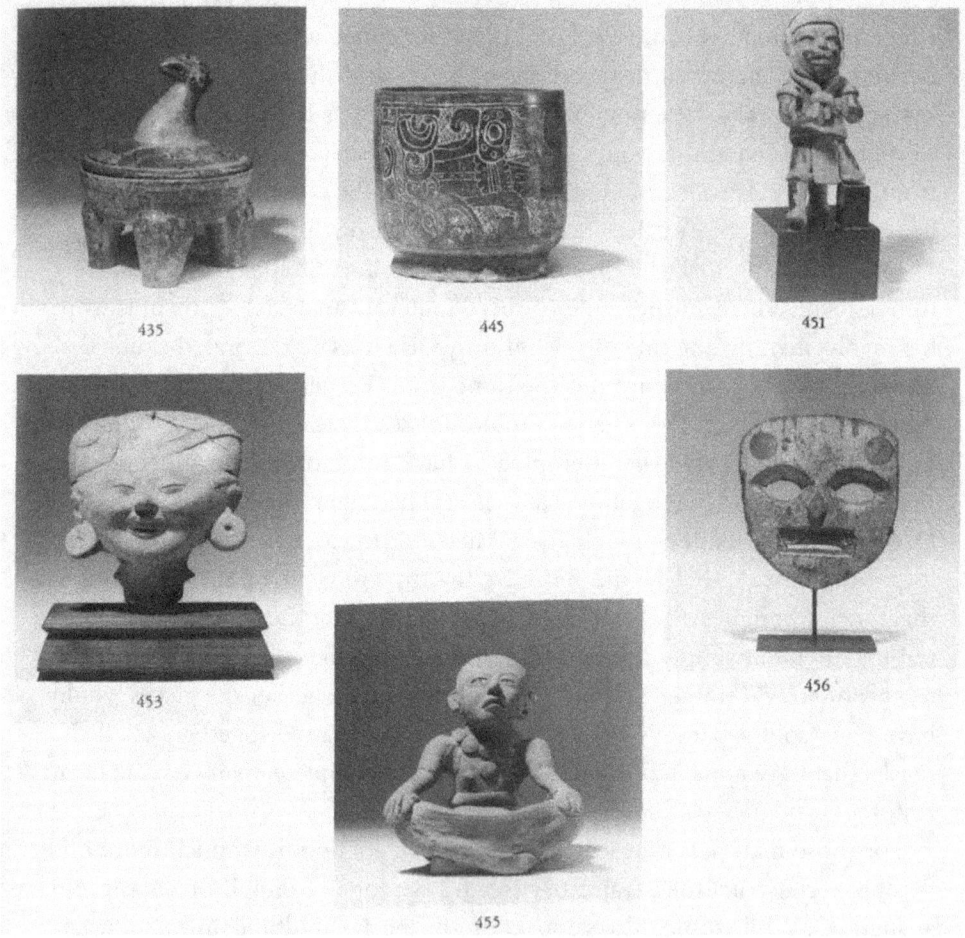

Figure 6.4. Mask (#456) as publicized for sale at auction in Sotheby Parke-Bernet's New York catalogue, February 24–25, 1981. Image by the author.

Some remarks can be made about other pieces that appeared at public auction. Knowing that the NMAI Stolper mask fragments were unearthed in 1967 and 1968, it can hardly be coincidence that a Parke-Bernet auction of April 28, 1968, lists "Two Mixtec Wooden Masks—Fragmentary face mask of flattened form, with large pierced eyes and mouth, and traces of mosaic inlay" (Parke-Bernet 1968, 26). Whether these are the two masks that, according to Stolper, are missing from the NMAI collection is uncertain. It seems somewhat improbable given that Stolper claims these had sold for $4,000 each. Additionally, as mentioned above, Stolper reports to Dockstader that one of the masks of the 1968 looting expedition was absolutely complete and sold for a huge price. While this may be the one that Rassiga brought to the Budapest museum, the Veranneman piece that was in the Emmerich galleries in 1972 (Berjonneau et al. 1985) is also a possible candidate.

Post-Depositional Life

Thus far in this chapter, I have attempted to reassemble collections that have been separated by the art market. The number of times the words "possibly," "hypothetically," and "maybe" are used in this article shows that this exercise is not straightforward and is far from definitive. Still, I hope to show that active provenance research can yield information on probable relations between objects from different museums. Concretely, this research sketches a couple of possible scenarios of where the corpus under study may have come from and how the material relates to each other.

For museum pieces, it can be expected that their post-depositional life begins at the moment that they are acquired by an institution. For pieces that still circulate on the market and are sold in galleries and auctions this is somewhat different. They do not (yet) have a post-depositional life, because they are never definitively deposited in one place. The post-depositional life of museum pieces often consists of periods of display and prolonged periods of time in storage, hidden away from the public eye. Because of this, much of the material in this corpus has never been on public display. Some of these collections were acquired by museums as study material, however, with the exception of the NMAI material (Scott n.d.), many pieces from this corpus have not been studied by academics until recently.

As far as can be gleaned from museum collections, the first collection in this corpus to come onto the market is from a cave that was found by Carl

A. Purpus which yielded a wealth of turquoise material that has been at the NMAI/Heye Foundation since the early twentieth century. This collection became available at a time when the market for pre-Columbian antiquities was not yet fully developed and the collector/looter of this material was a *bona fide* scientist working on botanical collections from Mexico, who sold his personal collection to a non-Mexican museum without the intervention of a dealer. After this, it takes more than forty years for any of this material to appear on the market or in museums. Interestingly, however, once it surfaced there was a six-year window (1966–1972) in which mosaic material started appearing at auctions and in galleries, and made its way into museum collections. After that explosion of material, it takes ten years for more of this material to surface. Much of this early 1980s material can, however, be traced back to a first documented acquisition in the 1960s. These 1980s pieces were also sold within a six-year window. After this, few new pieces came onto the market. A mask that did not surface earlier is at Sotheby's in 1998 and the Edward Merrin Gallery sold a mask around 2016. This mask can however be traced back to an original 1960s sale as well. We can thus assume that most, if not all, of this material was looted in the 1960s.

What then are the possible scenarios that we can sketch from all of this? At some point, probably in the mid-1960s, at least two caves or tombs were discovered in the Tehuacán area—the "Tomb known as Cueva del Tigre" and "Tomb 1." The contents of these tombs were sold in their entirety to the Brussels KMKG/MRAH by Emile Deletaille. Similar material was acquired, probably in Mexico, by Everett Rassiga around the same time. Also in this period, George Pepper acquired a collection of masks and ear plugs in Mexico. In 1967/68 Robert Stolper acquired a collection of relatively low-quality masks from Socorro Navarrete, a dealer in Veracruz. These were apparently the "leftovers" of a larger collection, as Stolper mentions that at least three masks are missing. While we cannot know if any of this material comes from the same location as that of Deletaille, it does seem probable that much of Rassiga's collection was found together. This is especially true for the Nelson-Atkins and Textile Museum collections (comprising the nonperishable and perishable materials, respectively) that were sold in the same year.

The fact that the Textile Museum and the KMKG/MRAH hold textile pieces that are virtually identical opens up the possibility that these pieces could also have come from the same context (see Montoya 2016 for a more in-depth discussion of these textile pieces). It is possible that the higher-quality material sold by Rassiga (the SLAM material and the Budapest mask) was part of the same collection and that these were separated for individual sale, considering their undoubtedly high monetary value. Conversely, the *amate*, fiber, and textile material that is found in the museum collections is entirely absent from auction catalogues. Moser's (1975) exploration of the Cueva de Ejutla located significant quantities of fiber, textile, and *amate* material in looters' debris, while the rest of the cave had been thoroughly stripped. Likewise, Johnson (1966/67) has written about several textiles and *amate* paper fragments that were looted from three caves in the Oaxaca-Puebla border region. These were left in the caves because "the 'treasure hunters' [. . .] did not consider [them] of 'value'" (Johnson 1966/67, 180). Apparently, these "specialist items" were only interesting for study collections in museums and did not present enough monetary value to be sold in auction, so they were not taken by looters. Naturally, the conservation problems that are associated with this type of material might well have contributed to this omission. It is unclear whether this means that the museum collections that do contain "non-sellable" items—corn cobs being the clearest example—were looted "on order" for dealers with a sale to a museum in mind.

Conclusions

In sum, it seems that all these acquisitions of turquoise mosaic and associated objects are in some way related. Either all of the material comes from the same cave or tomb, or the discovery of one of these caves sparks a surge of interest of looters in the region, which results in the recovery of more material. One factor that may have played a role in the appearance on the market of this material is the Tehuacán Valley Project, an archaeological project led by Richard MacNeish, which surveyed and excavated in the Tehuacán valley in the early 1960s. MacNeish describes multiple instances in which the project sparked looting of an archaeological site. For example, when discussing cave Tc34 he writes: "we left a piece of cotton cloth found in Zone B in the profile when we quit Friday night; when we returned Monday we found the cloth gone and our trench extended clear across the cave by looters. The looters had broken into the only two burial niches in the back of the cave and scattered the bones and the broken artifacts over the cave floor" (MacNeish 1972, 63).

As mentioned previously, looted caves with turquoise material abound in the Tehuacán Valley–Cuicatlán Cañada–Sierra Mazateca area. Examples include the "Cueva de Don Bonfilio" near Caltepec (Mastache 1975), the Cueva Cheve (Steele and Snavely 1997), the Puente Colosal (Urcid 2004), and the Cueva de Ejutla (Moser 1975).[4] From the salvage archaeology and exploration that took place in the Cueva de Ejutla it seems that this cave alone would have been large enough to provide the entire corpus under study here. The fact that Stolper mentions that the NMAI masks were found in the same cave in two different years, after it had also been explored by professional archaeologists, indicates that return visits to the same cave(s) took place and that separate collections can come from the same site. A rare glimpse into possible looting practices in the region is given in the case of Santa Ana Teloxtoc, in which a local recounts that a "gringo" came to the village around 1980 offering 8,000 pesos to anyone who would be willing to lead him to caves that contained cultural material, after which much of the material went missing (Rangel Plasencia 1989, 65). In the period it was fairly common that multiple dealers would be co-owners of pieces or would collectively fund looting expeditions (Michael Coe, pers. comm. 2017). Hence, it is quite possible that the loot from one particular find location was distributed among several dealers. At the same time, knowing that Mexico-based dealer Socorro Navarrete supplied Stolper with his material, it is possible that she, at one time, owned the whole lot and sold it in separate parts to North American and European dealers.

While it will most likely never be possible to definitively associate material from the art market with specific looted caves or tombs unless dealers decide to publish their archives, as far as these exist, it is not unthinkable that techniques such as DNA sequencing, stable isotope dietary analysis, C14 dating, and turquoise isotopic signatures might someday reveal links between materials that have been separated by the art market (see Thibodeau et al. 2018 for an example of this kind of study on this corpus). In the concrete case of this work, stable isotope and DNA analyses on the skeletal material could indicate possible relationships between the individuals whose remains are now in museums, and C14 dating or dendrochronology could produce dates for the different masks, informing us of their probable time of deposition in their original context. Similar research could be conducted on salvaged material from looted caves in an attempt to locate the origin of the materials. A project to study the KMKG/MRAH collections with these techniques is in its preparatory phase. At the same time, the fact that names of actual caves accompany a part of this collection creates possibilities for the identification of source locations. The Cueva del Tigre, for example, might correspond to the Cerro del Tigre, another name for the Cerro Colorado, a fortification that was part of pre-Colonial Tehuacán, which contains several caves with pre-Colonial material and associated stories about devils living in the cave (Castillo Tejero 2014). The "La Tambour cave" from which the Nelson-Atkins material supposedly came may well correspond to the Cerro Tambor, a few kilometers southwest of Tehuacán. Considering that much of the material from this corpus came onto the market in the late 1960s, those caves that were looted several years before 1966, the textiles of which were published by Johnson (1966/67), are also possible candidates for the provenience of at least some of the material treated here. MacNeish and Petersen (in MacNeish 1972) list four caves that contained looted burial chambers made of stone or wattle-and-daub constructions. Most of these are less than 3 kilometers outside of the town of Tehuacán and might correspond to the caves mentioned by Stolper as the source for the NMAI material.

In light of the constant development of analytic techniques, it is more important than ever to conduct thorough provenance research of looted collections in order to create a corpus that can be studied as a whole. Active provenance research should be standard practice in every museum. At the same time, I feel that field archaeologists should overcome their apprehension of working with museum material that lacks a definitive provenance. While we should always maintain a critical stance toward the art market and be wary of increasing the monetary value of objects that should not have monetary value in the first place, ignoring these objects deprives us of a wealth of possible information and precludes the possibility of reconstructing the contents and context of looted archaeological sites. This is especially true in areas such as the one under discussion here, in which no true archaeological excavation has found material similar to the large majority of the pieces that have been looted and are now part of museum collections.

Acknowledgments

This work would not have been possible without the help of the many museum archivists, curators, and conservators that supplied the material needed to compile the corpus discussed. I am thankful to Serge Lemaître (KMKG/ MRAH), Emily Kaplan, Patricia Nietfield, and Rachel Menyuk (NMAI), Amy Clarke (SLAM), Jessie Beyers (Nelson-Atkins Museum), Marie Gaida (Etnologisches Museum), János Gyármati (Neprajzi Múzeum), Ann Rowe (Textile

Museum, D.C.), Sue Bergh (CMA), and Yvonne Fleitmann (Israel Museum) for providing me with archival material and provenance information. I would like to thank Frances Berdan, Matthew Robb, and Mary Miller for their help with this project, and the editors of this volume for inviting me to contribute. Davide Domenici and an anonymous reviewer provided important suggestions on how to improve this article. Naturally, all remaining errors are my own.

Notes

1. A similar point was made in the 1980s by the United States Association of Art Museum Directors in response to the proposed introduction of the Cultural Property Repose Act (see Shestack 1999).

2. These pieces are found primarily in the collections of the British Museum (Carmichael 1970; McEwan et al. 2006), the Weltmuseum Wien (Feest 1990), the Pigorini National Museum of Prehistory and Ethnography, and the Danish National Museum. Saville's (1922) overview remains a thorough introduction to most of these early turquoise mosaic pieces.

3. While there is no room in this article to go into the actual cultural meaning of these pieces, considering the representation of turquoise-colored dogs (*xolocozcatl*) made of painted paper during the New Fire Ceremony in the codex Borbonicus (p. 71), and the well-established association between fire, the sun, and turquoise, it may well be that these turquoise mosaic pieces represent dogs, rather than jaguars.

4. Around the same time that the collections under discussion surfaced, several turquoise-mosaic decorated human skulls were acquired by museums in North America and Europe. Considering the number of caves that exist around Tehuacán, and the amount of turquoise mosaic found in them, it is not unthinkable that the discovery of a tomb/cave with a wealth of turquoise tesserae and skeletal material may have been the source for the creation of several turquoise mosaic-decorated skulls in the 1950s or 1960s (Berger 2013; Urcid 2010).

References Cited

Berger, Martin E. 2013. "Real, Fake or a Combination? Examining the Authenticity of a Mesoamerican Mosaic Skull." In *Creating Authenticity: Authentication Processes in Ethnographic Museums*, edited by Alexander Geurds and Laura Van Broekhoven, 11–37. Leiden: Sidestone Press.

Berjonneau, Gerald, Emile Deletaille, Jean-Louis Sonnery, and Michel Graulich. 1985. *Art précolombien, Mexique-Guatemala, Chefs d'Oeuvre Inédits*. Brussels: Editions Arts 135.

Bernal, Ignacio. 1949. "Exploraciones en Coixtlahuaca, Oaxaca." *Revista Mexicana de Estudios Antropológicos*: 5–76.

———. 1951. "Nuevos Descubrimientos en Acapulco." In *The Civilizations of Ancient America: Selected Papers of the XXIXth International Congress of Americanists*, edited by Sol Tax, 52–56. Chicago: University of Chicago Press.

Boone, Elizabeth Hill (editor). 1993. *Collecting the Pre-Columbian Past.* Washington, D.C.: Dumbarton Oaks Research Library and Collection.

Bruhns, Karen Olsen, and Nancy L. Kelker. 2010. *Faking Ancient Mesoamerica.* Walnut Creek, Calif.: Left Coast Press.

Carmichael, Elizabeth. 1970. *Turquoise Mosaics from Mexico.* London: British Museum Press.

Castillo Tejero, Noemi. 2014. "La fortaleza popoloca de Tepexi el Viejo, al sur del estado de Puebla." *Arqueología, segunda época:* 199–215.

Caygill, Marjorie. 2012. "Henry Christy, A. W. Franks and the British Museum's Turquoise Mosaics." In *Turquoise in Mexico and North America: Science, Conservation, Culture and Collections,* edited by J.C.H. King et al., 187–201. London: Archetype Publications.

Chase, Arlen F., Diane Z. Chase, and Harriot W. Topsey. 1988. "Archaeology and the Ethics of Collecting." *Archaeology* 41 (1): 56–60, 81.

Coe, Michael D. 1993. "From Huaquero to Connoisseur: The Early Market in Pre-Columbian Art." In *Collecting the Pre-Columbian Past: A Symposium at Dumbarton Oaks, 6th and 7th October 1990,* edited by Elizabeth Hill Boone, 271–290. Washington, D.C.: Dumbarton Oaks Research Library and Collection.

Coggins, Clemency. 1969 "Illicit Traffic of Pre-Columbian Antiquities." *Art Journal:* 94–114.

Domenici, Davide. 2016. "Máscaras, escudos y tablas con mosaicos de turquesa en Puebla y Oaxaca." *Arqueología mexicana* 141: 44–49.

———. 2017. "Missionary Gift Records of Mexican Objects in Early Modern Italy." In *The New World in Early Modern Italy, 1492–1750,* edited by Elizabeth Horodowich and Lia Markey, 86–102. Cambridge: Cambridge University Press.

Ekholm, Gordon, F. 1964. "The Problem of Fakes in Pre-Columbian Art." *Curator:* 19–32.

Feest, Christian. 1990. "Vienna's Mexican Treasures. Aztec, Mixtec, and Tarascan Works from 16th Century Austrian Collections." *Archiv für Völkerkunde* 44: 1–64.

Gallegos, Roberto. 1963. "Zaachila: The First Season's Work." *Archaeology* 16 (2): 226–233.

Graham, Ian. 2011. *The Road to Ruins.* Albuquerque: University of New Mexico Press.

Gyármati, János (editor). 2008. *'Taking Them Back to My Homeland . . . ': Hungarian Collectors; Non-European Collections of the Museum of Ethnography in a European context.* Budapest: Neprajzi Museum.

Johnson, Irmgard. 1966/67. "Miniature Garments Found in Mixteca Alta Caves, Mexico." *Folk* 8/9: 179–190.

King, Mary Elizabeth. 1979. *The Prehistoric Textile Industry of Mesoamerica.* Washington, D.C.: Dumbarton Oaks Research Library and Collection.

Levine, Marc N., and Lucha Martínez de Luna. 2013. "Museum Salvage: A Case Study of Mesoamerican Artifacts in Museum Collections and on the Antiquities Market." *Journal of Field Archaeology* 38: 264–276.

MacNeish, Richard S. (editor). 1972. *The Prehistory of the Tehuacan Valley.* Vol. 5. *Excavations and Reconnaissance.* Austin: University of Texas Press.

Martínez Tuñón, Antonio, and Nelly Robles Garcia. 2010. "Xatachío: un pequeño sitio monumental en la Mixteca Alta." *Arqueología, segunda época* 44: 73–92.

Mastache, Guadalupe. 1975. "Dos fragmentos de tejido decorados con la técnica de plangi." *Anales del INAH:* 251–260.

McEwan, Colin, Andrew Middleton, Caroline Cartwright, and Rebecca Stacey. 2006. *Turquoise Mosaics from Mexico*. Durham, N.C.: Duke University Press.

Merrin Galleries. 1966. *Pre-Columbian Art*. New York: Merrin Galleries.

Montoya, Julia. 2016. "Textiles y otros materiales arqueológicos del Valle de Tehuacán, México, en los Museos Reales de Arte e Historia (MRAH), Bruselas." In *PreColumbian Textile Conference VII / Jornadas de Textiles PreColombinos VII*, edited by Lena Bjerregaard and Ann Peters, 104–131. Lincoln, Nebr.: Zea Books.

Moser, Christopher L. 1975. "Cueva de Ejutla: Una Cueva Funerarie Pós-Clasica?" *Boletín del INAH* 14: 25–37.

Parke-Bernet Galleries. 1966. *Pre-Columbian Art, Auction of 26 April 1966*. New York.

———. 1968. *African, Oceanic, American Indian & Pre-Columbian Art from the Collection of Allan Frumkin (New York)*. New York.

Parsons, Lee A. 1980. *Pre-Columbian Art: The Morton D. May and the St. Louis Art Museum Collections*. New York: Harper and Row.

Rangel Plasencia, Carlos. 1989. "El hallazgo: una ventana hacia el pasado." In *Las Cuevas de Santa Ana Teloxto*, edited by Ernesto Vargas, 61–75. Mexico DF: UNAM.

Rincón Mautner, Carlos. 2005. "Sacred Caves and Rituals from the Northern Mixteca of Oaxaca, Mexico: New Revelations." In *In the Maw of the Earth Monster: Studies of Mesoamerican Ritual Cave Use*, edited by James A. Brady and Keith A. Prufer, 117–152. Austin: University of Texas Press.

Saville, Marshall. 1922. *Turquois Mosaic Art in Mexico*. New York: Museum of the American Indian, Heye Foundation.

Shestack, Alan. 1999. "The Museum and Cultural Property: The Transformation of Institutional Ethics." In *The Ethics of Collecting Cultural Property: Whose Culture? Whose Property?*, edited by Phyllis Mauch Messenger, 93–101. Albuquerque: University of New Mexico Press.

Sotheby's. 1981. *Pre-Columbian Art, Auction 24/25 February, 1981*. New York.

———. 1983. *Important Pre-Columbian Art, May 12 and 13, 1983*. New York.

———. 1987. *Pre-Columbian Art, 18 November 1987*. New York.

Steele, Janet F. 2005. "Pre-Hispanic Rain Ceremonies in Blade Cave, Sierra Mazateca, Oaxaca, Mexico." In *In the Maw of the Earth Monster: Mesoamerican Ritual Cave Use*, edited by J. Brady and K. Prufer, 91–116. Austin: University of Texas Press.

Steele, Janet F., and Ralph Snavely. 1997. "Cueva Cheve Tablet." *Journal of Cave and Karst Studies* 59 (1): 26–32.

Stolper, Robert. 1970. Robert Stolper to Frederick Dockstader, November 4, 1970. (Box 312, Folder 18). National Museum of the American Indian, Smithsonian Institution.

———. 1971a. Robert Stolper to Frederick Dockstader, June 28, 1971. (Box 312, Folder 18). National Museum of the American Indian, Smithsonian Institution.

———. 1971b. Robert Stolper to Frederick Dockstader, August 25, 1971. (Box 312, Folder 18). National Museum of the American Indian, Smithsonian Institution.

Taylor, Dicey. 1982. "Problems in the Study of Narrative Scenes on Classic Maya Vases." In *Falsifications and Misreconstructions of Pre-Columbian Art*, edited by Elizabeth P. Benson and Elizabeth H. Boone, 107–124. Washington, D.C.: Dumbarton Oaks.

Thibodeau A.M., L. López Luján, D. J. Killick, F. F. Berdan, and J. Ruiz. 2018. "Was Aztec and Mixtec Turquoise Mined in the American Southwest?" *Science Advances* 4(6): eaas9370.

Tremain, Cara Grace. 2017. "Fifty Years of Collecting: The Sale of Ancient Maya Antiquities at Sotheby's." *International Journal of Cultural Property* 24: 187–219.

Urcid, Javier. 2010. "Human Skulls with Mosaic Designs." In *Ancient Mexican Art at Dumbarton Oaks*, edited by Susan Toby Evans, 185–190. Washington, D.C.: Dumbarton Oaks Research Library and Collection.

———. 2004. "Sacred Landscapes and Social Memory: The Ñuiñe Inscriptions in the Ndaxagua Natural Tunnel, Tepelmeme, Oaxaca." *Report submitted to FAMSI.* November 2004. http://www.ancientamericas.org/sites/default/files/03068Urcid01.pdf (accessed July 16, 2017).

Vargas, Ernesto (editor). 1989. *Las máscaras de la cueva de Santa Ana Teloxtoc.* Mexico: UNAM.

7

Ancient Zapotec Material Culture
and the Antiquities Market

ADAM SELLEN

Beginning with the early colonizing explorers and continuing to later nine-teenth-century travelers, collectors, and archaeologists, Latin America's mate-rial culture has been acquired and incorporated into private and public muse-ums through processes that include looting, falsification, and contraband, as well as significantly less controversial arrangements such as official exchanges between museums and *partage* agreements. The latest installment in the ac-quisition boom is characterized by a new surge in private collections, fed by a robust market for cultural-historical material via the internet. Antiquities from most countries can now be acquired online from a seller anywhere in the world (Brodie 2015), placing renewed pressure on world heritage sites and their material evidence.

In contrast to this unrestrained activity to accumulate objects and profit from their sale are efforts in specialized fields to document material culture and to denounce its illegal procurement through online catalogues, blogs, and other assorted websites. It is not clear whether these efforts are putting the brake on the clandestine exchange of cultural materials or just adding to an abundance of electronic information, but in my view the digitization of mate-rial culture is laying the foundation for a new online community approach to preserving the past—a task that has traditionally been the responsibility of museums and law enforcement.

This chapter is the result of my own journey into the digital age through the creation of an online catalogue of archaeological effigy vessels from southwest Mexico—ceramic artifacts that are rich in iconographic detail and are an unparalleled source of information about ancient Mesoamerican society. The online catalogue of these vessels complements, and in a few instances can replace, cumbersome printed material that is often prohibitively expensive, inaccessible, and out of date. In general, internet databases are easily accessed and updated as new information comes forth. Furthermore, they can be searched inter-relationally and, as will be seen, can be used to keep track of material that has entered the vagaries of the international art market. Thus, they can play a central role not only in preserving and generating knowledge about the past, but also in stemming the illicit flow of material culture that has typically constituted one-way traffic, from poor to rich countries. Although I created the online catalogue of effigy vessels for academic purposes, over time it has become a peripheral barometer of the antiquities market.

For almost two decades now, in collaboration with a small group of researchers, I have been involved with identifying ancient Zapotec material culture in public and private collections, writing on its significance from a cultural and historical perspective, and in particular, studying how it has been collected (Sellen 2015, 2007, 2005a, 2005b; Sellen and König 2015; Urcid and Sellen 2009; Jennings and Sellen 2018). The main thrust of my work centers on ceramic effigies—commonly known as "urns"—because they are rich in iconographic information and their study opens a palatial window onto ancient Zapotec culture and society. Generally, they are associated with tombs or burials and can be objects ranging from 10 cm to almost a meter tall. Another feature of the urns is that they were often produced in series of four or five, corresponding to an ancient Mesoamerican belief that divided the world into five parts: four corners and the center.

Urns are found throughout the state of Oaxaca, in southwest Mexico, with a large concentration of materials coming from Monte Alban, the hilltop city of the ancient Zapotec that has received continuous archaeological attention since excavations began there in the 1930s. Yet, when one considers all the known urns in collections, relatively few have been found in controlled archaeological contexts compared with the hundreds of specimens that have either been looted or were retrieved during the nineteenth century, when archaeology was still in its infancy but the formation of amateur collections was at its height. Since that time, objects have been removed from Oaxaca to different museums in Mexico and around the world, and as a result of this process valuable contextual information has been invariably lost. Furthermore, there are a lot of fake urns in collections, confounding the archaeological record even more.

The online catalogue of urns came about because I was looking to create a reference with sufficient hard archaeological data and imagery to be able to say something about the variation in the iconography of Zapotec urns. But when I first proposed the study for my doctoral research,[1] I was discouraged because of the difficulty of assembling a reliable corpus, given the lack of archaeological data available from objects acquired from uncontrolled excavations and the notorious number of fakes in museums and catalogues. Despite the challenges involved, I set about creating a database that could do the following:

Separate the fakes from the genuine material
Illustrate the objects through line drawings, and
Provide as much contextual and historical information as possible about
    each artifact.

After the completion of my dissertation I offered the database to the Florida-based organization Foundation for the Advancement of Mesoamerican Studies, Inc. (FAMSI), which published it on their website in both Spanish and English.[2] To date it contains records detailing 570 objects, representing the largest collection of Zapotec effigy vessels in the world. This virtual museum gets a lot of visitors: a combined average for the English and Spanish sites is 7,000 visits a month. From feedback I have learned that the database is used by a variety of people in distinct professions: educators, archaeologists, art restorers, and even tattoo artists. Today it is also hosted on the website of the Los Angeles County Museum of Art (LACMA).[3] As the author of the database I can insert and update the data from any computer with internet access, and this feature represents one of the greatest advantages of an online catalogue, given that printed material is often prohibitively expensive and out of date.

At the end of the 1990s, when I began my search for objects to inform my doctoral research, the internet was not the best place to identify materials, and my sources were still published books and catalogues. For example, a singular Zapotec urn with glyphic information was published in *Pre-Columbian Art of Mexico* (Furst and Furst 1980) and its complex iconography was central to my investigation (fig. 7.1). I attempted to locate the artifact at the Munson-Williams-Proctor Institute in Utica, New York, where I had hoped to examine it, but I was told that the Institute had changed their priorities and, via an auction

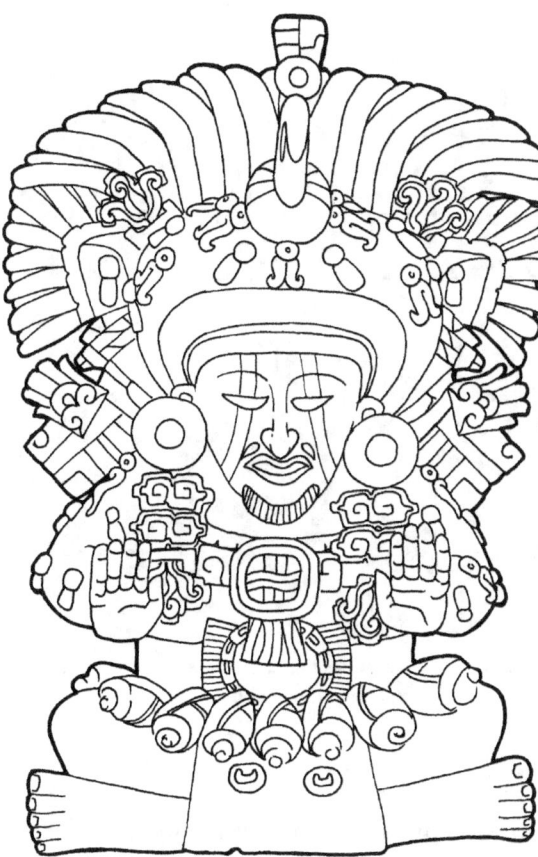

Figure 7.1. Zapotec urn. Formerly
at the Munson-Williams-Proctor
Institute in Utica, New York. Drawing
by Adam Sellen.

house, the urn had been sold to a private collector. While bibliographic materials are available online, as are entire museum collections, when a museum sells
off parts of their collection to private interests, often the only people tracking
these transactions are independent scholars.

Accordingly, another player in the web platform is the auction house. Since
the nineteenth century the ubiquitous Zapotec urn has been a favorite at
auction houses, and through their exchanges many objects in private collections—including early forgeries—made their way to prominent museums. For
example, the important American collector George Gustav Heye purchased
several lots of urns at an auction held at the Drouot Hotel in Paris in 1929.
Even though the majority of the objects he acquired were twentieth-century
creations, they ended up on the shelves of the Museum of the American Indian
he founded in New York (fig. 7.2). This museum was shuttered in 1989 and

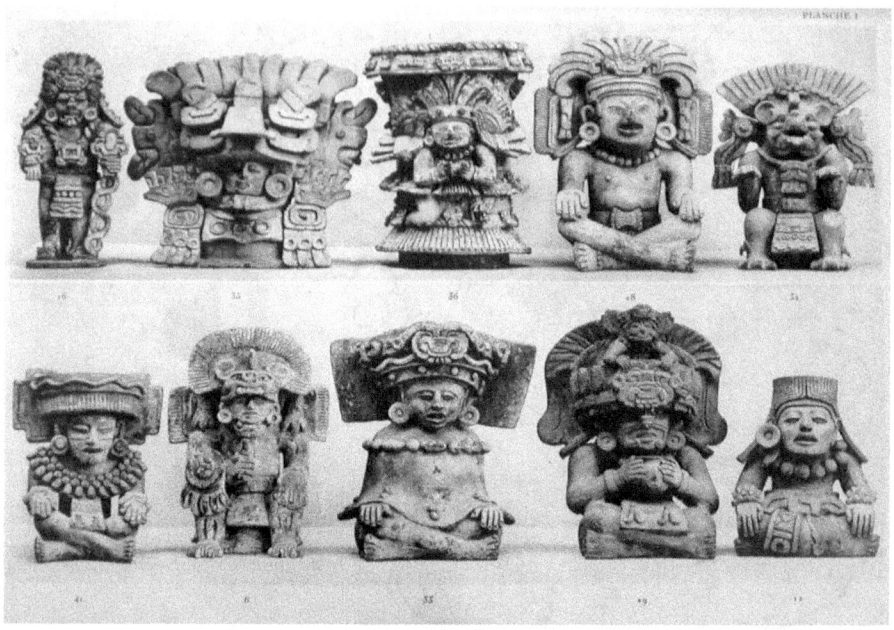

Figure 7.2. Plate 1, "Arts du Mexique Précolombien: ceramiques mixtèque, zapotèque, aztèque, etc." Auction catalogue in the Hotel Drouot, April 1929. Paris: Imprimie Lahure.

its collections were transferred to the Smithsonian Institution in Washington, D.C., where they have been cared for impeccably and are made available for study at the National Museum of the American Indian.[4]

The gradual migration of private collections to museums via auction houses, while hardly curbing the trade in illicit antiquities, at least meant that artifacts were ending up in museums where they could be properly cared for, publicly accessed, and even possibly repatriated (if, of course, they were not again sold into private hands). Unfortunately, this migration now rarely happens. Many museums are rightly reticent about acquiring materials that have been sold at auction given that provenance records can be falsified (Yates 2015, 37). And despite the accessibility of technologies like thermoluminescence (TL), forgeries of Zapotec urns remain undetected on many auction sites, perhaps because even TL results are being forged. Finally, museums rightly shun these materials simply because they do not want their reputations tarnished by purchase of artifacts that should never have left the country of origin in the first place.

Howard Leigh and the Museo Frissell in Oaxaca

Museums—one would suppose—are perhaps the best places to keep archaeological materials. To our collective sorrow we have learned that museums are
in fact not impervious to social and political change, nor to misdeeds committed by insiders. In 1959, Erwin Frissell, a lawyer and amateur American
collector who vacationed in Mitla, Oaxaca, and who owned the building that
had housed La Sorpresa, a legendary hotel in the center of town, transferred
his property and large archaeological collection to Mexico City College. The
site of the former hotel became the Museo Frissell and the Mexican government sanctioned its private operation under the auspices of the College. In
1965 the Museo Frissell acquired a collection from another American residing
in Mitla, an artist by the name of Howard Leigh. He was a life-long guest at
the Frissell home and had amassed a small but stunning collection of ancient
Zapotec artifacts (fig. 7.3).

Leigh, who was chronically short of cash, began to sell parts of his collection to deep-pocketed collectors in the United States, violating not only the

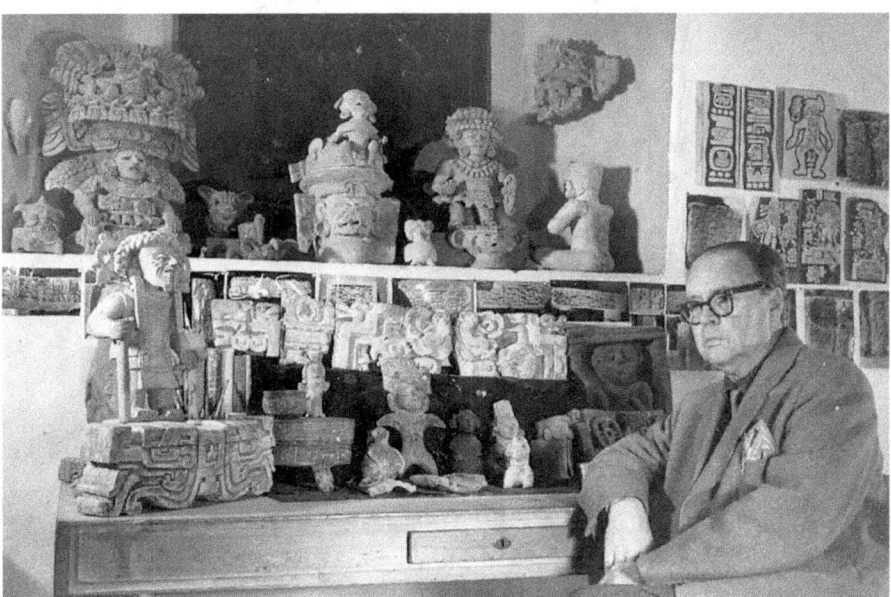

Figure 7.3. Howard Leigh and his archaeological collection in Mitla, Oaxaca, circa 1965. Photo
courtesy of Javier Urcid.

museum's declaration that they would not sell, nor be associated directly or indirectly with the sale of, pre-Hispanic artifacts,[5] but also the laws of Mexico (see below). In one case, he sold a Zapotec urn that was part of an identical series of four, because presumably under this logic he would still have other objects from the set. Sometime between 1965 and 1967 a very large urn (76.8 cm tall) was sold to a buyer by the name of "Davis" in New Orleans (fig. 7.4). Soon after, in 1968, it appeared in a catalogue from the Isaac Delgado Museum of Art in New Orleans, and in 1974 the object was put up for auction at Sotheby's Parke-Bernet. A year later the Canadian magnate George R. Gardiner acquired the urn for his personal collection from this auction house, and it is presently on display at the Gardiner Museum of Ceramic Art in Toronto, Canada—an institution he founded with his collection and that of his spouse.

The Gardiner urn story illustrates how objects can migrate—via the auction house and unscrupulous collectors—from museums in Mexico to public institutions in countries different from their culture of origin. I have documented these movements on the database because they constitute a crucial part of

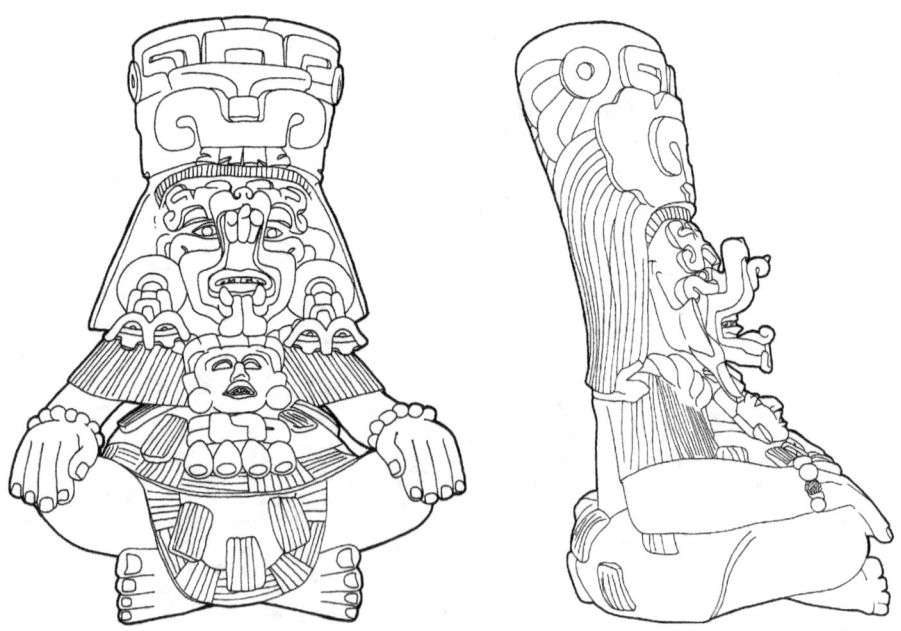

Figure 7.4. Zapotec urn from the Leigh collection. Gardiner Museum cat. 83.1.179. Drawing by Adam Sellen.

the life history of an object. In this case it is important to know that the urn is part of a series. Zapotec urns, especially those with Cociyo imagery, were often produced in matching sets of four or five, yet in a museum context it is rare to see these artifacts exhibited together. In fact, few museums possess complete matched sets of urns, and the reason has to do with how they have been collected. Beginning in the nineteenth century, when many collectors divested their collections, they often divided up the sets, because individual objects would fetch more money. Furthermore, the precarious archaeological context of the urns often resulted in one or more of the objects being damaged, and because some objects in the set were in better shape these could be sold at a premium. This practice extended into the twentieth century and was even common with museums that considered the matching urns "duplicates" that could be used for trade or donation. Even Mexico's National Museum has taken this position and allocated urns from excavated sets to bolster collections in smaller museums around the country.

The problem with this approach is that it violates the character of the artifacts, which should be considered together, as a whole, from the perspective of core beliefs in indigenous worldview and ritual practice. Furthermore, if we were to make an in-depth study of an object that was part of a set, information about the locations of the other objects in the series would be invaluable. However, reconstituting these sets is a difficult task. Many of the individual urns have followed circuitous routes between buyers and institutions before finally ending up in museums, principally in North America and Europe. In addition, locating the distinct parts of these sets can be a challenge because museums do not routinely make public all the materials they hold in their storerooms, especially if they are in a fragmented state. Because of this situation, the documentation of sets is a priority for the database and will be explored next.

A Zapotec Urn at the Archaeological Institute of America

Made public in Donna Yates's first-rate blog *Anonymous Swiss Collector*,[6] Mesoamerican and Egyptian antiquities in the care of the Archaeological Institute of America (AIA), Saint Louis Society, were de-accessioned and sold through the international auction house Bonhams on November 12, 2014. Among these materials, the one object that caught my interest was a Zapotec urn from lot 149 (sold for US$3,750).[7] According to the AIA's website, the society acquired the urn in gratitude for its support of the work of the Maya archaeologists Edgar Lee Hewett and Sylvanus Morley for the School of American Archaeology in Santa Fe, sometime in 1912. In 1943, the society loaned the urn to the Saint Louis Art Museum (SLAM) where it received the catalogue number E3051.73 and remained until 1990, when it was returned to the AIA.[8]

The SLAM's substantial holdings of Mesoamerican archaeology, acquired from the American magnate Morton D. May, include more than 100 Zapotec urns. In 1973 the art historian Philippa Shaplin, suspecting fakes among that collection, teamed up with David Zimmerman at the Center for Archaeometry at Washington University in St. Louis to test the urns with a novel new method known as thermoluminescence. They published their results a few years later (see Shaplin and Zimmerman 1978). This was the first time Zapotec ceramic effigies had ever been tested using this method and, while not part of the May collection, urn E3051.73 was also tested and confirmed to be ancient.[9] In addition to this important study, the urn's unique maize iconography was analyzed in Shaplin's master's thesis (1975), and also in Eubanks's published work *Corn in Clay* (1999).

In her blog, Yates says that the Mesoamerican objects in the Bonhams sale constituted a rare case of "legal" artifacts in the United States, and mentions that they were "clean," having been exported from their country of origin before legislation was enacted to protect them. Many members of the AIA also referred to these artifacts as "documented" and thus consider their sale "proper."[10] The distinction between "clean" and "documented" is difficult to understand, especially if these objects come from Mexico, and they probably do, because we have to consider that this country, since 1827, has enacted various types of legislation to protect its cultural heritage. These measures were created specifically to curb international interest in acquiring Mexican collections for foreign museums.[11] Later in the century this legislation included implementing a blanket prohibition in 1897 specifically making all ruins and artifacts property of the Nation.[12]

Because of these measures, had they been exported legally, a permit approved by the corresponding institution would have necessarily accompanied the objects, and in absence of that documentation, it can be surmised that the objects were most likely removed from Mexico illegally. Nonetheless, Yates rightly called into question the institute's motives for selling off parts of their collection and the repercussions of such sales in incentivizing the market in illicit antiquities. I would also add that public institutions and societies, by their very nature, have established a trust with their collections that includes proper stewardship—as outlined by ICOMOS—for the benefit of society and its development. Surely this would be evident to the AIA, a serious organization with a strict code of ethics and signatories to several international resolutions on the importation and acquisition of antiquities.[13] Yet recently, Michael Fuller, acting president of the AIA's Saint Louis Society, told the Joint Annual Meeting on January 10, 2015, that they had "tried hard in St. Louis to convince two local leading cultural institutions to accept the artifacts [referring to the Egyptian and Mesoamerican objects], keep them, and at least periodically display them. But after years of talks, both institutions refused."[14] However, correspondence between Fuller and Sidney Goldstein, associate director of the SLAM in 1990, suggests that this museum was all in favor of keeping the Zapotec urn and other artifacts, especially since they had housed them responsibly for more than 30 years, but the board at the society decided against transferring these objects into the museum's permanent care, arguing that they were part of their "heritage and assets" and that donating them would seriously jeopardize the future of the organization.[15]

Another unfortunate consequence of this sale has been its effect on research. De-accessioning and selling objects from the public to the private domain seriously diminishes the possibility that scholars can continue working with these artifacts. Sadly, I found out about this case too late. The Saint Louis Society's former urn is part of a set of at least two. The other is in a collection at the Royal Ontario Museum (ROM) and was acquired around the same time—in 1919—from collector Constantine Rickards, the British consul in Oaxaca (fig. 7.5). Early photographs of Rickards's collection in Oaxaca show the ROM urn (cat. 917.4.97) on the second shelf to the left, while on the top shelf there is a twentieth-century fake (HM 1908) that closely resembles the ancient artifact (fig. 7.6). It is still not clear whether Rickards also owned the urn that was in Saint Louis, but it is a strong possibility given the penchant of collectors to sell what they consider "duplicate" material. Since the ROM urn is more complete in the facemask and the headdress, and the former AIA urn gives us a better idea of the pot held by both hands and the lower section, we can now get a more complete picture of the object by combining the information from each urn. But how can we further investigate this aspect and other research questions (such as the traces of blue pigment on the headdress) when one of these pieces is now in private hands? And taking into account ancient Zapotec worldviews that sets should be considered one single artifact, what possibility do we have of reuniting these artifacts? We are left to rigorously document the object, place it on the database, and hope that some day it returns to a museum or other public collection.

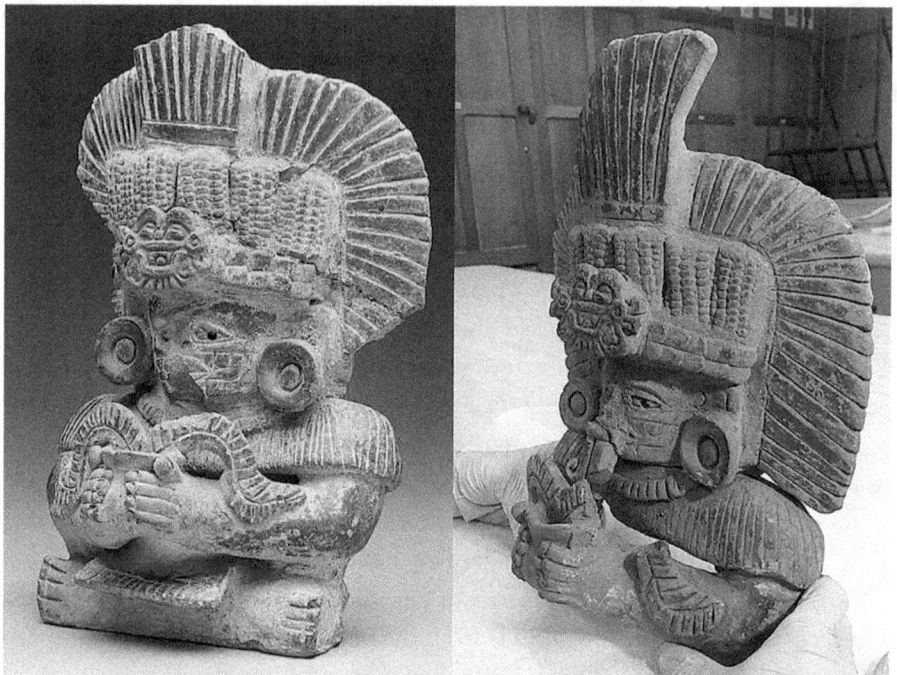

Figure 7.5. Comparison of the urn from the AIA, Saint Louis Society's collection, cat. E3051.73 (photo from Bonhams sale catalogue), with the Royal Ontario Museum's urn, cat. 917.4.97 (photo by Adam Sellen).

With these few cases I have demonstrated the success and pitfalls of documenting material culture online. As we have seen, landing in a museum hardly means that artifacts are safe from being circulated again in the private market. Museums in the United States, for example, can lose funding or reestablish priorities and sell parts of their collections. The renewed growth of private collections thanks to online sales is another disturbing trend cutting off the flow of artifacts to museums. These types of transactions are notoriously hard to document because online auctions houses conceal the identities of the buyers, so all we can do is remark on the fact that an object has surfaced for sale. If nothing else, my obsession with tracking Zapotec urns does help verify their very existence, and that effort is particularly important because Mesoamerican artifacts, especially those from the lesser-known cultures, are often overlooked in the discussion on the antiquities trade.

Tracking sales of archaeological materials is easier because of the online

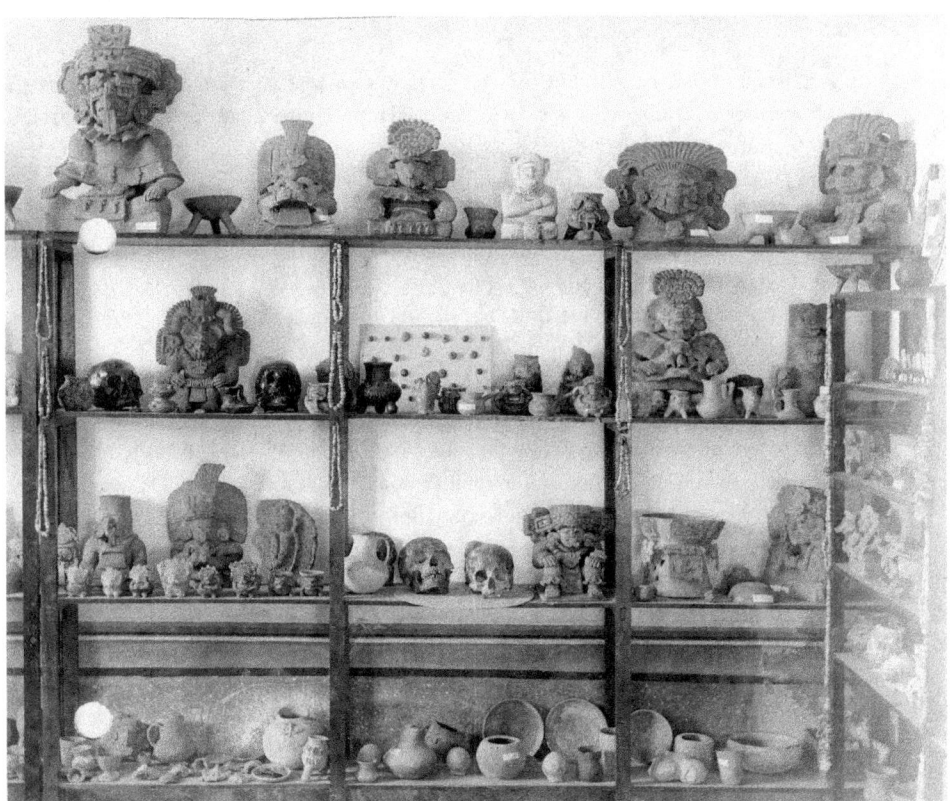

Figure 7.6. The Rickards collection in Oaxaca circa 1917. Photo from NWA archives, Royal Ontario Museum, Toronto, Canada.

experience, and this in turn creates a real advantage for database owners and bloggers who can update and add to them in an attempt to keep up with a digital landscape that is constantly changing. Yet this digital convenience is a double-edged sword, as I found out recently. Last year the French auction house Binoche et Giquello sold an elaborate urn (Lot 27, €410,000[16]) from a collection in Barcelona. In its promotional material, the auction house had cited my catalogue in the list of publications to provide scholarly background on the object; that is to say, to legitimize the object academically. This was never the intention of my database, but since it is in the public domain one wonders how to curb this type of use. A future plan of mine is to put a very strongly worded disclaimer on the website, so auction houses will not feel inclined to use this information freely.

Notes

1. Published under the title *El Cielo compartido. Deidades y ancestros en las vasijas efi-gie zapotecas*, serie Monografías 4. Centro Peninsular en Humanidades y Ciencias Sociales, UNAM, Merida, 2007.

2. http://www.famsi.org/research/zapotec/index.html

3. http://www.ancientamericas.org/collection/browse/492

4. An excellent study of the fakes in this collection is by Annette Neubert, *An Analysis of the Collection Histories of Fake Zapotec Urns at the National Museum of the American Indian*, unpublished Master's thesis on file at the Faculty of Columbian College of Arts and Sciences, George Washington University, 2012.

5. "Statement of Policy by the Executive Council of the Frissell Museum of Zapotecan Art," published in Paddock (1960, 6–7).

6. http://www.anonymousswisscollector.com/2014/10/archaeological-institute-of-america-st-louis-society-selling-meosamerican-antiquities-at-auction.html (accessed October 27, 2017).

7. https://www.bonhams.com/auctions/21802/lot/149/ (accessed October 27, 2017).

8. Personal communication with Amy Clark, Senior Research Assistant, Saint Louis Art Museum, November 2, 2017.

9. The 1978 publication did not include the specific TL results for object E3051.73. The author of that text obtained them from archival files that were kindly donated to me by Ms. Shaplin.

10. In text read by Michael Fuller, acting president of the AIA, Saint Louis Society, at the AIA Council Meeting on January 10, 2015, during the 116th Joint Annual Meeting, New Orleans, Louisiana. See http://users.stlcc.edu/mfuller/aia/press4.html.

11. For example, see the case of the French antiquities dealer Latour Allard who, in 1827, was caught red-handed trying to sell the Dupaix collection and was denounced by the Mexican commercial attaché in Paris, Tomás Murphy (Sellen 2015, 70–73).

12. Many laws have been passed (see Rico Mansard 2004, 353–355), beginning with Arancel para las aduanas marítimas y de frontera de la República Mexicana en el Capítulo IV, prohíbe la exportación de monumentos y antigüedades mexicanas (November 16, 1827), and culminating in the most important law of the century, declaring archaeological monuments property of the Nation: Decreto en que se reafirma la propiedad de la Nación sobre monumentos arqueológicos (May 11, 1897).

13. See https://www.archaeological.org/about/policies

14. See http://users.stlcc.edu/mfuller/aia/press4.html.

15. Michael Fuller to Sidney Goldman, February 16, 1990, SLAM archives.

16. http://www.binocheetgiquello.com/html/fiche.jsp?id=5727734

References Cited

Brodie, Neil. 2015. "The Internet Market in Antiquities." In *Countering Illicit Traffic In Cultural Goods: The Global Challenge Of Protecting The World's Heritage*, edited by France Desmarais, 11–20. Paris: ICOM.

Eubanks, Mary. 1999. *Corn in Clay*. Gainesville: University of Florida Press.

Furst, Jill Leslie, and Peter T. Furst. 1980. *Pre-Columbian Art of Mexico*. New York: Abbeville.

Jennings, Justin, and Adam Sellen (editors). 2018. *Real Fake? The Story of a Zapotec Urn*. Toronto: Royal Ontario Museum. Free Ebook available at: https://bit.ly/2AluMvw

Paddock, John (editor). 1960. "New Alliance of Oaxaca Area Cultural Institutions," *Boletín de Estudios Oaxaqueños* 15 (May 15): 1–9.

Rico Mansard, Luisa Fernanda. 2004. *Exhibir para educar. Objetos, colecciones y museos de la ciudad de México (1790–1910)*. Barcelona-Mexico: Ediciones Pomares, S.A.

Sellen, Adam. 2005a. "La colección arqueológica del Dr. Fernando Sologuren." *Acervos: Boletín de los Archivos y Bibliotecas de Oaxaca* 29 (7): 4–15.

———. 2005b. "The Lost Drummer of Ejutla: The Provenance, Iconography and Mysterious Disappearance of a Polychrome Zapotec Urn." *Baessler-Archiv* Band 51 (2003): 115–138.

———. 2007. *El Cielo compartido. Deidades y ancestros en las vasijas efigie zapotecas*. Serie Monografías 4. Merida: Centro Peninsular en Humanidades y Ciencias Sociales, UNAM.

———. 2015. *The Orphans of the Muse. Archaeological Collecting in Nineteenth-Century Oaxaca*. Merida: Centro Peninsular en Humanidades y Ciencias Sociales, UNAM.

Sellen, Adam, and Viola König. 2015. "Using Nineteenth-Century Data in Contemporary Archaeological Studies: The View from Oaxaca and Germany." In *Bridging the Gaps. Integrating Archaeology and History in Oaxaca, Mexico. A Volume in Memory of Bruce E. Byland,* edited by Danny Zborover and Peter Kroefges, 342–359. Boulder: University of Colorado Press.

Shaplin, Philippa D. 1975. *An Introduction to the Stylistic Study of Oaxacan Urns*. Unpublished M.A. Thesis, Wellesley College Department of Art, Boston.

Shaplin, Philippa D., and David Zimmerman. 1978. "Thermoluminescence and Style in the Authentication of Ceramic Sculpture from Oaxaca, Mexico." *Archaeometry* 20 (1): 47–54.

Urcid, Javier and Adam Sellen. 2009. "A Forgotten House of Ancestors from Ancient Xoxocotlán." *Baessler-Archiv* Band 56 (2008): 117–224.

Yates, Donna. 2015. "Illicit Cultural Property from Latin America: Looting, Trafficking, and Sale." In *Countering Illicit Traffic in Cultural Goods: The Global Challenge of Protecting The World's Heritage*, edited by France Desmarais, 33–45. Paris: ICOM.

8

Forgery and the Pre-Columbian Art Market

NANCY L. KELKER

Art forgery is not a new problem but one that seems to have become much worse in recent years. In fact, things have gotten so bad that *Artnet News* dubbed 2016 "The Year of the Fake" (Abrams 2018). This dubious honor was awarded after a string of forgeries involving Old Master artists were revealed, capturing media attention. But that was only a single year in what is quickly looking like the "Decade of the Fake," in which the annual reveal of some multimillion-dollar forgery scandal has become the norm. Still, one has to wonder, are forgeries really more common than ever before? Or are forgeries simply being discovered a bit more quickly than in the past? Although some would argue that the first forgeries were produced by the Phoenicians, the first accounts of art forgery date from the Renaissance, when a rising merchant class began buying and selling works of art. Until quite recently, it would take about 100 years for a forgery to become apparent as a product of the taste and cultural assumptions of its time. This may still be the case for the higher end or "good fakes," as the more skillful forgers seem to be getting better at producing works that fool experts and sometimes even confound science.

Considering the difficulties of producing "good fakes" in some genres of art, one has to wonder at the motivation of forgers. Why do they make fakes? Quite a number of studies have been done on forgeries of Western art in recent years and they suggest that there are potentially as many reasons for fakery as there are forgers. Sometimes, as in the cases of Han van Meegeren[1] and Eric Hebborn,[2] it is a matter of a failed artist seeking revenge on the critics who dismissed his talent. Others, for example, Shaun Greenhalgh,[3] John Myatt,[4] and Wolfgang Beltracchi,[5] have turned to art fakery because they had some degree of technical facility or "hand-skills" but either lacked the dedication or the creative "mind-skills" necessary to achieve success as professional artists. Most often, however, the motivation for art forgery is the same basic one that drew Willie Sutton to rob banks: "Because that's where the [easy] money is." This certainly seems to be the case for the vast majority of pre-Columbian antiquities forgers, who, as a whole, appear not to be concerned about issues of creative genius or the annoyance of receiving bad reviews from critics, although for some there may be considerable satisfaction in fooling the "experts."

As a criminal enterprise, art forgery offers several advantages over bank robbery. First, the risk of getting caught is minimal. Art crimes tend to be a low priority for law enforcement; for example, it took Scotland Yard 17 years to get around to arresting the Bolton Forgers even though one of their first victims had immediately reported the crime to police.[6] Second, should the forger be inept or unlucky enough to get arrested, the sentences typically handed down for these sorts of nonviolent white-collar crimes are often little more than a slap on the hand. For example, the Beltracchis received a six-year prison sentence and served only four years, throughout which they were released during the day to work unattended in their studio.[7] Rarely do forgers get sentenced to prison time, and even when they do, it is likely to be minimum security for periods seldom longer than three or four years, and with good behavior they are out in a matter of months. Third, the notoriety of being a convicted art forger seems to instill celebrity in a way that being a bank robber hasn't since the time of Bonnie and Clyde. A number of art forgers have gone on to write books (Beltracchi and Beltracchi 2014; Hebborn 1993, 1997; Greenhalgh 2017; Perenyi 2012), have movies made about them,[8] and used their fame to set up businesses selling their "gone straight" copies. Popular culture does love a "bad boy," particularly one who rips off the rich.

A Short History of Pre-Columbian Art Forgery

The history of pre-Columbian art forgery is not as well studied or filled with as many charming rogues as are found in Western art forgery, even though its history is nearly as long. The first forgery workshops in the New World are thought to have been inspired by the Aztecs, who often went out to the abandoned ruins of Tula and Teotihuacan to hunt for artifacts. Enterprising locals may have sought to satisfy market demand by creating ceramics and stone statuettes in imitation of ancient models. However, the earliest surviving examples of Mesoamerican and Andean forgeries date from the mid-sixteenth century;

these include Aztec-inspired pottery, decorated with a mix of indigenous and European motifs, and Inca-style wooden *keros* or "drinking cups" adorned with painted or carved zoomorphs borrowed from the art of earlier indigenous cultures. These hybrid pieces, possibly the first examples of American tourist art, were created as curiosities for the Spanish Colonial market. It has also been suggested that a cottage industry of forgeries may have developed during this era as a result of Spanish Missionary zeal. The Mendicant friars sent to convert the heathen Indians were intent on rooting out every form of Native idolatry; they manically burned thousands of painted manuscripts as well as destroying images and other religious objects. Apparently, upon arriving in a village, the friars tended to be torturously insistent that the Natives surrender their "idols," and it is thought that indigenous artisans, in an effort to protect their sacred objects as well as the lives and limbs of their people, produced large numbers of forgeries to be gleefully smashed and burned by the missionaries (Kelker and Bruhns 2010, 15).

The coming of independence from Spain in 1821 provided new business opportunities for forgers across Latin America as the borders of the formerly closed colonies were flung open to European and North American travelers and investment. Romantic accounts of treks though deepest jungle to lost cities, written by explorers such as John Stephens and Frederick Catherwood, Désiré Charnay, Guillermo Dupaix, and Augustus Le Plongeon, fueled interest in the New World, its ancient peoples, and the acquisition of pre-Columbian artifacts. These accounts not only helped to make the nineteenth and twentieth centuries into the golden age of pre-Columbian forgery, but also shaped the direction of those forgeries. Enterprising artisans looked at the drawings and early photographs illustrating these travelogues and gleaned from them the attitudes of their target market, knowing that works meeting those expectations would be easily accepted as more authentic than even the genuine article.

The first known forgery factories, located on Calle Tlatelolco in Mexico City, began producing their signature black wares even before the ink was dry on the Treaty of Córdoba. The Tlatelolco wares married European forms, such as pitchers, with quasi-Aztec ornamentation that seems to have been derived from stone sculpture rather than ceramics (fig. 8.1). The resulting works were about as far removed from the genuine Aztec artifacts they purported to be as the rings of Saturn are from Earth, but they were immensely popular and, as a result, there is hardly a museum in operation during that era that does not have at least one of these crude monstrosities hidden away in storage. The appeal of these especially dreadful fakes to collectors was not based on aesthetic merits because they had none, and that was exactly the point. The primitivism of the Tlatelolco pieces appealed because they reinforced the prevailing Eurocentric narratives of Western art as the only "real" art, and of white Europeans as the true inheritors of civilization. In some ways one has to admire the ingenuity of the Tlatelolco and other forgers in using the self-satisfied smugness of nineteenth-century Colonialists to sell them wagonload upon wagonload of the worst imaginable dross. As William Henry Holmes noted in the late 1880s, "It is very easy for the native artisan to imitate any of the older forms of ware; and there is no doubt that in many cases he has done so for the purposes of deceiving. A renewed impetus has been given to this fraudulent practice by the influx of tourists consequent upon the completion of numerous railways" (1886, 170).

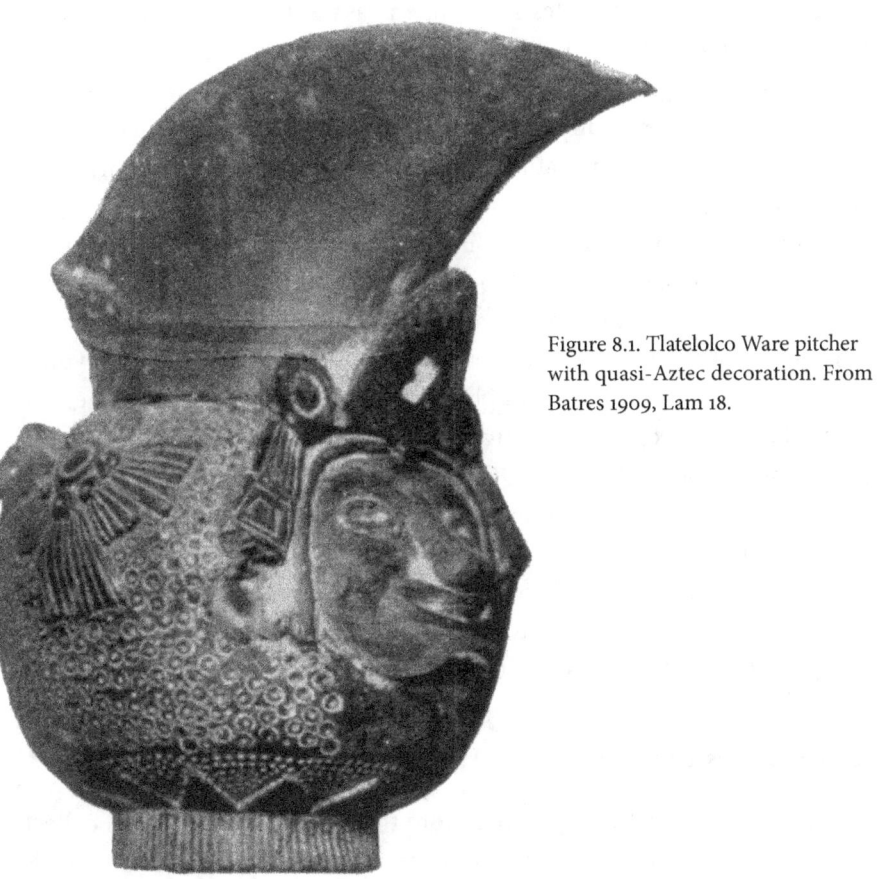

Figure 8.1. Tlatelolco Ware pitcher with quasi-Aztec decoration. From Batres 1909, Lam 18.

Forgery factories, first in Mexico, then in Peru, and subsequently in other Latin American countries, supplied the market with enough faux artifacts to fill innumerable curio cabinets as well as the storage shelves and display cases of some of the world's great museums. In 1909, Leopoldo Batres, one of Mexico's first archaeologists, published his pioneering study, *Antigüedades mejicanas falsificadas, falsificaciones y falsificadores*, which considered the forgery workshops then operating in the Mexico City area. His book covers the more common categories of forgeries offered on the market, from the long produced Tlatelolco Wares to faux Prehispanic codices, and a wide assortment of crude obsidian and alabaster fabrications. He also notes, all too briefly, the existing hierarchy in the forgery business but gives few details about specific forgers or the bottom-rung dealers who passed their wares up the ladder to those with the connections to sell to the wealthy foreigners. Instead Batres, having both an archaeologist's and an upper class Mexican's disdain for them, dismisses forgers as despicable lowlifes and "rude peasant[s] in the field." But even as the "Indian-peasant-forger" has remained the archetype, the business also attracted people of greater sophistication and connections in society. Batres also mentions that museum directors commissioned reproductions of museum objects and then sold them as authentic antiquities (Kelker and Bruhns 2010, 40; Batres 1909, 14).

While the majority of forgers have remained hidden in the shadows, the upper-echelon dealers who sold their wares are known to us from the museum acquisition and provenance records associated with some of the more egregious fakes of the era, including faux Zapotec urns (see Sellen this volume), crystal skulls, spurious obsidian plaques, mosaic skulls, and monumental Veracruz figures. Except for their involvement with forgeries, most would appear to be respectable professionals: Constantine George Rickard, a British Consular employee in Mexico, French antiquarian Eugène Boban, Alfredo Martinez Bustamante, a.k.a. the Tlacolula Pharmacist, and Fernando Sologuren, a physician. In the twentieth century, prominent dealers such as Alfred Stendahl, Helmut de Terra, and Robert L. Stolper sold some of the higher-end forgeries that made their way into major museums around the world.

"Same Indians, Same Clay?"

Upon being told that many of the more than 59,000 pieces in his collection of Mexican antiquities were recent forgeries, Mexican painter Diego Rivera is said to have remarked, "Same Indians, same clay" (Ruy-Sanchez Lacy 1995, 73). Rivera, like many others of his time and ours, romanticized forgers (and looters) as the same sort of simple brown-skinned Indians who peopled his murals; people who still lived as their ancestors had and who made works that were not imitations but continuations of ancient traditions. The motives of the looter and the forger are imagined to be basic subsistence; they rob tombs or make false antiquities as a means of eking out a living for themselves, their wives, and their children.

However, the reality is that most forgers are mestizos, living in modern homes in the modern world, in cities with running water and electricity (Bruhns and Kelker 2010, 36). Many are well educated, and some even attended art school; others learned their craft in government-sanctioned "authentic reproduction" workshops or trained in one of the major forgery ateliers. Forgers have been known to attend scholarly conferences and museum symposiums to keep abreast of the latest archaeological discoveries. For example, the discovery of Monte Alban Tomb 7 in 1931 was reported by news media around the world, and the National Geographic publication of Alfonso Caso's account of the excavations the following year did not escape the notice of enterprising forgers. One of the more spectacular finds from Tomb 7 was a mosaic-decorated human skull. The Tomb 7 skull apparently provided considerable stimulation for the forgery industry as collectors began to salivate over the find. Within a few years at least 10 human skulls with forged mosaic decoration, all appearing to be by the same atelier if not the same hand, as well as some spurious (allegedly Mixtec) mosaic masks began popping up on the market and in private and public collections, including the San Antonio Museum of Art (see Berger this volume for a discussion of Mixtec masks). Adorned and unadorned human skulls, both biologic and petrologic, are perennial favorites; after all, what conveys savagery and horrid rites better than a human skull?

But above all, forgers read books. Hasso von Winning's *Pre-Columbian Art of Mexico and Central America* (1968), one of the first big coffee-table books with lots of color pictures, must have been a boon to the industry. Indeed, there is hardly a museum or private collection in the United States that does not have at least one piece that seems to replicate the examples, not all of which are authentic, illustrated in von Winning's book. It remains unclear whether the publication inspired production of fakes based on the images in the book, or whether the images selected for the book by Alfred Stendahl included some of the more common forgeries of the era. Were von Winning and Stendahl aware that some of the pieces were not ancient? Probably; the author's experience with Hasso was that he could spot a fake at twenty paces, and mixing the faux in with the real is a not uncommon practice in the dealing world even today.

Forgers also read newspapers and magazines and watch television; they are aware of current social and cultural trends, popular media, and even the latest home-decorating fashions, all of which help them to anticipate the needs of their target audiences even though they may be thousands of miles away. Forgers are continually making slight adjustments to their faux wares to make them more attractive and thus increase their salability; for example, perennial sellers such as Colima and Jalisco dog figurines are even more adorable when these ceramic puppies are holding bones or sticks in their mouths just like modern pampered pets. Given that the exotic primitive has almost always been associated with the sexual and that the mammiferous fascination of certain wealthy American males is well known, some forgers in the last forty years or so have been augmenting the breasts of their female figurines in a range of styles from Jaina to Valdivia; instead of the small breasts characteristic of Indigenous Peoples and authentic works, they have become large, perky, and very much like those of a traditional Barbie doll. In what may be a case of what's sauce for the goose is sauce for the gander, exposed male genitalia are also becoming more common on forgeries; sometimes being added to figures in styles where anatomical correctness was rarely a feature of ancient works, as well as being rendered proportionally larger in those nonerotic styles where genitals were depicted.

Sometimes very specific market demographics are targeted by forgers. The media attention paid to the AIDS crisis in the 1980s inspired Ecuadorian forgers to create works, purported to be from the Manteño culture (ca. 800–1530 CE) designed to appeal to the gay market, which up to that point had been served mainly by purveyors of homoerotic Greek antiquities, real and otherwise. While erotic art was known from a few cultures in Peru, the Ecuadorian Manteño did not produce it. At about this same time, a resurgent American Creationist movement gave entrepreneurs in the vicinity of Ica, Peru, an opportunity to repurpose some old pieces from the 1960s, the Ica Stones, which purport to show dinosaurs interacting with humans. Although Basilio Uchuya had long ago confessed to fabricating the pieces that he passed on to a gullible local doctor as antiquities (Polidoro 2002), the Ica Stones continue to be presented in Evangelical Creationist publications as "proof" that science and evolution are wrong.

Monumental Veracruz, Lessons *Still Not* Learned

One of the first great forgery stories concerns Michelangelo Buonarroti, who is known to have created, when finances were tight, at least one, if not two, faux classical sculptures not as copies but as outright forgeries; however, being a Michelangelo, such indiscretions are taken as signs of his greatness. If Mexican art forgery has a Michelangelo, he is, without a doubt, Brigido Lara (b. 1942). Lara claims to have created more than 40,000 false Olmec, Maya, Aztec, and Veracruz pieces. How many of his false works are still standing spot-lit in museum display cases is unknown, since most were discovered only when he revealed having made them. Lara is best known for his monumental Veracruz figures, which neatly filled a scale void in the pre-Columbian ceramic corpus (fig. 8.2). Large-scale ceramic figures are rare, so when Lara's big ornate pieces—some more than 5 feet tall—began appearing on the market, dealers, collectors, and museums snapped them up; however, it was not simply their size that made Lara's works so desirable. Lara is a consummate craftsman and a highly original artist. In the manner of the great European master forgers,

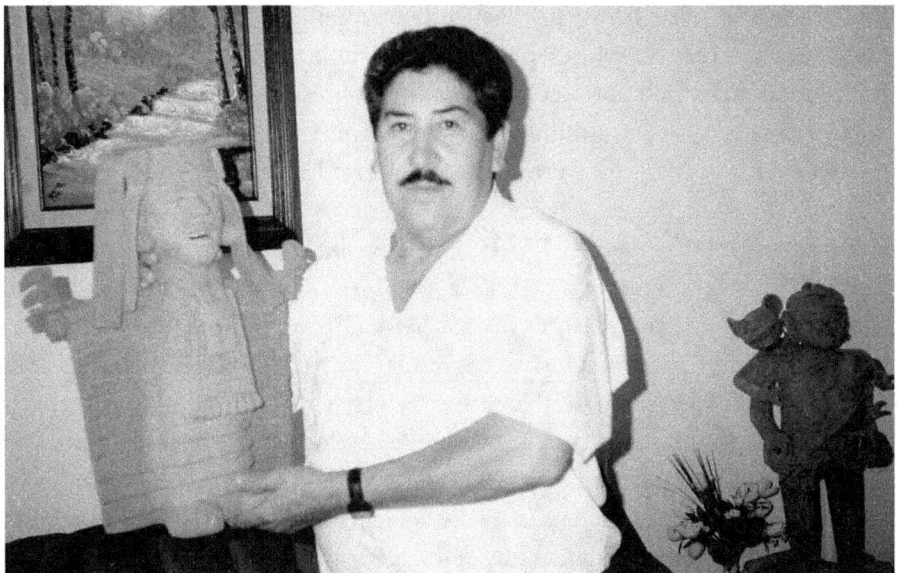

Figure 8.2. Brigido Lara holding a Veracruz-style statuette (note an El Zapotal–style figure in the background). Photo by Elayne Marquis, courtesy of Karen Olsen Bruhns.

he does not merely copy or make pastiches of known works but creates new works that the ancient peoples of Veracruz might have created if they had gotten around to it.

As are many forgers, Lara is vague about his training, claiming to be self-taught and having figured out how to create his forgeries through experimentation. While still a teenager, Lara apprenticed in what must have been a high-end forgery atelier in Mexico City, learning not only the importance of certain details in creating an aura of authenticity but also the techniques used to build large figural pieces. Ironically, Lara's skill as a forger was both his undoing and his salvation. In 1974, Lara and some of his associates were arrested as they were transporting several of his forged pieces. After experts from the Instituto Nacional de Arqueología e Historia (INAH) certified the seized works as genuine antiquities, Lara was charged with smuggling and sentenced to 10 years in prison. He ultimately secured his release by creating, under the watchful eyes of the prison guards, replicas of the mistaken antiquities, which when presented to the INAH experts were again certified as ancient.

Stories of forgers, even bad ones, fooling the experts at museums and academic institutions are stock-in-trade of the fakery game, often because the forgers design their works to meet the tests standardly run by experts to adjudge authenticity. Van Meegeren, a bad painter by any measure, was able to fool Vermeer experts whose primary test of authenticity was to check the dryness (hardness really) of the oil paint layer; he simply added powdered Bakelite to his medium, which produced the desired test response. When his canvases passed this test, expert blindness kicked in and the paintings were authenticated even though they were very far removed in quality from a genuine Vermeer.

Lara's forgeries presented INAH and later museum experts with a much more difficult task. Lara was obsessive about his craft, visiting archaeological sites where he saw not just the works that had been unearthed but also examples of ancient tools that he used as models to craft similar ones for his own use. He would search the local area for the clay sources used by the ancients and dig them for his creations. He even collected local ochers and the full color range of native cinnabars, from deepest vermillion to brick red, in order to have the exact shade of each used by the ancient artisans in a particular region. He convincingly aged his works by re-creating the natural discoloration and mineral deposition resulting from long periods of contact with the soil, treating the works with his own formulations of Portland cement, white lime, clay, urine, and sugar dissolved in hot water and sealed with Resistol 850 (Crossley and Wagner 1987, 99–100). Additional problems could have been presented by the materials Lara used. Clays from the Veracruz region give notoriously unreliable readings under thermoluminescence testing (not that any forensic tests were conducted by INAH). Finally, Lara, like the best European forgers, realized that forgeries of lesser-known artists (or styles) are more likely to be accepted by the experts than those of the better-known masters. In concentrating his major production on his home state of Veracruz, he was free to invent as he wished. The region had seen very little legitimate excavation and the archaeological work that had been done was poorly published. Consequently, Veracruz styles were known only superficially to the experts, meaning they had no solid frame of reference to evaluate Lara's works.

The revelation in 1987 that Lara's forgeries graced the collections of the Metropolitan Museum of Art (fig. 8.3), the St. Louis Museum of Art, and the Dallas Museum of Art (among what must be hundreds of other public and private collections) ought to have served as a cautionary tale for collectors of pre-Columbian art and for the institutions that accept donations, particularly those that violate ethical acquisitions practices. Although Lara's works are high-quality forgeries, they are not without red flags that should have given potential purchasers pause—they were large and unique types, unlike anything archaeologically known at the time. They had no record of provenance, leading dealers and collectors to assume they were looted and therefore genuine antiquities; however, smuggling should never be taken as de facto proof of authenticity. Smugglers, like some dealers, often mix real and faux in their offerings, and the author has personally seen seizures of smuggled artifacts that contained a good number of forgeries. Apparently, believing the works real, no one ever did even the most basic surface tests, which could have revealed the presence of polyvinyl acetate glues used to seal the surfaces.

Traditionally, few galleries or auction houses have made any pretense of conducting scientific examinations to validate the authenticity of the works they accept for sale, and certainly getting reliable results could be problematic in a world of for-hire testing labs. Recently, perhaps as a response to the ever-increasing number of "problematic works" on the market, Sotheby's hired former FBI expert James Martin to start an in-house Scientific Research Department (Pogrebin 2016). Still, for many dealers, authenticity is not the point; salability is. The first question to be asked by the dealer or

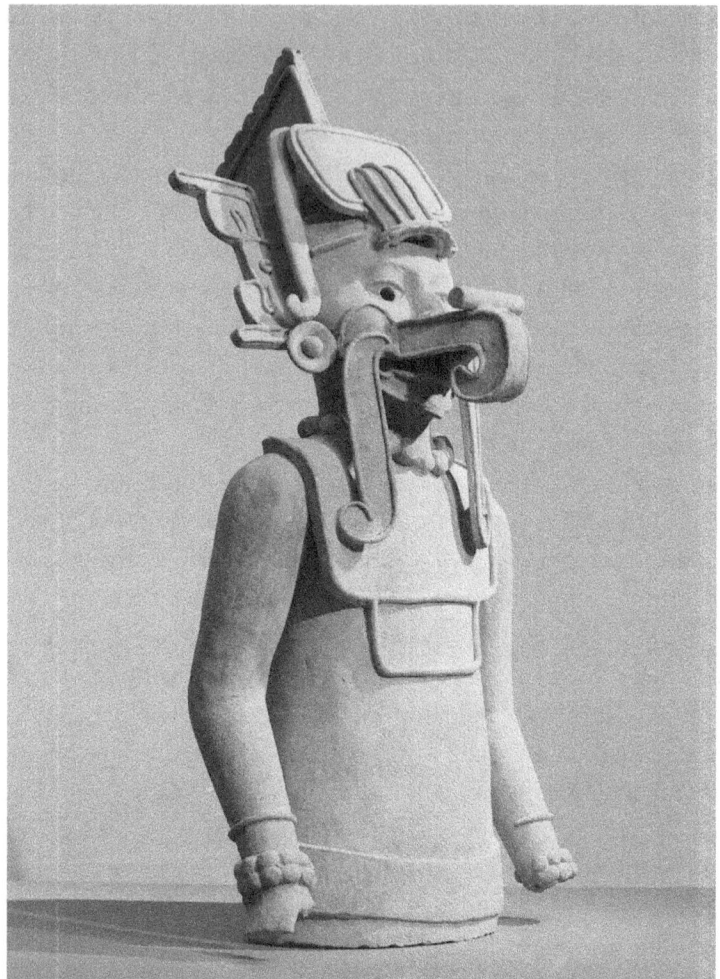

Figure 8.3. Ehecatl (Aztec Wind God) figure attributed to Brigido Lara. Public domain image courtesy of The Metropolitan Museum of Art, Michael C. Rockefeller Memorial Collection, Gift of Nelson A. Rockefeller, 1963.

auctioneer about any potential consignment is: "Will it sell?" If the answer is yes, then all other questions are moot. A few, perhaps, may ponder their still miniscule odds of being sued as a possible cost of doing business; however, the likelihood of the buyer discovering he or she has been "stung" is small, and recourse is limited by skillfully crafted "Terms of Sale" clauses that include five-year limits on canceling sales and warrant authenticity only to objects of named authorship, when bolded and capitalized in the sales listing. The expense of proving to the seller's satisfaction that the authorship is incorrect is to be borne by purchaser, and even if the buyer prevails, the most that can be recovered is the original sales price. Faced with these limits, the disillusioned purchaser most often conceals embarrassment over having been duped and simply puts the faux work up for sale again at the very same auction house that sold it to him. In this market version of samsara, the false works resold as genuine just keep circulating through the system until ultimately some rooked collector takes a tax write-off and donates his pieces to a museum. This simple fact accounts for the high numbers of fakes in museum pre-Columbian collections built through donations such as that of the San Francisco Mexican Museum, which was recently revealed to be 96% fake (Kinsella 2017).

While the Mexican Museum may be the most recent museum to have its fakes outed, it is not the only institution to suffer from an abundance of forgeries in its collection. In 1996, Thomas Hoving, lamenting the current state of the market, estimated that 40% of the works offered for sale to the Metropolitan Museum of Art during his tenure as director were "phonies or so hypocritically restored or so misattributed that they were just the same as forgeries" (1996, 17). He went on to speculate that the percentage had probably risen since then. Indeed, in 2014, *Artnet News* reported that Yann Walther of the Swiss Fine Art Expert Institute (FAEI) conservatively upped the estimate to 50% of the artwork on the market. Walther also stated that some 70–90% of the works examined by the FAEI were misattributed (Artnet News 2014). Such estimates, however, are market-wide generalizations; the forgery problem is much worse for particular segments of the market, specifically pre-Columbian, Chinese, Egyptian, and Classical antiquities being especially rife with fakes. Certainly, even the most cursory glance through the offerings of online auction and gallery catalogues will reveal an abundance of improbable works; in some cases, the proportion of obvious frauds hovers close to the 100% mark. Before spending $3.4 million on a life-size Maya figure wearing an Iroquois False Face Society mask, American Girl Doll ballet shoes, and carrying a hatchet, it would seem expedient given the current state of the market for a collector to spend some money, if not on forensic tests, then on some expert opinions. So where are the experts and why are they silent?

Traditionally, the experts of the art world were the connoisseurs; depending on the type of art under investigation, these individuals might have been academicians, museum curators, autodidactics, or all too often in the case of pre-Columbian art, the dealers themselves. Their decisions often had more to do with aesthetics than with science. If a work met the connoisseur's and the collector's concepts of beauty, it was deemed authentic, even if inconsistent with the stylistic canons of their presumed culture of origin in every way. Well into the twentieth century, few universities in the United States offered courses in pre-Columbian art, architecture, or archaeology, making nondealer "experts" hard to find. Today there are more programs, although there are indications of declining numbers as other areas gain momentary ascendance in the market and in academia. But, if Mark Jones (2017) is correct, academically trained "experts" may be ill-suited to the task of determining authenticity. Jones suggests in an article for the *Art Newspaper* that while plenty of research is being conducted in universities and national museums, very little of it is geared to developing the sort of expertise necessary to distinguish "the genuine from the false and make judgments about quality." Since the late 1970s the focus in many art history and archaeology programs has tilted toward the theoretical, and away from formalist analysis of the object and all those exercises that teach students to look and think about the materiality and style of artworks and to weigh the value of different types of evidence.

Although finding a qualified expert, as Jones suggests, may be difficult, they do exist even if their numbers are rarer in some fields of art history than others. However, many experts now refuse to authenticate works of art, and some are even hesitant to publish art historical analyses that touch on the authenticity of works due to retaliation from the market.[9] As the art market has become very big business involving syndicates of investors who collect art purely for profit, increasing financial and legal pressure has been brought to bear on scholars to suppress information that casts doubt on the authenticity of works. There has always been a certain unspoken rule among the old school connoisseurs that one expert does not publicly contradict the opinion of another, even if it is undeniably wrong, but the situation has become more sinister in the twenty-first century (see Alberge 2014). Experts who express a negative opinion on the authenticity of pricey works being offered on the market can find themselves being sued for ruinous amounts of money and their expertise challenged in court with piles of impressive-looking but essentially meaningless data (Alberge 2014). Unfortunately, the silencing of

experts whose opinions are inconvenient seems to be a widespread phenom-
enon both within and outside the art market and has been for many years
(see Easby and Colin 1968).

The Pre-Columbian Art Market in the Twenty-First Century

Global art sales have increased steadily since the beginning of the century,
topping a record $68 billion in 2014 (Kinsella 2017) and, even in the depths
of the Great Recession of the late 2000s, the fine art market performed better
overall than many other investment categories. Looking at art over a longer
time period, beginning in 1970, we find its performance as an alternative
asset class was pretty much equivalent to that of the S&P 500 and real estate
until 1986, when the market experienced a sharp increase. It topped out in
1990 and gradually declined until 2002, when it rebounded, experiencing a
downturn in 2009 before resuming its climb (Eurasia Review 2016).

The three biggest markets for fine art are the United States, with a 43%
share in 2015 (up 5% from 2013), the United Kingdom with a 21% global
share (64% within the European Union), and China with a 19% stake (down
5% from 2013). The remaining 17% is divided among the rest of the world
with France (6%) and Germany (2%) as the largest of these markets (Arkell
2016). As for what is currently selling in the global markets, the volume of
sales differs slightly from year to year as certain types of art either gain or
lose momentum with collectors, but a general breakdown by collecting category is as follows: Contemporary Art 40%, Modern 28%, Impressionist and
Post-Impressionist 13%, Old Masters 8%, Chinese Art 7%, and "Other" (Pre-
Columbian, Native American, African, Indian, Oceanic, Korean, Japanese,
etc.) approximately 5% of sales (Daniel 2016; see also Caines 2014).

The majority of art sales come through the two largest auction houses,
Christie's and Sotheby's, which, in 2012, controlled 37.9% and 34.7%, respectively, of the market (Maneker 2013). Together the two auction houses tend
to dominate the category markets in which they participate; for example, in
2014, they controlled 91% of contemporary art sales with Christie's taking a
55% share and Sotheby's 36% (Maneker 2014). Statistics on their participation
in the pre-Columbian art market are less accessible (see Tremain this volume
for sales of Maya antiquities at Sotheby's). Both houses entered the pre-Columbian market in the 1960s with annual spring and winter sales, but by the
1980s Sotheby's seems to have eclipsed its rival in the category. Indeed, there

were and continue to be some smaller auction houses, such as Bonham's, with stakes in the pre-Columbian market, but most have recorded annual sales under $200,000.

The Sotheby's auctions were generally two sessions with the higher-quality items being offered in the first and the lesser offerings in the second. These were often large sales, sometimes exceeding 600 lots, and generating in excess of $3 million annually. Christie's pre-Columbian auctions tended to be smaller sales, usually around 100 items, with results seldom exceeding six figures. Christie's discontinued annual sales of pre-Columbian art in 2007. Sotheby's remains the leading purveyor of pre-Columbian antiquities in the twenty-first century, boasting sales of $45 million for the category over the course of the last 15 years, with $17 million of that in the last five years.[10] This reflects an increase from average sales of $2.8 million during the first decade of the millennium, to $3.4 million during the post-recession recovery. However, Sotheby's current pre-Columbian sales are very different from those of the last century; they are no longer dedicated sales but are held in combination with auctions of African and Oceanic materials. In these mixed sales the number of pre-Columbian items offered is typically fewer than 100 pieces, with sold lots averaging 65%.

Earnings per item, however, have increased significantly over the prices achieved during the 1980s and 1990s, but this appears more likely the result of a general escalation in the art market rather than offerings of exceptional quality. Indeed, many of the lots offered in the two most recent New York sales were described as "old" pieces, originally sold by dealers, such as Edward Merrin, Everett Rassiga, Alphonse Jax, Andre Emmerich, and Earl Stendahl, before 1972, a common safe harbor date. The mixed auctions, lower lot volume, and the apparent recycling of old pieces, both real and otherwise, would almost seem to suggest that the market for high end pre-Columbian art is drying up or possibly disappearing underground. What a wonderful thing that would be in terms of reducing market demand for looted and forged art. In reality, however, the high-end market has simply shifted toward greener European pastures. With the exception of Germany, which tightened its antiquities laws in 2016, European nations are seen as having less encumbering laws, and as requiring less in the way of provenance documentation than the United States, making Europe a more profitable place in which to sell antiquities of all kinds (Pearlstein 2012). Certainly, the record prices paid for pre-Columbian items (some rather problematic ones at that!) at Christie's, Sotheby's, and Drouot's

Parisian auctions in the last two decades suggest that Paris has become the new market center.

In addition to brick-and-mortar sales locations, auction houses and high-end art galleries now have websites and employ online auctions as a means of reaching new customers. For places such as Christie's and Sotheby's, such sales are economical replacements for the old afternoon sales of the 1980s and 1990s as means of vending lower value items. Unfortunately, there are a lot of internet peddlers with less venerable names and decidedly less posh locations also offering high-volume sales of purported pre-Columbian items. The pieces offered by these bottom market dealers are frequently of highly dubious quality and this seems to be reflected in their prices. Still, most of these online sellers offer the prospective buyer an assurance of authenticity in a "just trust me" guarantee based solely on their many years of sales experience or their acquaintance with acknowledged but unnamed experts, or the fact that no one has ever returned a piece they sold as a "reproduction." Of course, they usually fail to mention that most Latin American countries have government-sponsored reproduction workshops that produce very good replicas of ancient pieces, marked accordingly. So it is a pretty safe bet that they have not had any "reproductions" returned. However, the phrasing is a verbal sleight-of-hand meant to mislead the prospective buyer into thinking the seller has never sold a fake, but that is highly improbable considering the high numbers of fakes regularly ending up in private and public collections.

Other than a change of venue for high-end sales, and the addition of the internet auction for the low end, very little seems to have changed in the art market, and none of it for the good. Collectors and collecting consortiums, anticipating high returns on a scarce commodity, are still buying pre-Columbian art and regularly setting new record high prices. Whether the pieces they are buying are genuine or not does not appear to be a concern since it is not difficult to find experts who will authenticate-to-order, or to silence dissenting experts with threats of lawsuits. The laws enacted since the 1970s to stop antiquities looting have had little effect on the market and this is unlikely to change (see Yates, this volume); the laws are simply an occasional inconvenience and regarded as a cost of doing business. Every so often a group of dealers will propose a new scheme for self-regulation, but having the foxes guard the henhouse has never worked out well, except for the foxes.

So what is the solution? There is no simple answer. First, better academic training of all scholars, but especially of art historians, is needed in the analysis of artworks and in ethical professional practices. Second, laws that protect the honest, fact-based opinions of experts from bullying lawsuits by dealers and collectors are definitely needed. Third, existing fraud and deceptive practices laws need to be applied to those who both create and vend forged art instead of treating them as some sort of popular culture antiheroes. Fourth and most importantly, efforts need to be made toward reducing the numbers of forgeries circulating in the international art market. Accomplishing this reduction would need phased-in requirements for forensic testing and evaluation by a panel of nondealer experts of all artworks prior to their inclusion in any sale, auction, or art fair. Of course, dealers will scream about the cost and inconvenience, but the alternative is more of what we have now. Some might argue that collectors spending millions on fakes is its own reward, and I would agree, except that those fakes ultimately end up in museum collections, get reproduced in textbooks, and go on to pollute another generation of scholars and scholarship.

Notes

1. For general information about the life and crimes of Han van Meegeren, see Kiely 2014, Davis 2006, Dolnick 2009, and the film "Van Meegeren's Fake Vermeers" by Hans Wessels, produced by the Museum Boijmans van Beuninger, Rotterdam.

2. See Alberge 2015 and Hebborn 1993.

3. For general information on Shaun Greenhalgh, see Harper 2017, Greenhalgh 2017, and the 2008 documentary *The Artful Codgers*, produced by Nick Hornby.

4. For the story of John Myatt and John Drew, see Salisbury 2010.

5. See Beltracchi and Beltracchi 2014 or the 2014 documentary *The Art of Forgery*, directed by Arne Birkenstock.

6. The Bolton Forgers were first reported to police in 1990 by art dealer Peter Nahum, who purchased their first successful forgery.

7. See the aforementioned documentary *The Art of Forgery*.

8. In addition to the aforementioned documentary *The Art of Forgery* about Wolfgang Beltracchi, see *F is for Fake* about Elmyr de Hory (1973, directed by Orson Welles), *Art and Craft* about Mark Landis (2014, directed by Sam Cullman), or Ken Perenys's self-promotional series *How to Fool the Experts and Laugh Your Way to the Bank* (2016). Additionally, *Ruins*, about the traffic in fakes, features Brigido Lara (1999, directed by Jesse Lerner).

9. Archaeologists who are members of the Society for American Archaeology, by contrast, observe a code of ethics that prohibits them from authenticating or appraising antiquities.

10. Sotheby's Pre-Columbian Department http://www.sothebys.com/en/departments/pre-columbian-art.html

References Cited

Abrams, Amah-Rose. 2018. The Year of the Fake: The 8 Biggest Forgery Controversies of 2016. *Artnet News*, December 27. https://news.artnet.com/art-world/biggest-art-forger-ies-2016-783464 (accessed February 4, 2019).

Alberge, Dalya. 2014. "Revealed: The Art Experts Who Pass Fakes as Authentic." *Guardian*, February 22. http://www.theguardian.com/artanddesign/2014/feb/23/art-scholars-dis-grace-forgeries (accessed March 25, 2018).

———. 2015. "Great Art Forger Continues to Ridicule Experts from Beyond the Grave." *Guardian*, August 24. https://www.theguardian.com/artanddesign/2015/aug/24/great-art-forger-continues-to-ridicule-experts-from-beyond-the-grave (accessed March 25, 2018).

Arkell, Roland. 2016. "Brexit: How Will the UK Art and Antiques Trade Vote?" *Appreciating Assets*, March 22. https://www.borro.com/uk/borro-blog/brexit-will-uk-art-antiques-trade-vote (accessed March 25, 2018).

Artnet News. 2014. "Over 50 Percent of Art is Fake." *Artnet News*, October 13. https://news.artnet.com/market/over-50-percent-of-art-is-fake-130821 (accessed March 25, 2018).

Batres, Leopoldo. 1909. *Antigüedades mejicanas falsificaciones y falsificadores*. México, DF: Imprenta de Fidencio S. Sorio.

Beltracchi, Helene, and Wolfgang Beltracchi. 2014. *Selbstporträt*. Reinbek: Rowohlt Verlag.

Bruhns, Karen O., and Nancy L. Kelker. 2010. *Faking the Ancient Andes*. Walnut Creek, Calif.: Left Coast Press.

Caines, Matthew. 2014. "International Art Market 2013: New Report Examines the Facts and Figures." *Guardian*, March 20. https://www.theguardian.com/culture-professionals-network/culture-professionals-blog/2014/mar/19/international-art-market-2013-facts-figures (accessed March 25, 2018).

Crossley, Mimi, and E. Logan Wagner. 1987. "Ask Mexico's Masterly Brigido Lara: Is It a Fake?" *Connoisseur* 217 (905): 98–103.

Daniel, Daria. 2016. "40 Percent of World Gallery Art Sales Made at Fairs and Other Key Findings in the TEFAF Art Market Report 2015." *Artnet News*, March 12. https://news.artnet.com/market/5-key-findings-from-tefaf-report-2015-276301 (accessed March 25, 2018).

Davis, Serena. 2006. "The Forger Who Fooled the World." *Telegraph*, August 5. https://www.telegraph.co.uk/culture/art/3654259/The-forger-who-fooled-the-world.html (accessed March 25, 2018).

Dolnick, Edward. 2009. *The Forger's Spell: A True Story of Vermeer, Nazis, and the Greatest Art Hoax of the Twentieth Century*. New York: Harper Perennial.

Easby, Dudley T., and Ralph F. Colin. 1968. "The Legal Aspects of Forgery and the Protection of the Expert." *Metropolitan Museum of Art Bulletin* 26 (6): 257–261.

Eurasia Review. 2016. "Is There a Bubble in the Art Market?" *Eurasia Review*, January 7. http://www.eurasiareview.com/07012016-is-there-a-bubble-in-the-art-market/ (accessed March 25, 2018).

Greenhalgh, Shaun. 2017. *A Forger's Tale: Confessions of the Bolton Forger*. Crow's Nest, Australia: Allen & Unwin.

Harper, Paul. 2017. "Artful Dodger: World's Most Infamous Art Forger Legally Sells Fake

Lowry-Style Paintings at Auction for Triple the Expected Value." *Sun*, February 21. https://www.thesun.co.uk/news/2917531/art-forger-sells-fake-lowry-paintings-auction-legal-shaun-greenhalgh/ (accessed March 25, 2018).

Hebborn, Eric. 1993. *Drawn to Trouble: Confessions of a Master Forger; A Memoir*. New York: Random House.

———. 1997. *Art Forger's Handbook*. New York: Overlook Books.

Holmes, William H. 1886. "The Trade in Spurious Mexican Antiquities," *Science* 7 (159): 170–182.

Hoving, Thomas P. F. 1996. *False Impressions: The Hunt for Big-Time Art Fakes*. New York: Simon & Schuster.

Jones, Mark. 2017. "Comment: Scholarly research is flourishing but curators' ability to judge an object's quality is not: Why museums are falling victim to fakers: expertise is undervalued and in decline." *Art Newspaper*, March 13. https://www.theartnewspaper.com/news/comment-scholarly-research-is-flourishing-but-curators-ability-to-judge-an-objects-quality-is-not (accessed March 25, 2018).

Kelker, Nancy L., and Karen O. Bruhns. 2010. *Faking Ancient Mesoamerica*. Walnut Creek, Calif.: Left Coast Press.

Kiely, Alexandra. 2014. "A Brief History of Art Forgery in Four Crazy Case Studies." *HeadStuff*, July 15. http://www.headstuff.org/2014/07/brief-history-art-forgery/ (accessed March 25, 2018).

Kinsella, Eileen. 2017. "A Staggering 96% of the Artifacts in San Francisco's Mexican Museum May be Fake." *Artnet News*, July 7. https://news.artnet.com/art-world/mexican-museums-artifacts-mostly-fake-1016198 (accessed March 25, 2018)

Maneker, Marion. 2013. "Artprice's Chart on 2012 Auction House Market Share." *Art Market Monitor*, March 19. https://www.artmarketmonitor.com/2013/03/19/artprices-chart-on-2012-auction-house-market-share/ (accessed March 25, 2018).

———. 2014. "Contemporary Art by Market Share." *Art Market Monitor*, October 1. https://www.artmarketmonitor.com/2014/10/01/contemporary-art-by-market-share/ (accessed March 25, 2018).

Pearlstein, William G. 2012. "Buying and Selling Antiquities in Today's Market." *Artnet Magazine*, June. http://www.artnet.com/magazineus/news/spencer/spencers-art-law-journal-7-17-12.asp

Perenyi, Ken. 2012. *Caveat Emptor: The Secret Life of an American Art Forger*. New York: Pegasus Books.

Pogrebin, Robin. 2016. "Sotheby's Hires Fraud Expert to Start New Research Department." *New York Times*, December 5. https://www.nytimes.com/2016/12/05/arts/design/sothebys-hires-fraud-expert-james-martin-orion-analytical.html (accessed March 25, 2018).

Polidoro, Massimo. 2002. "Ica Stones: Yabba-Dabba-Do! Notes on a Strange World." *Skeptical Inquirer* 26 (5). https://www.csicop.org/si/show/ica_stones_yabba-dabba-do (accessed March 25, 2018).

Ruy-Sánchez Lacy, Alberto. 1995. "A Labyrinth of Echoes." *Artes de México: La Falsificación y sus Espejos* 28: 73.

Salisbury, Laney. 2010. *Provenance: How a Con Man and a Forger Rewrote the History of Modern Art*. London: Penguin Books.

von Winning, Hasso. 1968. *Pre-Columbian Art of Mexico and Central America*. New York: Harry N. Abrams.

9

The Many Lives of Maya Antiquities

Tracking Distribution and Redistribution
through Auction Catalogues

CARA G. TREMAIN

Glossy sales catalogues published by high-end auction houses present a seemingly endless supply of antiquities for purchase from around the world. These catalogues offer insight into market trends and allow the volume of antiquities being bought and sold at auction to be monitored. At a time when the internet auction market is growing (e.g., Brodie 2015) but cannot be effectively monitored in the same manner as traditional auction house sales, it is important to record and share data from available print catalogues. Using the results of a systematic study of Maya antiquities at auction from sales catalogues that cover a period of more than 50 years (see Tremain 2017 for a full analysis), this chapter explores the distribution and redistribution of antiquities through the public auction market. Studies such as these, although time consuming and hampered by the difficulties of accessing information, are important for an understanding of the past and current market in antiquities.

Pre-Columbian Sales at Sotheby's

Sotheby's is one of the largest auction houses in the world. The company began in London in 1744 as a modest business specializing in the sale of books (Herrmann 1981, 4). The name of the company can be traced back to John Sotheby, who joined the auction house in 1778 after Samuel Baker, the original founder, passed away (Herrmann 1981, 12). Although the grandson of John Sotheby died in 1861, and with him the final line of the family name in the company, the remaining partners appreciated the importance of maintaining the Sotheby's name for the firm (Herrmann 1981, 49). Following the end of the First World War, the North American market opened up and the company began trading in New York. In 1964 they purchased rival New York auction house Parke-Bernet (Herrmann 1981, 349)—the largest fine art auction house in the United States at the time. Until 1971, the New York sales were advertised as taking place under "Parke-Bernet Galleries Inc., affiliated with Sotheby and Co. London," but from early 1972 onward the designation changed to Sotheby's Parke-Bernet Inc. In the late 1980s the company removed the Parke-Bernet Inc. designation and became known in both London and New York simply as Sotheby's.

Currently, the company has in excess of 50 departments and conducts auctions in more than 40 countries around the world. According to its website, Sotheby's annual worldwide sales turnover is currently in excess of $4 billion.[1] Private sales are also an important element of the company's business model, and Sotheby's reported private sales totaling more than $650 million in 2015 (Brady 2016). The Pre-Columbian[2] department, which has been active since 1980 (though Pre-Columbian antiquities have been sold at Sotheby's since the 1960s), claims to have achieved close to $45 million since the early 2000s.[3] The interest in purchasing Pre-Columbian antiquities at auction has increased throughout the years, so much so that it has become a recognized category of investment for art collectors (Tarmy 2015).

Pre-Columbian antiquities were initially sold through Sotheby's in both New York and London. In fact, the author's research demonstrates that up until the establishment of the Pre-Columbian Art Department in 1980, there were 191 sales including antiquities from Latin America in both London and New York (though only 116 included "Pre-Columbian" in the sale title). However, North America has long been the dominant market for Pre-Columbian antiquities—likely due to its proximity to the cultural area. The sales catalogues also reflect this dominant market, since it is the New York catalogues, rather than the London catalogues, that were first supplemented with photographs and lengthy descriptions of lots (see fig. 6.4 for an example of lots advertised at a New York auction in 1981). The Peter Watson (1997) scandal, which exposed the company's illegal exportation of old master paintings from Italy, led to the cessation of antiquities sales in London. The last recorded London auction that included Pre-Columbian antiquities appears to have been in 1992.

Throughout the 1980s and 1990s "Pre-Columbian Art" became a stand-alone sale at Sotheby's, likely owing to the great quantities of antiquities from Latin America on the market at that time. Yates (2006, 4–5) has suggested that the creation of independent Pre-Columbian sales indicates that these antiquities were no longer regarded as "primitive" forms of art. Prior to being sold in dedicated auctions marketed as "Pre-Columbian Art," antiquities from Latin America were sold in auctions of various titles including "Tribal Art" and "Primitive Art." The first auction titled simply "Pre-Columbian Art" took place on March 6th, 1971, in New York. Presently, Pre-Columbian antiquities are sold almost exclusively from the New York office as part of the annual auctions of African and Oceanic Art. Since 2001, annual sales in New York have taken place in May, but from the late 1980s until the millennium, biannual sales took place in May and November. Of the Sotheby's sales containing Maya antiquities[4] studied by the author, only one (the Barbier-Mueller Paris auction on March 22–23, 2013) was located outside New York or London.

The author's concentration on the sale of Maya antiquities at Sotheby's revealed that the first occurrence of a Maya antiquity was in the "Indian, Oceanic, American and African Art" auction in London on February 11, 1963. Just as Elizabeth Gilgan's (2001) research demonstrated, the author found that the 1980s offered the greatest quantity ($n = 1,341$) of Maya antiquities for sale at Sotheby's (see table 9.1).

Table 9.1. Total number of lots with Maya antiquities, and total number of Maya antiquities offered for sale at Sotheby's from 1963 to 2018

Year	Total Lots	Total Antiquities
1963–1969	161	188
1970–1979	455	539
1980–1989	1,258	1,341
1990–1999	1,087	1,256
2000–2009	223	247
2010–2018	93	95
Total	**3,277**	**3,666**

Interestingly, the decade with the height of sales also correlates with the time when sales catalogues changed significantly and became glossy color marketing tools. Sales have been steadily decreasing in number since the 1980s; from 2000 to 2009, just 247 Maya antiquities were offered for sale. In the past two years sales of Maya antiquities have reduced dramatically, with a sole antiquity (a painted ceramic) offered for sale in 2017 and six antiquities (including painted ceramics, a figurine, and pendants made from greenstone and shell) offered for sale in 2018.

As table 9.1 demonstrates, the quantity of Maya antiquities for sale from 2010 to 2018 is the lowest in the history of Sotheby's since the 1960s. The decrease in the number of Maya antiquities may reflect a shift from public to private (or "invisible" [Nørskov 2002, 291]) sales. This trend toward private sales may also be true of Italian and South American antiquities, as Lobay (2006) and Yates (2006, 39) have suggested. Alternatively, collectors may be keeping antiquities in their collections for longer periods of time and not offering them for sale at auction as frequently as they did in the past. Or, there may be other reasons fewer Pre-Columbian antiquities are making it to market (perhaps Sotheby's is focusing on higher-value antiquities and reducing the sale of lower-value antiquities).

The website of the Pre-Columbian Art department facilitates the search of past sales, since it allows for specific words or terms to be searched, enabling prospective buyers and any other visitors to the website to locate information about specific lots (lots can consist of a single antiquity, several antiquities of the same media, or antiquities of mixed media). Holders of Sothebys.com membership accounts, which are free to create, can also view extended information about lots such as condition reports. Information about Pre-Columbian sales dating back to the early 2000s is accessible via the Sotheby's website, but auctions preceding this time are generally available only in print format.

As the author (Tremain 2017, 195) and other scholars (Levine and Martínez de Luna 2013, 265; Gilgan 2001, 78) have demonstrated, it can be very difficult to track down and acquire print sales catalogues because they are in the holdings of many different institutions across the globe. Furthermore, there is a disparity of information that can be sourced from print catalogues; early catalogues (ca. 1960s) lacked photographs and had minimal lot descriptions whereas later catalogues (mid-1980s and later) included color photographs and lengthier descriptions about lots. As an example, a catalogue from the early 1960s would contain eight or more lots on a single page but without photographs of any of the lots. In contrast, a catalogue from the 1980s would advertise only one or two lots on a single page, usually with a full-page color photograph of at least one of the lots. Lobay (2006, 66–67) has described this change as one from mere "shopping lists" that catered to a wholesale venue, to catalogues that catered primarily to retail-based operations geared for private buyers.

The author's original study (Tremain 2017) was based on an investigation of Maya antiquities appearing in 150 Sotheby's catalogues, dating from 1963 to 2016. A total of 3,270 lots and 3,659 antiquities were recorded, which exceeded the number of Maya antiquities studied by other scholars by more than 300 (Gilgan [2001] recorded 3,300, while Levine and Martínez de Luna [2013] recorded 3,263). Adding the 2017 and 2018 data to these figures (which, as explained above, consist of seven antiquities) gives a more accurate number of 3,277 lots and 3,666 antiquities offered for sale at Sotheby's over a 55-year period (see table 9.1). As discussed below, some of the antiquities were resold on more than one occasion.

Of the lots offered for sale, it is not clear how many sold because of the lack of sales data. The author was originally able to access sales data for 78 auctions from 1966 to 2016, which demonstrated that 74% (n = 1,649) of the lots sold. Six of the seven Maya antiquities in the 2017 and 2018 auctions also sold (the highest price realized was $81,250 for a small greenstone plaque). Of all the recorded public auctions at Sotheby's since the mid-1960s, the highest price realized for a single Maya antiquity was $432,000 for a figurine in 2007 (the equivalent of $523,816 in 2018) and the lowest was just $40 for a painted ceramic in 1980 (the equivalent of $118 in 2018).[5]

Provenance and Provenience at Sotheby's

Antiquities sold through Sotheby's Pre-Columbian Art Department are almost exclusively unprovenienced—meaning that their original context is unknown. It is important to keep in mind that the auction market itself is a legal apparatus through which to trade goods; whether the goods sold through the market are legal themselves is another matter altogether. Despite growing regulations restricting the export of antiquities from Latin America, Sotheby's has continued to market and sell antiquities from Mexico and its southern neighbors. Situations such as this occur because an importing country may not be under any obligation to enforce the laws of the country from which the antiquity was exported. However, Sotheby's is required to perform due diligence into the provenance (history of ownership) of an antiquity to ensure it does not will-ingly sell illegally smuggled items.

Sotheby's staff have maintained that the company stringently checks every item it sells to make sure it has been purchased and transported over bor-ders legally (Grillo 2004), and they claim Sotheby's "will not sell property if it knows that it was illegally exported or imported unless irregularities can be legally rectified before the sale" (Lobay 2006, 56). The difference between legal and illegal antiquities is by no means easy to distinguish (Brodie 2006, 53), and Sotheby's staff have admitted the company does "make mistakes" (Honan 1995). An example in which the company clearly made a mistake is the case of the Cambodian Duryodhana statue, which was put up for auction in New York in 2011. Despite Sotheby's being advised that the statue had been looted decades earlier and that Cambodia was well aware of its theft, the company decided to proceed with its sale (Hauser-Schäublin 2017). Fortunately, it was blocked from auction and eventually returned to Cambodia in 2014.

Unless accompanied by special permission and paperwork, antiquities sold through Sotheby's are usually expected to have a pre-1970 import date so they are in line with the United Nations Educational, Scientific, and Cultural Orga-nization's (UNESCO) Convention on the Means of Prohibiting and Preventing the Illicit Import, Export and Transfer of Ownership of Cultural Property. The Convention was adopted on November 14, 1970, and officially came into force on April 24, 1972. Although the date of 1970 has no legal significance, since the Convention is an agreement between UNESCO member states and not a law, it marks an ethical watershed toward the acceptance of unprovenienced antiquities (Brodie 2014a, 440; Gerstenblith 2013). As of 2018, 138 countries have signed the Convention,[6] but wealthy market-dominated countries such as the United States and the United Kingdom were much slower to formally recognize the Convention (having signed in 1983 and 2002, respectively) than poorer countries whose heritage was at risk.

Prior to the UNESCO Convention, several Latin American countries cre-ated national laws to protect their cultural heritage. For example, as early as 1947 Guatemala passed the Ley Sobre Proteccion y Conservacion de los Mon-umentos, Objectos Arqueologicos, Historicos y Tipicos, which declares that archaeological, historic, and artistic objects are protected by the state and con-sidered part of the country's national treasure.[7] In the same year as the adop-tion of the UNESCO Convention, Mexico and the United States established a Treaty of Co-operation to aid Mexico in recovering illegally exported materials (Coggins 1998, 58, 63). In 1972 Mexico also passed the Ley Federal Sobre Monumentos y Zonas Arqueológicos, Artísticos e Históricos, which declared that artifacts and monuments were considered property of the Mexican nation. Emergency import restrictions and Memoranda of Understanding were later established by several Latin American countries (see Tremain 2017, 193).

Despite national laws such as those outlined above, there continues to be an international demand for unprovenienced Latin American antiquities—as the continued sale of unprovenienced Pre-Columbian antiquities at Sotheby's demonstrates. British collectors Sir Robert and Lisa Sainsbury, founders of the Sainsbury Centre for Visual Arts, admitted understanding the legality of purchasing such antiquities when they explained that "the stuff [that] came out of Mexico, one didn't ask how it had got out . . . the people who broke the law were the people who brought it over the border presumably" (Cioni 2014, 32). Clearly, the aesthetic desire and/or profits driving the purchase of unprovenienced antiquities have largely outweighed the concern about illegality or threats to cultural heritage.

In addition to the lack of provenience, the vast majority of Maya antiquities sold through Sotheby's also lack provenance information. As Yates (2016, 176) explains, auction houses are under no obligation to reveal the identities of the individuals who buy and sell at auction. People who consign items may not want to reveal their sale to family members, or they may not want to publicize their name for fear of theft (Lobay 2006, 56). Provenance information in a sales catalogue may include the name of a previous owner, or the name of a dealer or museum from which an antiquity was purchased. In some instances, information regarding the length of time an antiquity has been part of a collection is also offered. The author recorded both the instances in which the names of current owners were provided for Maya antiquities in sales catalogues, as well as information about their provenance (i.e., past ownership). The names of current owners of Maya antiquities appear as early as 1963 and have continued to appear, albeit sporadically, in sales up until the present day. Information about the provenance of antiquities first appeared in 1966, again in 1970, and then not again until 1980. This information is particularly interesting because it provides an insight into the collecting trends of individuals such as artist Andy Warhol and actor Vincent Price.[8]

Provenance information appears more frequently and in greater quantity from 1984 onward. In some instances, such as the 2013 Barbier-Mueller Paris auction mentioned previously, the entire sale is the property of one specific owner. Such auctions offer a glimpse into the range, type, and number of an-tiquities that private collectors have amassed over the years. They also provide information about where and from whom they have bought certain antiquities in their collection. Sales of individual collections containing Pre-Columbian antiquities are perhaps becoming more common at Sotheby's, since the sole 2017 auction and the most recent 2018 auction with Pre-Columbian antiquities ("The Collection of Edwin and Cherie Silver" and "The Collection of Howard and Saretta Barnet," respectively) were both the property of individual own-ers. Fortunately, the provenance of all the Maya antiquities in both auctions was provided and therefore helps to re-create the history of ownership. While provenance in no way replaces, or makes up for, lack of provenience, it helps to understand market trends.

In some instances, prior Sotheby's sales are offered as provenance in cata-logues, likely because they demonstrate that antiquities have been on the mar-ket for a certain length of time.[9] This marketing tactic may prove particularly useful if it can help to establish a pre-1970 import date, while allowing previous owners to remain anonymous. However, in some instances prior sales are also omitted from catalogues—likely to disguise the failure of a sale. As Tremain (2017, 209) has demonstrated with a particular lot from a 1985 auction, the fail-ure of the lot to sell at an auction from the previous year was omitted from the catalogue. Interestingly, the failure to sell appears to have had a direct impact on the estimated price—dropping $3,000 from the previous year. The lower es-timate, and perhaps omission of the failure to sell in the previous year, secured a sale in the 1985 auction.

Unfortunately, especially in early catalogues, provenance and current own-ership information is often too vague to be of use even when it is provided. For example, lots in early catalogues (from the 1960s especially) were described as being "from the collection of a lady" or "property of a private collector." This ambiguity has continued through time and appears to be an accepted condi-tion of purchasing antiquities at auction (Stoll 2004, 138). For example, in the May 14, 2018, "Art of Africa, Oceania, and the Americas" auction, all three of the Maya antiquities offered for sale had no specific owners listed and were instead described as being from "private" collections—one in Europe, one in Florida, and one simply in America (all three did have varying amounts of information about past ownership, however).

Neil Brodie (2014b) has suggested that auction houses have no real incentive to reform their policies on disclosing provenance, allowing such anonymity to continue to flourish in the market. The lack of provenance could be considered surprising when epithets such as "from the collection of" or "previously sold at" appear to be an indicator of authenticity and value (Fay 2011, 452). Similarly, de-accessioned antiquities from museum collections have often been regarded as prestigious and valuable (Washburn 1987, 28; Pfeffer 2014, 3). The value that provenance can bring to antiquities is partly the reason there have been instances of false provenance in sales catalogues (Yates 2015, 78; Herrmann 1981, 158–163).

Brodie (2014a) attempted to test whether collectors discriminate against poorly provenanced or unprovenanced antiquities, and whether they pay higher prices for well-provenanced pieces, but found no strong evidence to support the idea that provenance influences the sale of an antiquity. Similarly, Daniels et al. (2014) undertook a study of Pre-Columbian antiquities in Sotheby's and Christie's sales catalogues from 2000 to 2010 to determine whether antiquities sold with a provenance had a price premium. They calculated an 80% premium on antiquities with provenance that pre-dated 1970, and an 18% premium on antiquities without a provenance.

Although it is often difficult to separate the influence of aesthetics and object quality from provenance (Brodie 2014a, 430), it is likely that the longer an antiquity has been in a private collection the more desirable (and thus expensive) it will be. For example, the highest sale price achieved for a Maya antiquity in 2016 was for a figurine with a removable headdress. It sold for $125,000 with a provenance described simply as "acquired in the 1960s." Despite the vague provenance, it suggests the antiquity may have been part of a collection since the 1960s and therefore off the market for roughly 50 years. It is likely the antiquity reached a high sale price not only because it had increased in value over time, but also because it was reentering the market after a long period of unattainability. As Sotheby's staff have explained, "the longer that something is off the market, the better."[10]

Indeed, as the author has demonstrated (Tremain 2017), lengthy or detailed provenance information is by no means necessary to achieve a high sale price at auction. The author was able to demonstrate that only 19% ($n = 605$ lots) of Maya antiquities offered for sale through Sotheby's since the 1960s had their current owner listed, while a mere 13% ($n = 419$ lots) had specific provenance information. Consequently, a staggering 81% of lots contained no information about the current owner and 87% of the lots were devoid of any meaningful provenance. Such high numbers of unprovenanced Maya antiquities correspond to studies of other antiquities sold at Sotheby's (Davis 2011; Yates 2006).

Of the seven antiquities offered for sale in 2017 and 2018, all had some form of provenance information provided but only four had their current owner listed.

Market Redistribution

While the author's initial research was aimed at collecting data covering a wide range of categories, certain trends in the sale of Maya antiquities became obvious—particularly concerning painted ceramics. Being a visually distinctive category of antiquity, particularly because the majority have unique decoration on their exterior, their movement into and out of the marketplace can be carefully monitored. Reconstructing the provenance of Maya ceramics is particularly important considering their valued place among the collections of some of the world's most famous museums. Figure 9.1 is an

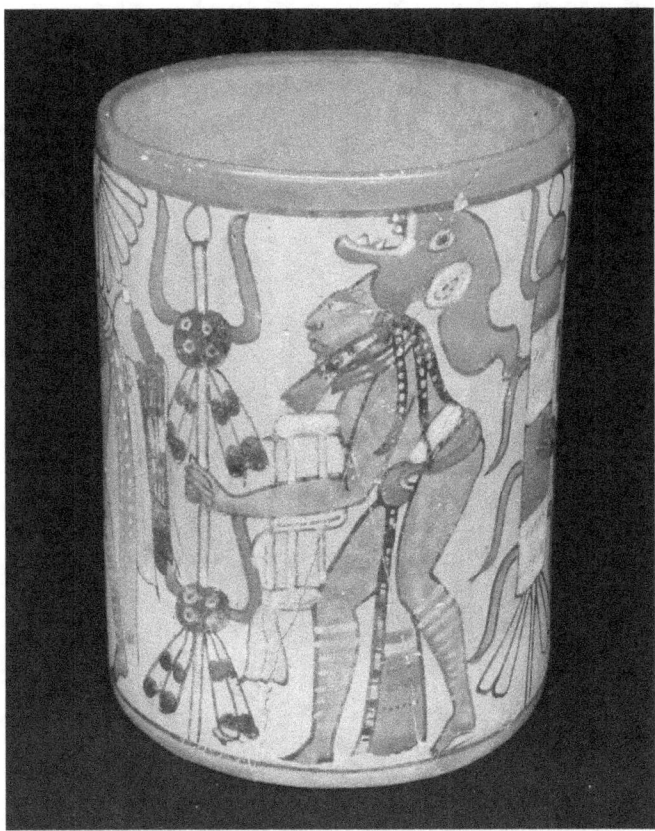

Figure 9.1. Cylindrical vase from the National Museum of the American Indian, Smithsonian Institution (catalog number 244089.000). Used with permission.

example of one of many Maya ceramics that has entered a museum collection with very limited provenance information. This particular ceramic, presently in the collections of the Smithsonian Institution's National Museum of the American Indian (NMAI), is known to have been acquired by the museum (along with several other Pre-Columbian objects) via an exchange with antiquities dealer Robert Huber[11] in 1971. No other information about its provenance is known.

What is interesting is that Huber's name appears only once in association with Maya antiquities in more than 50 years of Sotheby's sales.[12] As an active and well-known dealer, it is curious that his name is so noticeably absent—especially considering that he and his wife have described themselves as having "friendly relations with a variety of auctions" (Heritage Auction Galleries 2010). What is even more curious is that the auction in which his name appears clearly states that he and his wife sold the antiquity in question through Sotheby's public auction 20 years previously. As current owners of the antiquity at that time, they likely made a conscious decision to omit their names from the sales catalogue. Such anonymity hampers the ability to reconstruct provenance information, which is why alternative ways of tracking sales and shifts in ownership is necessary. The remainder of this chapter will concentrate on the redistribution of Maya ceramics at auction, how their marketing changes through time, and what can be learned about their sale through the study of auction catalogues.

Based on the study of sales catalogues from the 1960s onward, the author was able to identify 36 Maya ceramics that have been resold through Sotheby's on at least two occasions (table 9.2). The most common Maya antiquities offered for sale at auction were in fact ceramics ($n = 1,967$, including the 2017

Table 9.2. Maya ceramics identified by the author as being sold on more than one occasion at Sotheby's (auctions and lot numbers are organized chronologically)

Lot Number	Auction
Lot 89/ 213	July 12, 1977; May 10, 1980
Lot 249/ 196	November 10, 1979; November 23–24, 1982
Lot 250/ 231	November 10, 1979; May 9, 2006
Lot 227/ 168/ 114	May 10, 1980; November 20, 1989; May 16, 1995
Lot 149/ 282	February 25, 1981; May 17, 2002

Lot Number	Auction
Lot 182/ 191	May 9, 1981; May 28, 1997
Lot 224/ 338/ 301	December 5, 1981; November 27–28, 1984; November 11, 2004
Lot 217/ 219	December 5, 1981; November 18, 1991
Lot 229/ 176	December 5, 1981; November 23, 1992
Lot 227/ 84	December 5, 1981; May 17, 1993
Lot 221/ 279	December 5, 1981; November 11, 2004
Lot 225/ 160	June 12, 1982; May 19, 1992
Lot 221/ 260	June 12, 1982; May 15, 2003
Lot 19/ 318	March 22, 1983; November 19, 1990
Lot 193/ 99/ 152	May 12–13, 1983; November 26, 1985; May 19, 1992
Lot 194/ 81	May 12–13, 1983; May 14, 1991
Lot 192/ 101/ 69	May 12–13, 1983; November 18, 1991; May 15, 2015
Lot 196/ 288	May 12–13, 1983; November 11, 2004
Lot 328/ 79	November 27–28, 1984; November 26, 1985
Lot 355/ 283	November 27–28, 1984; November 11, 2004
Lot 123/ 115	May 31, 1985; May 20, 1986
Lot 99/ 190	May 31, 1985; June 2, 1999
Lot 89/ 133	November 26, 1985; November 24, 1986
Lot 222/ 413	November 18, 1987; June 2, 1999
Lot 117/ 296	May 2, 1990; May 14, 1991
Lot 111/ 484/ 326	May 2, 1990; November 18, 1991; May 17, 1994
Lot 197/ 74	November 18, 1991; May 15, 2015
Lot 159/ 144	May 19, 1992; November 22, 1993
Lot 158/ 74	May 19, 1992; November 22, 1999
Lot 85/ 161	May 17, 1993; November 24, 1997
Lot 153/ 183	November 15, 1994; November 25, 1996
Lot 158/ 73	November 15, 1994; May 15, 2015
Lot 169/ 79	November 20, 1995; November 22, 1999
Lot 157/ 217	May 18, 2000; May 9, 2006
Lot 540/ 122	May 19, 2001; March 22–23, 2013
Lot 261/ 124	May 15, 2003; May 7, 2016

and 2018 auction data), with painted ceramics constituting the most popular type of ceramic ($n = 966$, including the 2017 and 2018 auction data). The stark contrast between high numbers of decorative ceramics and very low numbers of plain ceramics ($n = 8$) demonstrates that undecorated ceramics are generally regarded as less valuable than highly decorative types (see Tremain 2017, tables 4 and 5 for complete data concerning ceramics).

Perhaps the most interesting instance in which a ceramic has been resold at Sotheby's on more than one occasion concerns an incised ceramic that first appeared as lot 193 in the "Important Pre-Columbian Art" auction of May 12–13, 1983, in New York. The lot had an estimate of $15,000–$20,000 and was not accompanied with any current ownership or past provenance information. It was not listed with a sale price in the available sales data, which might have been a result of the lot failing to sell. It is of course possible that the lot was withdrawn from the sale, or it was sold in a private sale following the public sale (a common practice for lots that do not reach their reserve price [Lobay 2006, 52]).

In 1985 the ceramic was again offered for sale at Sotheby's, this time as lot 99 in the "Pre-Columbian Art" auction of November 26, 1985, in New York. As well as the estimate changing to $10,000–$12,000, the description of the ceramic was much lengthier compared with that provided in the 1983 catalogue. Additionally, while the lot was photographed alongside two other lots in 1983, the 1985 catalogue included a much larger, stand-alone, photograph of the lot. Finally, the accompanying information also changed; it was presented as "Property of an American Institution" and the provenance given as "Cedric Marks collection." Despite a lower estimate, different photograph, and the addition of owner and provenance information, the lot may have failed to sell because it was once again not accompanied by a sale price in the sales data.

The ceramic entered the market for a third time as lot 152 in the "Pre-Columbian Art" auction of May 19, 1992, in New York. The estimate of the lot dropped for a second time, to $6,000–$8,000, and the owner and provenance information also changed: it was presented as "Property of the Manoogian Collection" and the provenance provided was "Mr. and Mrs. Peter Wray Collection." Since publication of the author's original study in 2017, sales data have been located for this auction and reveal that the lot sold for $3,850 (only 19% of its high-end estimate in 1983).

What this particular case study demonstrates is that the change in the description of lots, the lowering of their estimates, and the manner in which they are advertised are likely marketing tactics aimed at securing a sale. Owner and provenance information may also be introduced in catalogues, and perhaps even altered, following an unsuccessful sale to increase the perceived value of antiquities. However, the addition of collectors or collections that are relatively unknown is unlikely to add value to an antiquity.

Regardless of the reason for additions or changes to lot descriptions, the sales catalogues suggest a relationship between redistribution of Maya antiquities and information about owner and provenance. Specifically, the information provided for the ceramic discussed previously appears to suggest that it was purchased by the unspecified "American Institution" from Cedric Marks some time after the 1983 auction and prior to the 1985 auction. Subsequent to the 1985 auction, the Wrays are alleged to have purchased the ceramic from this same American Institution. The ceramic then reportedly entered the Manoogian collection before coming back to the public market in 1992. If the information provided is true, it is evidence of at least three different owners of the ceramic in the space of eight years, with ownership averaging just over two and a half years per owner.

Tracking the distribution and redistribution of Maya ceramics is also a method of tracing the movement of objects out of private collections and into public collections. An interesting case in point is the movement of 21 Maya antiquities (including 17 painted ceramics) from the "Pre-Columbian Art" auction on November 18, 1991, in New York into the collection of the Museo de America in Madrid. At the time the antiquities were offered for sale through Sotheby's, the museum was organizing the reinstallation of its permanent exhibition. Having very few Maya artifacts in the collection—specifically a complete lack of painted ceramics—led to the decision to acquire the antiquities at auction (Andrés Gutiérrez Usillos, pers. comm. 2016). The museum was unable to personally purchase the antiquities, but at the Spanish Ministry of Culture there is a department to acquire patrimonial objects on behalf of museums.

In total, the purchase price of the 21 antiquities was in excess of $140,000. Five of the 21 antiquities purchased had the name of the current owner listed (three from the same collector), while four additional antiquities had a vague owner listed such as "Florida Private Collector." One of the five antiquities with an owner listed also had provenance information provided, and interestingly both the owner and provenance are identical to that provided for lot 152 in the 1992 New York auction discussed previously. This speaks to the apparent value that certain collectors add to antiquities, and explains why the names of certain collectors appear more frequently in sales catalogues than others.

While it appears that more than 70% of the antiquities purchased for the museum are lacking available provenance information, the museum may have somehow acquired this information through private conversations with Sotheby's as a form of due diligence (the author was unable to establish whether or not this was the case). What is positive about the movement of the antiquities from various private collections into one public collection, is that they are now available for the public to view and researchers to study.[13] If the museum had been unable to organize the purchase, the antiquities would likely have remained hidden from public view in numerous private collections around the world. Only one of the ceramics purchased by the museum had been previously photographed by Justin Kerr (see K5033)[14] and was therefore accessible to view on his online portfolio of Maya antiquities, which means that 95% of the antiquities were previously largely inaccessible to the public and scholars alike.

Tracking the distribution and redistribution of Maya antiquities at Sotheby's demonstrates that the market is opaque, with a general lack of information on ownership and provenance. With auction sales shifting toward online arenas, it will become more and more difficult to track sales in the future and easier and easier for buyers and sellers to remain anonymous. The repercussions of this can be devastating. It increases the likelihood that illegally excavated items and fakes and forgeries will continue to penetrate the market, and it impedes the ability of researchers to understand the market in antiquities and monitor trends and changes through time.

Just as we should not ignore unprovenanced objects, we should also not ignore the ways in which they are bought and sold. Creating a "culture of vigilance" (Lobay 2006, 103) around the open market, by monitoring objects that have passed and continue to pass through, is essential for understanding the global demand for antiquities. This is of course a short-term solution to the longer-term goal of changing the attitudes of collectors and the regulations for antiquities sales. By continuing to investigate and examine auction sales, it is possible to increase awareness of the relationship of the legal market to the sale of illicit and faked/forged antiquities. Only by increasing awareness can we hope to educate others about the unethical and illegal side of the antiquities market and work together to reduce demand and push for improved legislation.

Acknowledgments

The research on which the author's original study was based was undertaken partly as a Pre-Doctoral resident at Dumbarton Oaks, and as a Pre-Doctoral Fellow at the Smithsonian's National Museum of the American Indian. The majority of the sales catalogues used in the study were made available through interlibrary loans at the University of Calgary. For the specific research undertaken in this chapter, Katharina Stoll kindly provided very useful information about the auction house market for which I am very grateful. Finally, Donna Yates provided sales data for auctions in 1991 and 1992 that the author had previously been unable to locate.

Notes

1. https://www.sothebys.com/en/about/our-history?locale=en

2. For consistency throughout the chapter, the capitalized "Pre-Columbian" is used even when the term is not part of a name or title.

3. http://www.sothebys.com/en/departments/pre-columbian-art.html

4. Lots specifically designated as "Mayan" were included, but antiquities that were clearly mislabeled or from peripheral regions were excluded.

5. USD prices were adjusted to the 2018 inflation rate using the United States Department of Labor CPI Inflation Calculator (http://www.bls.gov/data/inflation_calculator.htm), rounded to the nearest dollar.

6. http://www.unesco.org/eri/la/convention.asp?KO=13039&language=E

7. http://www.unesco.org/culture/natlaws/media/pdf/guatemala/guatemala_decree 425_1966_engtof.pdf

8. For example, "The Andy Warhol Collection" sold at Sotheby's in 1988 was described as including "objects from Mexico and Pre-Columbian Art" and lot 321 in the May 17, 1994, "Pre-Columbian Art" auction was described as "Property from the Estate of Vincent L. Price."

9. Watson and Todeschini (2007, 137–138) have demonstrated that antiquities dealer Giacomo Medici consigned dozens of antiquities at Sotheby's auctions that he then purchased back from himself; doing so would secure an auction house sale provenance.

10. Julian Dawes, Sotheby's TV, The Value of Art, Episode 4: Provenance. https://www.youtube.com/watch?v=K56EhgfCDjs (accessed November 5, 2017).

11. Robert (Bob) Huber and his wife Marianne are the owners of Huber Primitive Art in Dixon, Illinois. In addition to the NMAI, they have sold Maya ceramics to the British Museum, the Denver Art Museum, and the National Museum of Scotland. Huber is also associated with selling looted pieces of Piedras Negras Stela 3 to the Brooklyn Museum. See: https://www.anonymousswisscollector.com/2014/04/two-pots-two-stories-vignette-on-the-looting-of-guatemalas-maya-past.html

12. Huber and his wife's name appear as part of the provenance information for lot 113, a Maya stone hacha, sold in the "African, Oceanic and Pre-Columbian Art" auction on May 7, 2016. The information also reveals that they were the owners of the hacha when it was sold at Sotheby's as lot 179 in the "Pre-Columbian Art" auction on November 25, 1996.

13. The 21 Maya antiquities purchased from the 1991 Sotheby's auction are available to view in the museum's online collection by entering 1991/11/* into the search field at http://ceres.mcu.es/pages/SimpleSearch?Museo=MAM

14. See Justin Kerr's Maya Vase database at http://research.mayavase.com/kerrmaya.html

References Cited

Brady, Anna. 2016. "What do Auction House Private Sales Mean for Collectors and the Art Market?" *Apollo: The International Art Magazine*, August 4. https://www.apollo-magazine.com/what-do-auction-house-private-sales-mean-for-collectors-and-the-art-market/

Brodie, Neil. 2006. "An Archaeologist's View of the Trade in Unprovenanced Antiquities." In *Art and Cultural Heritage: Law, Policy, and Practice*, edited by Barbara T. Hoffman, 52–63. New York: Cambridge University Press.

———. 2014a. "Provenance and Price: Autoregulation of the Antiquities Market?" *European Journal on Criminal Policy and Research* 20 (4): 427–444.

———. 2014b. "Auction Houses and the Antiquities Trade." In *3rd International Conference of Experts on the Return of Cultural Property*, edited by S. Choulia-Kapeloni, 63–73. Athens: Archaeological Receipts Fund.

———. 2015. "The Internet Market in Pre-Columbian Antiquities." In *Cultural Property Crime: An Overview and Analysis on Contemporary Perspectives and Trends*, edited by Joris Kila and Marc Balcells, 237–262. Leiden: Brill.

Cioni, Enrico. 2014. "From John Hewett to John Stokes: How Robert and Lisa Sainsbury Assembled their Collection of Pre-Columbian Art." M.A. Thesis, University of East Anglia.

Coggins, Clemency. 1998. "United States Cultural Property Legislation: Observation of a Combatant." *International Journal of Cultural Property* 7 (1): 52–68.

Daniels, Brian, Sasha Renninger, and Richard Leventhal. 2014. "Evaluating the Impact of Archaeological Context on the Antiquities Market: A Case Study." Paper presented at the Society for American Archaeology 79th Annual Meeting. Austin, Texas, April 26, 2014.

Davis, Tess. 2011. "Supply and Demand: Exposing the Illicit Trade in Cambodian Antiquities through a Study of Sotheby's Auction House." *Crime, Law, and Social Change* 56 (2): 155–174.

Fay, Emily. 2011. "Virtual Artifacts: eBay, Antiquities, and Authenticity." *Journal of Contemporary Criminal Justice* 27 (4): 449–464.

Gerstenblith, Patty. 2013. "The Meaning of 1970 for the Acquisition of Archaeological Objects." *Journal of Field Archaeology* 38 (4): 364–373.

Gilgan, Elizabeth. 2001. "Looting and the Market for Maya Objects: a Belizean Perspective." In *Trade in Illicit Antiquities: The Destruction of the World's Archaeological Heritage*, edited by Neil Brodie, Jennifer Doole, and Colin Renfrew, 73–87. Cambridge: McDonald Institute Monographs.

Grillo, Ioan. 2004. "'Red List' Drawn to Help Recover Stolen Art." http://www.chron.com/entertainment/article/Red-list-drawn-to-help-recover-stolen-art-1984216.php (accessed July 8, 2016).

Hauser-Schäublin, Brigitta. 2017. "Looted, Trafficked, Donated and Returned: The Twisted Tracks of Cambodian Antiquities." In *Cultural Property and Contested Ownership: The Trafficking of Artefacts and the Quest for Restitution*, edited by Brigitta Hauser-Schäublin and Lyndel V. Prott, 64–84. London: Routledge.

Heritage Auction Galleries. 2010. Pre-Columbian Art Auction, Catalog #6506. December 5, 2010, New York. https://bit.ly/2TyJYoI (accessed February 4, 2019).

Herrmann, Frank. 1981. *Sotheby's: Portrait of An Auction House*. New York: W.W. Norton and Company.

Honan, William H. 1995. "Rare Pre-Columbian Relics, at Any Cost." *The New York Times*, July 31.

Levine, Marc N., and Lucha Martínez de Luna. 2013. "Museum Salvage: A Case Study of Mesoamerican Artifacts in Museum Collections and on the Antiquities Market." *Journal of Field Archaeology* 38 (3): 264–276.

Lobay, Gordon Brock. 2006. "Objects and Objectivity: An Archaeology of Auctions. Central Italian Antiquities at Bonhams, Christie's and Sotheby's 1970–2005." Unpublished Ph.D. Dissertation, Department of Archaeology, University of Cambridge.

Nørskov, Vinnie. 2002. "Greek Vases for Sale: Some Statistical Evidence." In *Illicit Antiquities: The Theft of Culture and the Extinction of Archaeology*, edited by Neil Brodie and Kathryn Walker-Tubb, 23–37. London: Routledge.

Pfeffer, Eva A. 2014. "From Auction to Gallery: Sotheby's Private Sales Development." M.A. Thesis, Sotheby's Institute of Art.

Stoll, Michael. 2004. *Whose Art is This, Anyway?* http://www.michaelstoll.com/writings/deyoung.htm (accessed November 5, 2017).

Tarmy, James. 2015. *The Smarter Way to Invest in Art*. http://www.bloomberg.com/news/articles/2015-03-19/art-investing-smart-buys-are-overlooked-underappreciated-works (accessed July 8, 2016).

Tremain, Cara G. 2017. "Fifty Years of Collecting: The Sale of Ancient Maya Antiquities at Sotheby's." *International Journal of Cultural Property* 24 (2): 187–219.

Washburn, Wilcomb E. 1987. "Increasing our Knowledge of Pre-Columbian Civilizations by Not Collecting Pre-Columbian Objects." In *Pre-Columbian Collections in European Museums*, edited by Anne-Marie Hocquenghem, Peter Tamási and Christiane Villain-Gandossi, 28–35. Budapest: Akadémiai Kiadó.

Watson, Peter. 1997. *Sotheby's: Inside Story*. London: Bloomsbury.

Watson, Peter and Cecilia Todeschini. 2007. *The Medici Conspiracy: The Illicit Journey of Looted Antiquities, From Italy's Tomb Raiders to the World's Greatest Museum*. New York: Public Affairs.

Yates, Donna. 2006. "South America on the Block: The Changing Face of Pre-Columbian Antiquities Auctions in Response to International Law." MPhil Thesis, University of Cambridge.

———. 2015. "Value and Doubt: The Persuasive Power of 'Authenticity' in the Antiquities Market." *PARSE* 2: 71–84.

———. 2016. "Museums, Collectors, and Value Manipulation: Tax Fraud through Donation of Antiquities." *Journal of Financial Crime* 23 (1): 173–186.

10

Failures and Consequences of Antiquities
Antitrafficking Policy in Mesoamerica

DONNA YATES

Is Cultural Property Policy Working?

Few countries have enacted legislation that provides blanket protection against the import of looted antiquities from other countries (Brodie and Renfrew 2005, 347), meaning that international conventions such as the 1970 UNESCO convention serve as the backbone of our global efforts to regulate the looting, trafficking, and sale of illicit antiquities. It has been more than four decades since the drafting of this convention, yet few practical evaluations of the successes or failures of this and other policy interventions within targeted local contexts have been made.

What is the on-the-ground result of policy interventions into the looting and trafficking of cultural objects? How do we measure success and failure? Are there unforeseen consequences to our regulation decisions? These are some of the most important questions to ask about our past and present attempt to disrupt the global illicit trade in antiquities, and they are among the most difficult to answer.

While reviews of the UNESCO convention have been conducted, they tend to be inward looking. They discuss the convention itself and rarely focus on the on-the-ground effects of the legislation. Success is marked in number of objects returned or through the number of countries that have signed the convention, rather than in the number of criminals caught or number of archaeological sites effectively protected.

For example, Prott's 2011 evaluation of the UNESCO convention considers success to be that so many countries signed on, that some museums accepted it, that it has encouraged training workshops, that it has inspired other conventions, and that some countries have changed their law to match the convention's wording (Prott 2011, 3). However commendable many of these successes are, none relate directly to the reduction of the looting and trafficking of antiquities, the disruption of trafficking networks, or the demonstrable protection of cultural sites. Prott's evaluation of the weaknesses of the convention are more telling: the drafting is clumsy, it does not mesh well with local and civil law, it is not retrospective, and nothing compels states that sign it to do anything at all (Prott 2011, 4–5). Even these measures of weakness are inward focused and do not address the practicalities of preventing looting and disrupting antiquities trafficking.

To accurately assess the effects of regulation on the illicit trafficking of antiquities, we must seek information from all points in the trafficking chain: source, transit, and market. We must look at the whole picture. By assessing just one aspect of the trade, we risk crediting policy measures for the effects of something else. A shift in market tastes, improved on-the-ground policing, or depletion of antiquities supply might cause a reduction in antiquities seizures or looting that could mistakenly be assigned to successful policy. Furthermore, if we do not evaluate the effects of policy on the ground, we also risk neglecting to fully assess unforeseen consequences of our policy decisions. Policy that is effective at disrupting the market might actually inspire more or different looting at supply.

In this chapter I will assess the effects of policy decisions intended to regulate the flow of looted Maya antiquities into the United States since the 1970 UNESCO convention. Emerging from this assessment is a picture of effective regulation, unforeseen consequences, and a subsequent failure to properly respond. A 1972 U.S. law effectively reduced the incidence of theft of Maya sculpture, but it encouraged the growth of a market for looted Maya vases and other small, portable objects. Further policy decisions based on the discourse of the UNESCO convention were not effective in reducing the looting and trafficking of these objects.

The results of a shift from policy focused on objects (object-specific regulation) to policy focused on country to country partnerships (country-specific regulation) can be seen on the ground, on the market, and in what little evidence we have for illicit antiquities transit in the Maya region. Our policy interventions to prevent the looting, trafficking, and sale of cultural objects may not be working and we must reassess them.

The Market for the Maya

The ancient Maya occupied large parts of Mexico, Guatemala, Belize, Honduras, and El Salvador from about 2000 BC up to the Spanish Conquest. Especially during the Classic period (approximately AD 250–900), their iconography and artistic execution excelled. Maya art first drew the attention of the adventurers of the nineteenth century, then the archaeologists of the early twentieth century. By the middle of the twentieth century, the Maya were "discovered" by the art market as well, with devastating consequences.

In the nineteenth century few museums or individuals collected Maya antiquities. Although some Maya objects left Central America for the United States or Europe as ethnographic curios, Maya art, being entirely non-Western, did not appeal to the market. In a Europe and United States obsessed with the perceived, if mistaken, origins of European exceptionalism, there was no place for Maya imagery of the lords of the hours of the night, sky serpents, and jaguar babies. Furthermore, the Maya were largely unknown at this time. Many Maya cities were truly "lost": swallowed by the jungle and unknown to even the modern Indigenous people of the region. The writings of John Lloyd Stephens (1841, 1843) and the drawings of Frederick Catherwood in the 1840s exposed many Maya cities to the outside world, but archaeologists did not arrive until the end of the decade (Yates 2013). Nonspecialist and art market attention was far behind them.

That is not to say that there were no nineteenth-century Maya antiquities collections. There were, but they tended to be "local," the product of the hobbies of wealthy Mexicans or European expatriates who lived near Maya sites. These people skirted the line between collector and investigator, and for the most part their collections drifted into anthropological museums abroad.

With the growth of such artistic movements as Dadaism and Surrealism in the early 1900s, the art world's emphasis on "Classic" forms was replaced with an examination of form in general. The most popular artists of this period began to draw on the non-Western for inspiration: Africa, the Pacific, Asia, and Latin America. As the art market caught up, these non-Western traditions were lumped together under such racist and deplorable descriptors as "primitive," "native," and "tribal" art. These traditions are in no way related to each other, and such a collapsing of geography and function belittles the cultural meaning of the pieces (Brodie 2011, 410). By the 1950s several prominent and deep-pocketed collectors appeared, such as Nelson Rockefeller, whose collection eventually became the Museum of Primitive Art which, in turn, became the core of the Metropolitan Museum of Art's non-Western collections, including Mesoamerica. There was suddenly a lot of money to be made off the Maya.

By the time the art market noticed the Maya, all the Maya countries had enacted legislation that claimed at least a degree of state ownership of ancient objects and banned the extraction and export of antiquities without a permit. Permits were only to be granted to credentialed archaeologists from well-known academic institutions. There was no fully legal way to buy Maya antiquities by the time collectors and museums in the United States became interested in them. Yet where there is demand, a supply is found. The end result was the widespread, destructive, and illegal looting of nearly every Maya site.

Stealing Stelae: Problem Recognized, Problem Solved?

Much of the mid-twentieth-century demand for Maya art in the United States was focused on sculptural items, particularly stone stelae. These massive pieces were erected throughout the Maya region during the Classic period and served important social, political, and ritual functions. Many portray lords in full regalia and/or long inscriptions which record significant events. Stelae are prominent at many sites, and because they often have clear dates carved on them, they were a focus of early archaeologists who wished to understand the temporal sequence of Maya sites. Hundreds of stelae were recorded in photos, drawings, casts, and writings in the first half of the twentieth century and became well known in academic circles (e.g., Morley 1937–38). Archaeologists rarely removed stelae from their original context largely because of their size. Little was done to protect them, as no one predicted widespread stelae looting: theft was thought to be unlikely.

Sadly, this was not the case. Starting in the 1950s but intensifying in the 1960s, demand grew among United States–based museums and collectors for Maya sculpture and thus ensued a period in which they were systematically looted (Coggins 1969, 94; 1998, 52; Robertson 1972, 147). Looters, sometimes directly employed by intermediaries or dealers, moved through the jungle locating stelae, hieroglyphic staircases, and stone ball-court markers. To ease transport, stelae either were broken into multiple pieces via toppling or through application of heat, or were thinned using saws (Coggins 1969,

94; Graham 1988, 123; Robertson 1972, 147; Sheets 1973, 317). These practices mutilated the sculptures, destroying the carved edges and sometimes shattering them into unrecognizable fragments. The pieces were then taken out of the jungle, trafficked into market countries such as the United States, and then purchased by collectors and museums (Robertson 1972, 151).

Archaeologists returning to sites would find sculptures such as stelae badly damaged or missing altogether. United States–based sales catalogues contained sculptures from Maya sites that archaeologists had not even discovered yet (Robertson 1972, 147). Well-recorded Maya stelae would suddenly appear on display (thinner, and in multiple pieces) in major U.S. museums. Coggins (1969, 94) likened the Mayanists' experience of these appearances to the way a Classical archaeologist would feel if the local museum had suddenly and secretly purchased the Arch of Titus. Archaeological sites were not the only casualties of this looting. In 1971 Pedro Arturo Sierra, an assistant to archaeologist Ian Graham, was killed when the two came across men looting a stela at La Naya, Guatemala (Robertson 1972, 147). In 1971 Merle Greene Robertson and her research team were detained by men with submachine guns who were sawing stelae at Itsimté, Guatemala (Robertson 1972, 147). It was impossible for collectors and museums not to know that the stelae they purchased were looted: the fragments display saw marks, and many appear in situ in academic publications. They bought them anyway.

It is clear that the primary market for looted Maya sculpture was the United States (Gutchen 1983, 225), and that action within the United States was needed to stem the flow of stolen objects. In 1972, as a direct result of effective lobbying by archaeologists, the United States enacted Public Law No. 92–587 (Regulation of Importation of Pre-Columbian Monumental or Architectural Sculpture or Murals) in an effort to prevent the movement of illicit Pre-Columbian antiquities into the United States. Under this law no ancient Mesoamerican sculpture, mural, or architectural item is allowed to enter the United States without an official permit from its country of origin. As none of the Maya countries issue such export permits for anything other than museum loans or scientific study, and certainly not for market purposes, this law prevents the import of these types of Maya objects into the United States for the purpose of sale. The law is "effectively enforced without creating a cumbersome and intrusive customs regime" (Bator 1982, 334).

The 1972 law is what I term "object-specific": the focus is not on the country of origin of the piece, rather on the piece itself; this is an important distinction. To risk simplifying a complex situation, ancient borders do not reflect modern borders (Yates 2015a, 2015b). Although, for example, Guatemala claims that all archaeological objects are property of the state, and although the United States, more or less, recognizes the sovereign right of Guatemala to do so, proving that a looted and trafficked Maya object from Guatemala is stolen property to the satisfaction of a U.S. court is nearly impossible. One barrier to doing so is proving that the piece left Guatemala after the date on which Guatemala claimed all antiquities as state property. Without, say, time-stamped photographs of the object in Guatemala after that date, how can one prove that an unprovenanced object left that country 10 years ago or 100 years ago? More challenging is proving that an antiquity is from Guatemala in the first place if archaeologists have not previously recorded it. Although regional styles exist among Maya pieces, it is almost impossible to state for a fact that a looted Maya object came from Guatemala and not from Belize or Mexico. In banning the import of any Maya sculpture that does not have an export permit, even when the country of origin is undetermined, these issues are avoided. The sculpture itself is contraband in the United States and, in theory, no specific country needs to prove that it is their property to prevent further trafficking and sale.

By most accounts, this law has been effective. While the law does not apply to markets for stelae beyond the United States, removing the primary market for these pieces was a significant achievement (Bator 1982, 333). Contemporary commentators detected an immediate drop in the appearance of Maya sculptures on the U.S. market and a reduction of stelae theft at Maya sites (Coggins 1976, 14; 1998, 53; Bator 1982, 334; Gutchen 1983). Museums and collectors could no longer publicly acquire Maya sculptures in the United States without serious backlash. Not only did demand plummet in response, so did supply. It appears that this law has served its intended purpose and effectively disrupted the looting of Maya sculpture and the trafficking of these objects into the United States. Unfortunately, the 1972 law has had an entirely unforeseen consequence on the ground in the Maya region.

Vase Looting: Devastating Response to Policy Decisions?

Maya ceramics range from plain utilitarian wares, the sort of pots used for everyday cooking, to elaborately decorated cylindrical tall-sided vases, often with painted scenes and writing. Although likely used in life, they are most often found in ritual deposits and tombs. These vases display a number of iconographic styles, some thought to be regional and others temporal. The distribution of different styles of Maya decorative pottery is poorly understood as a result of the intense looting of these objects.

It is difficult, perhaps even impossible, to definitively say that a looted Maya vase came from a specific archaeological site. We know from legitimate archaeological excavations that the Maya exchanged vessels over great distances and across modern borders. Even in an extreme case where a looted vase is inscribed with the name of a known Maya polity, there is no way to tell whether the vase was actually deposited at that location or whether it traveled in ancient times to a different polity. For a particularly strong example of this quandary, see Reents-Budet's (1994) discussion of the Buena Vista vase excavated at the site of Buena Vista (Belize) but bearing the emblem glyph of Naranjo (Guatemala).

Although widespread demand for Maya sculpture in the United States dried up after 1972, the public popularity of the Maya increased. Significant advances in the decipherment of Maya writing provided tantalizing new information that captivated public imagination (Coe 1992; Graham 1988; Schele and Friedel 1990) and the Maya were incorporated into the various popular New Age movements of the era (e.g., von Däniken 1968). Museums sought to increase their Maya holdings due to public interest, and collectors did not abandon the Maya. Again, where there is demand, a supply is found.

The 1972 law was strong, but it applied only to certain types of Maya objects: sculpture, architectural elements, and murals. This left smaller, portable Maya antiquities unprotected. Jade masks, incised shells, decorative vases, and other smaller items did not require a permit to enter the United States. As the market for stelae waned, the market for Maya vases boomed (Coggins 1976, 14; 1998, 53; Bator 1982, 334). Maya ceramics were not unpopular before 1972: Coggins (1969, 98), citing observations made by archaeologist E. Wyllys Andrews, notes the existence of vase looting bands in Campeche before the law went into effect. But after the 1972 law prevented the easy import of monuments, commentators note that Maya vases began appearing more frequently in sales catalogues at higher prices, and that looters began to focus their efforts on them.

Indeed, the influx of Maya vases post-1972 was not only visible in the U.S. market, it could also be seen on the ground. Stelae looting looks very different from vase looting. Although the mutilation of a stela for transport is upsetting, in most cases only the stela and its associated deposits are damaged in the looting process, because stelae were usually placed in open plazas or platforms, near but not within buildings. Vases, however, tend to be found in tombs which, in turn, are found deep within Maya buildings. To loot a Maya vase, one must usually tunnel into a large ancient building (Coggins 1976, 15). Maya structures that have been looted for vases and other small items are trenched and pitted like Swiss cheese (Pendergast and Graham 1981, 16). Some have been completely bisected. Once looted in this manner, they can collapse in on themselves. At times, they have reportedly collapsed on looters.

Before the 1970s the looting of graves within temples had been done "casually and opportunistically" (Coggins 1998, 55). Following the 1972 law, archaeologists increasingly reported the existence of looting gangs targeting and tunneling into the structures at Maya sites. They also began to record the proliferation of looter trenches, digging conducted on a scale not previously seen. There is evidence that intermediaries directly funded large looting ventures that combed the Maya region for pottery (Sheets 1973, 318; Yates 2012). Locals in difficult financial situations could reasonably engage in pottery looting for side income; although trenching a temple is hard work, vases are extremely portable, unlike stelae, and do not require special equipment for removal or transport (Paredes Maury 1999). During this time, nearly every known Maya site was looted, as were countless unknown sites. At some sites, such as Ka'Kabish in Belize, every structure was partially destroyed by this wave of looting (Pendergast 1991, 89). The site continues to suffer from looting today, despite local attempts to guard the area (C. Tremain, pers. comm. 2017). Furthermore, around 75% of the building groups at the site of Ixtontón, Guatemala, had been cut by looters' trenches before 1985, when the site was first located by archaeologists (Laporte and Torres 1988, 53). At the site of Naranjo, Guatemala, Fialko (2005) has documented more than 270 tunnels and trenches.

Despite the success of the 1972 law at preventing the import of looted stelae into the United States, and despite the massive and detectable increase in vase looting, no object-specific legislation was enacted to prevent the movement of looted portable Maya antiquities. This is most likely because a different type of cultural property protection regime had been adopted: what I term country-specific regulation.

The 1970 UNESCO convention was ratified by the United States in 1972 and implemented in 1983. In general, the convention is focused on the rights, responsibilities, and jurisdictions of the states party to it. It promotes state-to-state cooperation for the return of looted and stolen cultural property but offers limited suggestions for state-to-state cooperation for the prevention of trafficking. Some countries that have implemented the convention have done so in a manner that requires the development of bilateral and multilateral agreements, with the United States as a prominent example. Under U.S. implementation, a country that is a signatory to the convention notifies the United States that they have a looting problem, provides proof that the United States is a major receiver of these artifacts, and requests import restrictions on a list of artifact types. After a lengthy process the United States and the requesting country sign a Memorandum of Understanding (MOU) that promises that the United States will restrict the import of the listed types of antiquities for a period of five years (renewable) while requesting country attempts to stabilize the situation on the ground.

These MOUs are country-specific: the objects stopped at the U.S. border must be shown to have come from a country that shares a cultural property agreement with the United States. Only Maya vases from countries that have a cultural property MOU require a valid export permit to be allowed into the United States. Vases from countries that do not have an MOU with the United States do not require an export permit.

In theory, a vase with an undetermined country of origin may be able to slip through. As previously discussed, it is impossible to say for certain from which modern country a looted Maya vase came, there is always doubt, and it is possible that traffickers and dealers use this to their advantage (see Gilgan 2001). There were certainly opportunities to cast such doubt on the origins of looted Maya vases. Although at the time of writing all Maya countries have a cultural property MOU with the United States, they did not all obtain MOUs at once. Belize, a major source of Maya vases, was only able to obtain an MOU with the United States in 2013.

Following implementation of these country-specific regulations, no reduction in the appearance of Maya vases on the United States market is observable (Gilgan 2001, 80). By many accounts, major vase looting operations continued in the Maya region well into the 2000s. Pendergast (1991, 89) even documented an increase in the looting of Maya sites for vases in the late 1980s and early 1990s, 20 years after the passing of the 1972 monuments law and 10 years after the U.S. implementation of the UNESCO convention. It should be said that there appears to have been a significant decline in vase looting in recent years; yet this does not seem to be the result of effective regulation. Instead, trafficking of other regional commodities, particularly narcotics, lumber, and other forest products, has become a more lucrative focus of time and energy (Yates 2014, 2015a, 2015b) and it is possible most Maya sites have been gutted, the resource largely exhausted.

Success of Object-Specific and Failure of Country-Specific Regulation

In this case it seems clear that object-specific regulation worked and country-specific regulation did not. Banning the import of all Maya stelae lacking permits into the United States, regardless of country of origin, has drastically reduced the number of looted stelae that enter the country and also the number of stelae that are looted in the first place. Restricting the import of Maya vases based on country of origin and existence of a cultural property MOU does not seem to have reduced the number of looted vases entering the United States, nor has it reduced the incidence of site looting. Yet the model on which our current international regulatory regime is based is mostly country-specific.

Under many regulatory regimes, the person in possession of an object is assumed to be that object's owner unless someone can prove otherwise to the satisfaction of the law. Object-specific regulation considers antiquities to be a particular class of property that rests outside this usual assumption about possession and ownership. By simply adding another criterion before ownership can be assumed (an export permit), object-specific regulation acknowledges the significant potential for illegality in the movement of antiquities. This burden of producing a valid export permit should be negligible for a rightful owner but almost insurmountable for a trafficker.

Other types of objects are treated this way under existing international regulation. The most relevant example to this discussion is the extensive list of flora and fauna whose movement across borders is banned by the Convention on International Trade in Endangered Species of Wild Fauna and Flora (CITES). There are no circumstances under which various types of orchids, rhino horns, elephant tusks, and other protected natural goods can move from one signatory country to another without a permit. Permits are granted only for scientific and educational purposes and, even then, after considerable work on the part of the person seeking to export the material. The underlying assumption of this object-specific ban on the movement of natural objects is that biodiversity and extinction are global issues, not country-specific issues, and thus require global regulation. To ban the import of elephant tusks from one country but not those from another, the thinking goes, would do little to prevent the poaching of elephants. It also might encourage poachers to launder their tusks through countries with weaker regulatory regimes. These are exactly the type of consequences seen in the trafficking of antiquities with country-specific regulation in place.

Like conservation of the natural world, the protection of cultural heritage is of global, not country-specific concern. If we accept that there exists a cultural heritage of humanity, which UNESCO certainly does, country-specific regulation of the movement of antiquities appears to fall far short of the mark. If all of humanity is the cultural inheritor of the glory of the ancient Maya, why should the prevention of the looting of Maya objects be left to the shifting political situations of the governments of just two countries? Why do those who wish to own antiquities privately get the benefit of very little doubt while the collective good of humanity is left to suffer in the equation? We must reassess both our priorities and our policy.

Policy Reassessment

To say that the model put forth by the 1970 UNESCO convention does not work is potentially devastating and certainly hyperbolic. The Convention is simply good at achieving some goals, and not good at achieving others. It is not particularly good at dealing with the actual trafficking of objects, the in-between space where cultural property moves from jurisdiction to jurisdiction, losing its demonstrable connection to source. Yet, at this international level, connection to source remains a core component of stopping smuggled objects at borders and effecting cultural property return.

For example, recent moves toward global restrictions on the movement of objects from Syria and Iraq such as UN Security Council Resolution 2199 (2015), retain all the assumptions, and thus all the limitations of country-specific regulation. The UNSCR assumes that it is possible to distinguish Iraqi and Syrian objects from those that originate in neighboring countries (it often is not). It also assumes that it is possible to distinguish antiquities looted during recent conflict from those that were looted beforehand (it almost always is not). Such regulation is expensive at best, though even with infinite resources, the contextual information tying the piece to a specific country of origin is both unrecoverable and required to effect return. At worst, it is simply unenforceable. It is possible that country-specific regulation is now entrenched.

Yet hope is not lost. Although a CITES-style global object-specific ban on the movement of antiquities might be unrealistic, individual countries can enact object-specific legislation, and some market countries appear to be doing just that. In 2016, for example, Germany reformed its cultural property law, which now, among other things, prohibits "imports of unlawfully exported cultural property from other States and introduce[s] licensing procedures for cultural property to be exported from Germany" (Beauftragte der Bundesregierung für Kultur und Medien, 2016). A 2016 summary report of the Act distributed by Germany's Federal Government Commissioner for Culture and the Media states:

> The new Act stipulates that cultural property that was unlawfully exported from another States Party to the UNESCO 1970 Convention before the Convention entered into force in Germany, i.e. 2007, is considered to have been unlawfully imported into Germany if, upon import, no documents are presented that prove that the cultural property has been lawfully exported from the respective State.

Thus, cultural objects, no matter their origin, that do not have an export license are "considered to have been unlawfully removed" (Beauftragte der Bundesregierung für Kultur und Medien, 2016). This law appears to be object-specific and represents one of the first times a market country has enacted such policy on a large scale. At the time of writing, the effects of Germany's law remain to be seen.

However, the effects of the U.S. ban on the import of Maya stelae are clear. The 1972 law removed the primary location of demand from the trafficking chain and noticeably reduced stelae looting. Market countries that wish to stem the flow of illicit antiquities should consider requiring the presentation of a valid export permit in all cases of import and sale. While this places a burden on the market country, the cost of checking the existence of a permit is certainly less than either full investigations into suspected trafficking or lengthy legal cases of repatriation. Indeed, the 1972 law banning the import of stelae without permits has not caused a significant financial or logistical burden for the United States. The way forward is simple: no permit, no entry, no sale.

Policymakers and policy advisors must focus on artifacts, not countries of origin. Object-specific regulation is rare but potentially quite effective. Country-specific regulation is common but questionable. Our regulatory paradigm must shift if we hope to protect cultural property on the ground and prevent trafficking.

Acknowledgments

The author has received funding for this research from the European Research Council under the European Union's Seventh Framework Programme (FP7/2007–2013)/erc Grant agreement no. 283873 gtico, the Leverhulme Trust, and the Fulbright Program.

References Cited

Bator, Paul M. 1982. "An Essay on the International Trade in Art." *Stanford Law Review* 34 (2): 275–384.

Beauftragte der Bundesregierung für Kultur und Medien. 2016. *Key aspects of the new Act on the Protection of Cultural Property in Germany.* https://www.bundesregierung.de/Content/DE/_Anlagen/BKM/2016/2016-09-23-kulturgutschutz-informationen-englisch.pdf?__blob=publicationFile&v=2 (accessed November 1, 2016) AND https://web.archive.org/web/20171102120922/https://www.bundesregierung.de/Content/DE/_Anlagen/BKM/2016/2016-09-23-kulturgutschutz-informationen-englisch.pdf?__blob=publicationFile&v=2

Brodie, Neil. 2011. "Congenial Bedfellows? The Academy and the Antiquities Trade." *Journal of Contemporary Criminal Justice* 27 (4): 408–437.

Brodie, Neil and Colin Renfrew. 2005. "Looting and the World's Archaeological Heritage: The Inadequate Response." *Annual Review of Anthropology* 34: 343–361.

Coe, Michael. 1992. *Breaking the Maya Code.* New York: Thames and Hudson.

Coggins, Clemency C. 1969. "Illicit Traffic of Pre-Columbian Antiquities." *Art Journal* 29 (1): 94, 96, 98, 114.

———. 1976. "New Legislation to Control the International Traffic in Antiquities." *Archaeology* 29 (1): 14–15.

———. 1998. "United States Cultural Property Legislation: Observations of a Combatant." *International Journal of Cultural Property* 7 (1): 52–68.

Fialko, Vilma. 2005. "Archaeological Research and Rescue Project at Naranjo: Emerging Documentation in Naranjo's Palacio de la Realeza, Petén." *FAMSI.* http://www.famsi.org/reports/05005/05005Fialko01.pdf (accessed November 1, 2016) AND https://web.archive.org/web/20161127232508/http://www.famsi.org/reports/05005/05005Fialko01.pdf

Gilgan, Elizabeth. 2001. "Looting and the Market for Maya Objects: a Belizean Perspective."

In *Trade in Illicit Antiquities: The Destruction of the World's Archaeological Heritage*, edited by Neil Brodie, Jennifer Doole, and Colin Renfrew, 73–87. Cambridge: McDonald Institute Monographs.

Graham, Ian. 1988. "Homeless Hieroglyphs." *Antiquity* 62: 122–126.

Gutchen, Mark A. 1983. "The Destruction of Archaeological Resources in Belize, Central America." *Journal of Field Archaeology* 10: 217–227.

Laporte, Juan P. and Rolando Torres. 1988. "Reconocimiento en Ixtonton, Dolores." Reporte 1, *Atlas Arqueológico de Guatemala*. Guatemala City: Instituto de Antropología e Historia.

Morley, Sylvanus G. 1937–38. *The Inscriptions of the Peten*, 5 vols. Publication 437. Washington D.C.: Carnegie Institution of Washington.

Paredes Maury, Sofia. 1999. "Surviving in the Rainforest: The Realities of Looting in the Rural Villages of El Petén, Guatemala." *FAMSI*. https://www.famsi.org/reports/95096/9 5096ParedesMaury01.pdf (accessed November 1, 2016) AND https://web.archive.org/ web/20150216200439/http://www.famsi.org/reports/95096/95096ParedesMaury01.pdf

Pendergast, David M. 1991. "And the Loot Goes On: Winning Some Battles, But Not the War." *Journal of Field Archaeology* 18: 89–95.

Pendergast, David M., and Elizabeth Graham. 1981. "Fighting a Looting Battle: Xunantunich, Belize." *Archaeology* 34 (4): 12–19.

Prott, Lyndel V. 2011. *Strengths and Weaknesses of the 1970 Convention: An Evaluation 40 years after Its Adoption*. Background paper. Paris: UNESCO.

Reents-Budet, Dorie. 1994. *Painting the Maya Universe: Royal Ceramics of the Classic Period*. Durham, N.C.: Duke University Press.

Robertson, Merle G. 1972. "Monument Thievery in Mesoamerica." *American Antiquity* 37 (2): 147–155.

Schele, Linda and David A. Friedel. 1990. *A Forest of Kings: The Untold Story of the Ancient Maya*. New York: William Morrow.

Sheets, Payson. 1973. "The Pillage of Prehistory." *American Antiquity* 38 (3): 317–320.

Stephens, John L. 1841. *Incidents of Travel in Central America, Chiapas and Yucatán*. New York: Harper and Brothers.

———. 1843. *Incidents of Travel in Yucatán*. New York: Harper and Brothers.

Von Däniken, Eric. 1968. *Chariots of the Gods?* New York: Putnam.

Yates, Donna. 2012. "November Collection of Maya Pottery." *Trafficking Culture Encyclopedia*. http://traffickingculture.org/case_note/november-collection-of-maya-pottery (accessed November 1, 2018 AND https://web.archive.org/web/20160404224723/http://trafficking-culture.org/case_note/november-collection-of-maya-pottery/

———. 2013. "Publication as Preservation: A Remote Maya Site in the Early 20th Century." In *From Plunder to Preservation: Britain and the Heritage of Empire, 1800–1950*, edited by Astrid Swenson and Paul Mandler, 217–239. Oxford: Oxford University Press.

———. 2014. "Displacement, Deforestation, and Drugs: Antiquities Trafficking and the Narcotics Support Economies of Guatemala." In *Cultural Property Crimes: An Overview and Analysis on Contemporary Perspectives and Trends*, edited by Joris Kila and Marc Balcells, 23–36. Liden: Brill.

———. 2015a. "Reality and Practicality: Challenges to Effective Cultural Property Policy on the Ground in Latin America." *International Journal of Cultural Property* 22 (2–3): 337–356.

———. 2015b. "Illicit Cultural Property from Latin America: Looting, Trafficking, and Sale." In *Countering Illicit Traffic in Cultural Goods: The Global Challenge of Protecting the World's Heritage*, edited by France Desmarais. Paris: ICOM.

Contributors

MARTIN BERGER is curator for Central and South America at the National Museum of World Cultures, The Netherlands, and curator for the Paul and Dora Janssen-Arts collection of Pre-Columbian Art at the Museum aan de Stroom in Antwerp, Belgium.

ALLISON R. DAVIS is a cultural property research analyst in the Cultural Heritage Center at the U.S. Department of State. She works with foreign governments and nongovernmental stakeholders to combat cultural property looting and trafficking in the Americas.

JAMES A. DOYLE is assistant curator for Art of the Ancient Americas at the Metropolitan Museum of Art, New York. Doyle's focus is the ancient Maya.

ROSEMARY A. JOYCE received her PhD from the University of Illinois-Urbana and is currently professor of anthropology at the University of California. She continues research on Honduran collections in museums throughout Europe and the Americas.

NANCY L. KELKER is professor of art history, specializing in the art of the non-Western world, and a former associate curator of pre-Columbian and Latin American art at the San Antonio Museum of Art. She is the author of several articles, exhibition catalogues, and books.

GUIDO KREMPEL is an independent researcher who studied cultural anthropology with a focus on the ancient Americas and prehistoric and protohistoric archaeology at the University of Bonn, Germany. His current works include a publication series on Maya ceramics of unknown provenance, and a corpus of Maya monuments.

CHRISTINA LUKE is associate professor of archaeology and history of art at Koç University in Istanbul, adjunct associate professor in the Archaeology Program at Boston University, and a consulting scholar with the Cultural Heritage Center at the University of Pennsylvania. She also serves as editor of the *Journal of Field Archaeology*.

SOFÍA PAREDES MAURY is currently executive director of La Ruta Maya Foundation. She has a BA degree in Maya archaeology from the Universidad del Valle de Guatemala and an MA degree in museum studies and Latin and Caribbean studies from the Graduate School of Arts & Science, New York University.

ADAM SELLEN is senior researcher in the Peninsular Centre for Humanities and Social Sciences at the Universidad Nacional Autónoma de México. He specializes in the ancient cultures of Oaxaca with a focus on the iconography of Zapotec urns.

CARA G. TREMAIN is an instructor in the Department of Sociology and Anthropology at Langara College in Vancouver, British Columbia. She specializes in ancient Maya archaeology, and her current research focuses on Mesoamerican antiquities within museum collections and on the auction market.

DONNA YATES is associate professor of criminology in the Faculty of Law at Maastricht University, The Netherlands.

Index

Page numbers in *italics* refer to illustrations.

Maya Studies

EDITED BY DIANE Z. CHASE AND ARLEN F. CHASE

Salt: White Gold of the Ancient Maya, by Heather McKillop (2002)

Archaeology and Ethnohistory of Iximché, by C. Roger Nance, Stephen L. Whittington, and Barbara E. Borg (2003)

The Ancient Maya of the Belize Valley: Half a Century of Archaeological Research, edited by James F. Garber (2004; first paperback edition, 2011)

Unconquered Lacandon Maya: Ethnohistory and Archaeology of Indigenous Culture Change, by Joel W. Palka (2005)

Chocolate in Mesoamerica: A Cultural History of Cacao, edited by Cameron L. McNeil (2006; first paperback edition, 2009)

Maya Christians and Their Churches in Sixteenth-Century Belize, by Elizabeth Graham (2011; first paperback edition, 2020)

Chan: An Ancient Maya Farming Community, edited by Cynthia Robin (2012; first paperback edition, 2013)

Motul de San José: Politics, History, and Economy in a Classic Maya Polity, edited by Antonia E. Foias and Kitty F. Emery (2012; first paperback edition, 2015)

Ancient Maya Pottery: Classification, Analysis, and Interpretation, edited by James John Aimers (2013; first paperback edition, 2014)

Ancient Maya Political Dynamics, by Antonia E. Foias (2013; first paperback edition, 2014)

Ritual, Violence, and the Fall of the Classic Maya Kings, edited by Gyles Iannone, Brett A. Houk, and Sonja A. Schwake (2016; first paperback edition, 2018)

Perspectives on the Ancient Maya of Chetumal Bay, edited by Debra S. Walker (2016)

Maya E Groups: Calendars, Astronomy, and Urbanism in the Early Lowlands, edited by David A. Freidel, Arlen F. Chase, Anne S. Dowd, and Jerry Murdock (2017; first paperback edition, 2020)

War Owl Falling: Innovation, Creativity, and Culture Change in Ancient Maya Society, by Markus Eberl (2017)

Pathways to Complexity: A View from the Maya Lowlands, edited by M. Kathryn Brown and George J. Bey III (2018; first paperback edition, 2021)

Water, Cacao, and the Early Maya of Chocolá, by Jonathan Kaplan and Federico Paredes Umaña (2018)

Maya Salt Works, by Heather McKillop (2019)

The Market for Mesoamerica: Reflections on the Sale of Pre-Columbian Antiquities, edited by Cara G. Tremain and Donna Yates (2019; first paperback edition, 2023)

Migrations in Late Mesoamerica, edited by Christopher S. Beekman (2019)

Approaches to Monumental Landscapes of the Ancient Maya, edited by Brett A. Houk, Barbara Arroyo, and Terry G. Powis (2020)

The Real Business of Ancient Maya Economies: From Farmers' Fields to Rulers' Realms, edited by Marilyn A. Masson, David A. Freidel, and Arthur A. Demarest (2020)

Maya Kingship: Rupture and Transformation from Classic to Postclassic Times, edited by
Tsubasa Okoshi, Arlen F. Chase, Philippe Nondédéo, and M. Charlotte Arnauld (2021)
*Lacandón Maya in the Twenty-First Century: Indigenous Knowledge and Conservation in
Mexico's Tropical Rainforest,* by James D. Nations (2023)
The Materialization of Time in the Ancient Maya World: Mythic History and Ritual Order,
edited by David A. Freidel, Arlen F. Chase, Anne S. Dowd, and Jerry Murdock (2023)
El Perú-Waka': New Archaeological Perspectives on the Kingdom of the Centipede, edited by
Keith Eppich, Damien B. Marken, and David Freidel (2024)

www.ingramcontent.com/pod-product-compliance
Lightning Source LLC
Chambersburg PA
CBHW070417290526
45791CB00005B/1733